P9-CQM-278

FRIED TWINKIES BUCKLE BUNNIES & BULL RIDERS

FRIED TWINKIES BUCKLE BUNNIES &BULL RIDERS

A YEAR INSIDE THE PROFESSIONAL BULL RIDERS TOUR

JOSH PETER

RODALE

Mention of specific companies, organizations, or authorities in this book
does not imply endorsement by the author or publisher, nor does mention of
specific companies, organizations, or authorities imply that they endorse this book,
its author, or the publisher.

Internet addresses and telephone numbers given in this book
were accurate at the time it went to press.

© 2005 by Josh Peter

All rights reserved. No part of this publication may be reproduced or transmitted
in any form or by any means, electronic or mechanical, including photocopying,
recording, or any other information storage and retrieval system,
without the written permission of the publisher.

Printed in the United States of America

Rodale Inc. makes every effort to use acid-free ♾, recycled paper ♻.

Photographs by Beiron Andersson; fried Twinkie photograph by Barry Sweet

Book design by Drew Frantzen

Library of Congress Cataloging-in-Publication Data

Peter, Josh.
 Fried twinkies, buckle bunnies, and bull riders : a year inside the professional bull riders
tour / Josh Peter.
    p.   cm.
 Includes index.
 ISBN-13 978–1–59486–119–2 hardcover
 ISBN-10 1–59486–119–6 hardcover
  1. Bull riding.   2. Professional Bull Riders, Inc.   I. Title.
 GV1834.45.B84P48   2005
 791.8'4—dc22   2005017297

Distributed to the trade by Holtzbrinck Publishers

2   4   6   8   10   9   7   5   3   1   hardcover

We inspire and enable people to improve their lives and the world around them
For more of our products visit **rodalestore.com** or call 800-848-4735

For my beloved wife, Vanessa,
and my beautiful little Taurus, Norah

CONTENTS

ACKNOWLEDGMENTS

First and foremost, a big thanks to all of the bull riders, especially those who advised me against getting on a bull. As Adriano Moraes put it, "At your age, you'll probably die."

Simply writing about bulls required an incredible support team that included Frank Scatoni and Greg Dinkin, the best agents a writer could have; Pete Fornatale, my talented and tireless editor; all of the hard-working folks at Rodale, who not only published this book but helped make it something of which I'm especially proud; friends like Phyllis Shnaider and Charles Billings, who provided unyielding optimism; and my entire family, but especially my wife and my mother, who believed in me even when I didn't. And that's just the beginning of my gratitude.

This book could not have been written without the generosity of the PBR; without the support of David Meeks and Doug Tatum, my bosses at the *Times-Picayune*; or without the help of the Outdoor Life Network—especially Matt Vinick, who must have spent half of the year responding to my requests for videotapes. It also would have been much less fun to write without the camaraderie and friendship of people like Todd Pierce, Jinx Clower, Tandy Freeman, Joe Loverro, Leah Garcia, Brett Haber, Brandon Bates, Beiron Andersson, and countless others.

Additional thanks to Chris McManes, for his friendship and keen eye; Gail Woerner, for her dedication to rodeo history; Sharon Mahrley, for her stewardship of the Lane Frost Web site; and to all of the other men and women dedicated to giving bull riding and rodeo the attention and publicity they so richly deserve.

ONE

MAKE 'EM SHIVER

"If the PBR don't get your fire going, your wood is wet."
—*Larry Seamans, Texan and ardent bull riding fan*

Las Vegas, Nevada
Saturday & Sunday, November 8 & 9, 2003

Climbing into the 6-foot-deep, coffin-shaped metal chute, Chris Shivers lowered himself onto the back of Silver Select, a 1,600-pound bull. He wrapped a custom-made bull rope around his left hand and with his right hand pounded closed his gloved fist. Then he tightened his legs against the bull and called for the gate with a shout of "Go."

The chute gate swung open, and out they burst, man and beast.

Ropes of saliva shot from Silver Select's nostrils as he bucked and whirled and leapt and shook. The crowd of more than 16,000 inside the Thomas & Mack Center loved it, all the more because the rider aboard the furious bull at the Professional Bull Riders' World Finals was Shivers, a baby-faced 24-year-old from Louisiana and the reigning hero and heartthrob of the PBR. "Make us Shiver!" read a handmade sign. That's exactly what happened as the crowd cheered, shouted, and . . . gasped.

Shivers was hung up.

He'd tumbled off the right side of Silver Select with his hand caught in the bull rope. As Silver Select twisted and spun, Shivers looked like he was caught in a blender. What happened next was a blur.

His left hand ripped free of the bull rope, the bull knocked him face-first into the dirt, Shivers crawled away, reaching his feet and staggering for safety.

Out of danger, Shivers grimaced as he clutched his right arm. The medical staff hustled to his aid. Wincing as he walked out of the arena with the assistance of a trainer, he managed to tip his cowboy hat as if to assure the fans he was okay. Tentative applause rippled through the crowd.

Bull riders are no ordinary men. To see that, one need look no further than the beasts they attempt to stay on for 8 seconds. The bulls, weighing up to 2,200 pounds, go by names like Dippin' Rampage, Tombstone, and McNasty—and have dispositions to match. The baddest of the lot was Little Yellow Jacket, a 1,700-pound monster who'd been voted Bull of the Year for the second straight season. But the riders, if not as strong as the bulls, were just as tough.

At the 2003 finals, one rider was competing with a partially collapsed lung; another was back less than 4 weeks after suffering a broken rib and punctured lung; yet another was climbing aboard bulls 5 months after suffering a skull fracture that required emergency brain surgery. Now, on the eve of the last day of the finals, Silver Select had pounded Shivers's back, strained his left arm, and stomped on his right arm.

Less than 24 hours later, Shivers returned to the arena, ignored the pain, and climbed onto Tar Baby. He felt every bit of Tar Baby's 2,000 pounds beneath him as the bull leaned against the back of the chute. The bull thrashed and reared as Shivers made his wrap, weaving the rope between the ring finger and pinkie of his left hand—a "suicide wrap," they call it, because running the rope between the two fingers makes it harder for the bull to pull it out of a rider's hand but also harder for the cowboy to let go. About half of the PBR's riders use the suicide wrap and risk dangerous hang-ups.

Shivers fidgeted, trying to get comfortable on the anxious bull; and with Tar Baby still wriggling, he called for the gate.

"Go."

The bull lunged forward with a savage buck, his massive head plunging down and his hind legs kicking high into the air. Shivers stayed centered. And when Tar Baby cut hard to the right, Shivers cut with him. At the last instant, the bull reversed directions. But Shivers anticipated the move, and . . . *Yes.*

The buzzer had sounded. Shivers, pulling the tail of his rope and easing out of the suicide wrap, had ridden the 2,000-pound beast.

Bailing out to the right, Shivers landed on all fours, popped to his feet, and broke into a huge grin as he jogged away from the bull. Then he threw his cowboy hat into the air, an exclamation point following the ride that clinched the 2003 season championship. In the world of bull riding, his financial reward would be unprecedented.

In the beginning, the reward was bragging rights. Rodeo sprung up in the Southwest, an outgrowth from the men on horseback who appeared on the dusty plains after the Civil War ended in 1865. Fueled by liquor and pride, the cowboys boasted about their skills, and arguments led to exhibitions. In full swing by the 1930s, organized rodeos featured calf roping, steer wrestling, bareback riding, and saddle bronc riding. The bull riding always came last, because promoters knew the most dangerous event would hold the crowds for the entire show. Yet the top bull riders competed for just enough money to stay on a circuit replete with liquor, gambling, and accommodating women. That began to change in 1992, when 20 riders seeking more money and input broke away from the Professional Rodeo Cowboys Association (PRCA), which for 50 years had controlled pro rodeo. The riders pitched in $1,000 apiece with the idea of starting their own tour—the Professional Bull Riders, Inc. A decade later, at the 2003 finals, came a watershed moment: Shivers, the newly crowned champion, taking home a $1 million bonus, the first in rodeo history.

In addition to the fans watching that last day of the 2003 finals inside the Thomas & Mack Center, more than two million television viewers watched on NBC, certifying bull riding as one of America's fastest-growing spectator sports. The sport appealed to those who loved to watch danger and the accompanying wrecks. In fact, some saw the PBR as the next NASCAR. But PBR executives still felt they needed a superstar. On November 9, 2003, inside the Thomas & Mack Center, it looked as if they'd found him.

With his pale blue eyes, light brown hair, and stubble-free face, Chris Shivers looked closer to 18 than 24. He stood only 5 feet 5 inches tall. But in the world of bull riding, he was a giant. "The Tiger Woods of our sport" is what the PBR's chief executive officer called him.

Shivers grew up in the two-stoplight farming community of Jonesville in central Louisiana. Every year his father, Glynn, took him to the Black River Roundup, the town's annual rodeo, and every year Chris waited for the bulls. What a sight: cowboys sitting astride bulls built like railroad cars, the tough men gripping their braided ropes and holding on for dear life as the 1-ton animals bucked and the crowd frantically cheered. From the day he watched his first rodeo, Shivers wanted to ride a bull and make the crowd cheer.

When he was 12, he and a friend used rope to rig a metal barrel to four trees, and presto—they had their own bull. One boy sat on the barrel while the other pulled on the rope to simulate bucking action. They spent hours riding that barrel; and when Shivers turned 13, his father let him ride the real thing.

It was a spring night in 1992. They drove 2 hours and pulled into the dirt parking lot at the wooden bullring in Bastrop, Louisiana. Glynn Shivers signed the liability waiver, and Chris climbed aboard M1, a black and white bull. The chute gate opened. M1 lunged forward. Almost as soon as the ride started, it ended, with Shivers tumbling to the ground.

But he stood up, dusted off his jeans, and grinned. The adrenaline that shot through his body had produced a sensation he'd never experienced, the greatest sensation imaginable. Some riders said it made them feel more alive. For little Chris Shivers, it made him feel like a man.

He continued to ride despite his parents' fears, and he rode with flair—small carriage upright, free hand whipping high and hard, spurring with his right foot. At 16, he won the Louisiana state high school bull riding championship. He also competed on a professional rodeo circuit in Louisiana and won a $17,000 truck. Soon Shivers was making $30,000 to $40,000 a year, about as much as his father made operating a backhoe.

The day he turned 18, he joined the PBR as one of more than 500 riders vying for a spot on the Built Ford Tough Series (BFTS). They were coveted spots, awarded to the riders ranked in the top 45 based on total earnings in PBR events. Shivers climbed behind the wheel of his truck and set out for the PBR's minor leagues, a two-tier circuit spread out across America's back roads.

In less than a month, he'd won enough money to crack the top 45.

Three years later, Shivers had an agent, a Web site, endorsement deals, and, after winning the 2000 PBR title, the prized gold buckle encrusted with diamonds that's awarded to the world champion. He was profiled in *Newsweek, Sports Illustrated,* and *USA Today* and inducted into *Rolling Stone* magazine's Sports Hall of Fame. Yet he was a reluctant star, dreading media appearances or being away from home for more than a few days at a time. He felt most comfortable on his ranch in Jonesville and passed the time roping calves and hunting wild hogs. But after he won his second PBR championship on November 9, 2003, it seemed as though there was no place Shivers would rather be than on center stage in the Thomas & Mack Center. He stared at the oversize winner's check and the numbers in black marker that, next to "Amount," read: "$1,000,000."

"I just can't get my eyes off all them zeros," Shivers said.

But eventually he would turn his attention to the '04 season and the riders who stood in the way of his becoming the first three-time PBR champion. The only other rider capable of doing it first was Adriano Moraes, but the notion of the 33-year-old Brazilian's winning another title looked remote at best. During the 2003 season, Moraes's gift had all but vanished.

He'd fallen off so many bulls in a row that he'd lost count. During one televised event, a commentator declared that Moraes should retire. Not just any commentator, mind you, but Tuff Hedeman—the four-time world champion and bull riding icon.

The charismatic Brazilian turned combustible. After getting bucked off one bull, he punched a sponsorship sign and broke his hand. He snapped at his wife and their three young sons. Despite having won PBR championships in 1994 and 2001, he began to wonder whether maybe it really was time to quit. And Shivers thought his main competition would come from the rider who'd chased him throughout 2003.

No one eyed the PBR throne more hungrily than Justin McBride, the lean Oklahoman who had finished runner-up to Shivers as the PBR's reserve world champion. Having finished in the top five in each of the past three seasons yet with no world championship to show for it, Justin McBride had become Justin *McBridesmaid*—and in some ways the perfect foil to Shivers.

Shivers spoke in a reserved, quiet tone, while McBride's foghorn voice served as the regular soundtrack inside the PBR's locker room. McBride expressed pride in not having brushed his hair for 2 years and, depending on the occasion, used the expression "fart stick" as an insult or a term of endearment. He was 24, with a narrow face and deep blue eyes, and was pure cowboy: a drinker, a gambler, and a chronic cusser.

On the road he brought his acoustic guitar and entertained his buddies with crude songs. Some riders worked with coaching gurus, studied videotape, and talked ceaselessly about technique. McBride broke down the nuances of his sport like this: "All it is, is holding on for 8 seconds."

It was only a matter of time, veteran riders told him, and that time looked imminent on October 5, 2003.

That day in Atlantic City, with three regular-season events left before the finals, he overtook Shivers in the standings. The race was on. In Grand Rapids, Michigan, the next week, entering the championship round, Shivers had slipped back in front of McBride by the thinnest of margins—a single point. But now McBride was settling on top of Mission Pack with a chance to regain the lead. He'd never heard of the bull but, once out of the chute, realized the sucker was a fierce bucker. After a few straight-ahead jumps, Mission Pack kicked up his hindquarters and gave them a twist, spinning McBride over the right side. McBride slammed to the dirt, and an instant later Mission Pack's right hind hoof slammed McBride.

X-rays showed he had a broken rib and punctured right lung. Laid up in a hospital bed, McBride wept out of frustration.

Back home in Elk City, Oklahoma, where he had moved with his parents, he was too sore to brush his teeth or dress himself. His girlfriend, Michelle Beadle, bathed him for 2½ weeks. But when x-rays showed the hole in his punctured lung had closed, the pain was irrelevant. Shivers had widened his lead, but McBride still had a shot at the championship. With his ribs heavily wrapped, he headed to Las Vegas.

On the first night of the 2003 finals, McBride not only stayed on Moody Blues for the required 8 seconds but also rode him for the highest score of the round. Two days later, on the last day of the finals, McBride was within striking distance of Shivers. But in the final round, he got bucked off Mossy Oak Mudslinger; and Shivers, riding Tar Baby earlier that day, clinched the championship.

If only McBride had been healthy, the experts said, surely he would have captured the elusive gold buckle, making him a clear top contender for the 2004 championship. But during the 2003 season, everybody—Shivers, McBride, and Moraes included—had taken note of Mike Lee. He was a 20-year-old Texan with undeniable talent and the unmistakable air of an outsider. One of the things that set him apart was the protective helmet with a titanium face guard he wore in a culture where most riders frowned upon the headgear and wore only cowboy hats. Yet the headgear may have saved Lee's life.

In May 2003, at a rodeo in Arkansas, Lee suffered a head-to-head collision with a bull. He wanted to go straight home that night, but his mother insisted he go to the hospital. She, too, probably saved his life. Blood had settled on Lee's brain, and doctors performed emergency surgery. The zipperlike scar on the right side of his skull provides a reminder of the near-fatal wreck.

At the time of the injury, Lee was in third place in the standings and chasing Shivers and McBride. The neurosurgeon told him he'd need 6 to 8 months of recuperation before he could ride again—provided he still had the heart for it. Lee returned to action in 3 months.

Though out of the race for the championship by the time he returned to action, Lee finished the season in sixth place, won more than $90,000, and stayed on 62 percent of his bulls—the best riding percentage of the 2003 season. Cody Custer, a onetime champion, was among those predicting Lee would be a future superstar. Others wondered if he could stand up to the pressure.

At the 2003 finals, Lee had successfully ridden only one of four bulls. But no one was tougher on Lee than Mike himself. He was a perfectionist, a devout Christian, and the most reclusive rider on tour. With his head down, he walked past most people as if they didn't exist. Fellow riders knew he was talented but also suspected he was troubled. Most of them just had no idea why.

As mysterious as Lee was a cowboy-themed billboard that, during the 2003 finals, towered within sight of the Thomas & Mack Center. "Deep-Fried Twinkies," it advertised, competing for attention with flashing neon lights and towering casinos dominating the skyline in a city overrun with buckle bunnies, as female rodeo groupies are known. Bull riding and the Twinkie, both quintessentially American. But the placement of the billboard was as incongruous as, well, the sight of bull riders swaggering into a packed arena to the sound of blaring rock music, pyrotechnics, and explosions, courtesy of the PBR.

The quest to learn more about deep-fried Twinkies, buckle bunnies, and bull riders was about to begin, and so was the PBR's 2004 season. It would start in Jacksonville, Florida, with Shivers aiming to become the tour's first three-time champion. With McBride hoping to end his hard luck. With Moraes wondering if he could revive his career. With

Lee wanting to prove he could ride under pressure. With Little Yellow Jacket bucking for an unprecedented third Bull of the Year award. And with political tension between a bull riding icon and the tour's chief executive officer threatening to pull apart everything the riders had worked for over the past decade.

At stake was nothing less than the $1 million bonus, the prized gold buckle, and the future of the PBR.

TWO

THE MARATHON BEGINS

⊛

Jacksonville, Florida
Saturday, December 27, 2003

Ninety minutes before the start of the season opener, Justin
McBride and three other riders sat side by side at a table,
signing autographs. The single-file line of fans snaked out
of view. It included fathers and sons dressed in cowboy
outfits, single mothers wearing too-tight jeans, preteen
girls caked with eye shadow, and buckle bunnies clad in
spaghetti-string tops.

The requests came fast and furious.

"Is it okay to take your picture, Justin?"

"As long as you don't think it'll break your camera."

"Can I give you a hug?"

McBride stood up and obliged.

"This is the man. This is Justin McBride," a father told his young son. "Shake his hand."

McBride's calloused right hand extended across the table.

The riders stayed on their best behavior, even if some of the fans didn't. Cindy Jones and Angie Bass, two middle-aged women, ogled the riders. Jones explained that their husbands were somewhere in the woods. "They're hunting deer, and we're hunting cowboys," she said, adding that they watched the PBR on TV, but this was their first live event. "We want to smell the bulls. We want to get that close."

One step inside the arena was all it took. The place smelled of dirt, sweat, and manure. It was a pleasantly familiar smell for McBride, who 20 minutes later headed down to the arena floor for a question-and-answer session in front of about 100 fans. Kaleb McNeil, a 7-year-old boy dressed from head to toe in cowboy gear, asked a question that McBride strained to hear.

"He wants to know how you can handle those bulls," the boy's mother said.

McBride grinned.

"That's something I'm still trying to figure out," he said. "I think we're all still learning. I don't think it's a sport you can ever have completely figured out."

With the Q-and-A session over and less than an hour to go before the scheduled seven o'clock start of the Florida Times-Union Invitational, McBride headed back to the locker room. Walking up from behind, he wrapped his arms around Chris Shivers and squeezed.

Shivers whipped around. The two stood face-to-face.

"Cocksucker," McBride said, breaking the silence.

They exchanged grins like long-lost brothers. Almost 2 months had passed since their season-long duel ended, and it'd been 5 weeks since they'd seen each other. In fact, no rider had seen McBride during the 5 weeks following the postfinals all-star event. For those who asked, he explained his disappearance. First, he'd taken refuge deep in the woods in Elk City. Still healing from his rib and lung injuries, McBride had been too sore to pull back the bow and arrow he used to hunt deer. Didn't matter. He was hunting for peace of mind. Three weeks later, he'd flown to Italy with his girlfriend. The thing he liked best about the 2½-week trip was that none of the Italians knew who he was or asked him when he was going to finally win a championship. McBride didn't want to talk about the 2003 season or his injuries, didn't want to talk about bull riding at all. But from the moment he stepped into the locker room in Jacksonville, his voice boomed at its regular volume.

Not everybody appreciated the obscenity-laced soundtrack. It was a small locker room, and in it gathered a diverse group of young men. The beer drinkers and the born-agains. The faithful and the philanderers. Those seeking eternal life in heaven and those looking to raise hell. There they all were, dressed in their starched jeans and starched Western shirts, rubbing rosin onto their custom-made bull ropes and removing the lint from their cowboy hats, the PBR's top riders all squeezed inside the same locker room deep in the bowels of Veterans Memorial Arena.

This is where it all began. The 2004 season. The chase for $1 million.

From the entryway of the locker room, a handful of PBR officials surveyed the surroundings. The contingent of riders included Australians, Brazilians, Canadians, a Mexican, and, of course, the Americans. They would spend much of the next 10 months together, hopscotching the country, sharing hotel rooms, and enduring broken ribs, busted lips, and broken dreams. From this motley group would come the next world champion.

But one of the best-known riders was missing. Adriano Moraes was nowhere to be seen. Word was, on the way to the airport in Moraes's home country of Brazil, his truck had broken down. In 2003 he'd qualified for the finals but finished the season 29th, humiliating for the two-time champion. He'd left the finals in Las Vegas vowing to come back stronger than ever. But now some wondered if he was coming back at all.

As the seven o'clock start grew near, the riders grew quiet and looked up. Tuff Hedeman, president of the PBR and among the best riders ever, stood before them. "Y'all know the rules," he said, "so I'm not going to go over them now."

The basics were simple: The clock started when a bull's shoulder or hip crossed the plane of the chute. If the rider stayed on for 8 seconds without touching the bull with his free hand, without touching the ground, and without allowing the bull rope to come out of his hand, he qualified for a score. Two judges, allotted 25 points each to score the rider's performance, looked for good control, body position, and how well he stayed centered over the bull throughout the ride; and spurring the bull earned extra points. The same judges, allotted another 25 points each to score the bull's performance, looked for speed, power, and directional changes, such as a drop in the front end, a kick from the back end, and action when airborne. The scores were combined for a potential total of 100 points, with a 90-point ride the mark of excellence.

At the end of the season, the top 45 riders ranked by total earnings qualified for the finals in Las Vegas. But it was the points, with up to 600 available to each rider at a 1-day event and up to 900 available to each rider at a 2-day event, that would determine the world champion.

Unlike the 1-day event in Jacksonville that kicked off the start of the 2004 season, all but five of the 27 regular-season events ran 2 days, with a minimum purse of $80,130. Four of those events were Bullnanzas, premiere stops that predated the PBR and were vital to the tour's early growth. But Hedeman had no time to review those details as the scheduled introductions for the season opener approached.

The bulls were waiting. So was a sellout crowd of more than 12,000. It was showtime.

With the fringe of their colorful leather chaps swishing and the star-shaped rowels on their spurs clink-clink-clinking on the concrete floor, the bull riders paraded out of the locker room and down the concrete tunnel. They were greeted by explosions, pyrotechnics, and blaring rock music. "This ain't a rodeo," the PA announcer thundered. "This is the one and only PBR!"

The smell of smoke from the extinguished fireworks mingled with the smell of bull manure as Bart Jackson settled onto Drifter for the first ride of the year. Both needed a solid performance in the worst way.

Jackson, a Mississippi native with a stare colder than dry ice and 2 weeks from turning 24, had missed 4 months the previous season with a broken foot and broken collarbone and finished the year by getting bucked off on 10 of his last 11 rides. Drifter had been successfully ridden 10 consecutive times—a sure way for a bull to end his bucking career. The gate opened, and Drifter came out as if he knew he was headed for the slaughterhouse. Feebly jumping and kicking in a circle to the right, the 1,500-pound bull looked as ferocious as an overgrown calf. Jackson coasted to the buzzer for a 78.5-point score, and Mike Lee followed with an 86-point ride on Happy Jack. Two riders out . . . two qualified scores . . . it all looked so easy. Then came the face-plants, the thud landings, and the painful reality. Over the next 15 rides, 11 bulls won the battle, tossing the rider before the buzzer. That was more like it in the lopsided mismatch of man versus beast.

Without coaches, they went through their own preride rituals. Some, like Lee, sought seclusion. But most of the 45 riders waited on the metal deck that was sandwiched between the back pens and the chutes. There they squatted and stretched their groins, went through simulated bull ride moves, helped each other pull up the slack of the bull ropes, shouted encouragement, and burned off nervous energy. Tobacco juice fell like raindrops, and those in search of a nicotine buzz had no trouble finding it.

"Have any chew?" one rider asked another.

"Does a one-legged duck swim in circles?" he replied.

"Does a pond ripple when a duck farts?" countered the other.

Out came the tin of Copenhagen.

When it was time to ride, each man zipped up his black protective vest, jammed in his mouthpiece, climbed into the chute, and settled on top of the beast. With his rosin-coated bull rope wrapped around the bull's midsection and cowbells tied to the end of the bull rope so the rope would fall rather than getting tangled when released, the rider pulled up the slack, made his hand wrap, and waited for the stock contractor to wrap the flank strap around the bull's hindquarters.

Then came the rider's signal—a nod or "Let's go, boys" or simply

"Go"—and the gateman swung open the chute gate. The clock started, and so did the violent dance.

Of the first 18 riders, only eight managed to stay on their bulls for 8 seconds, and it was no surprise to those familiar with the greatest mismatch in sports. The average rider failed to stay on more than half of the time. But the man up next was no average rider.

Sitting atop Extreme, Chris Shivers tried to get settled as the bull shifted in the chute. Shivers slapped the bull on the back, slapped him again, and reset the tail end of his bull rope. With the bull as steady as he'd get, Shivers signaled with a "Let's go," and the chute gate swung open.

Springing out from its hindquarters, Extreme dive-bombed, then lunged again before a full second had elapsed. Shivers leaned forward, up on his rope, chin down, free hand at a 90-degree angle—textbook. But the white bull with brown spots was just getting started. He spun hard to the right, away from Shivers's riding hand, and unleashed a series of bucks as he picked up speed. The kicks sent the bull's back end high into the air and each time jerked Shivers a little more off center.

Down he went, Shivers sailing off the side of the bull before the 8-second buzzer sounded. He popped back on his feet and hustled to the side. The three bullfighters—not to be confused with the barrelman, who was responsible for entertaining the crowd—stood ready to intervene if the bull went after Shivers. Apparently satisfied with his victory, Extreme exited through the center gate and went back to the holding pens.

Moments later the gateman moved in front of the chute holding Slider, a brown and white speckled bull. He was unridden in 13 attempts, but straddled atop his back now was Justin McBride. The bull rocked and thrashed in the chute, and McBride waited for the right moment before giving his quick nod to the gateman.

The chute gate swung open, and the bull charged out and turned back to the left, knocking McBride out of the pocket. Three jumps later, the bull rope slid through McBride's right hand, and he slipped off the back end of Slider before the 8-second buzzer sounded. McBride crawled to a metal fence between the chutes and pulled himself to his feet, but he had company.

Unlike the bull Shivers rode, this one wanted more. Ignoring the outstretched hand of a bullfighter, Slider zeroed in on McBride, shoved his stubby horns into the rider's gut, and pinned him against the metal fence. Standing on the deck behind the chutes, a rider threw his cowboy hat, which bounced off the giant bull like a BB pellet would've bounced off King Kong's chest.

McBride wriggled free and staggered off with his hand over his right eye as the bullfighters distracted the bull and led him out of the center gate. Just like that, the top two riders from 2003 were done for the night. Neither would make the championship round featuring the 15 riders with the highest scores from the first round.

The championship round, also known as the short-go, featured not only the night's top-scoring riders but also the PBR's fiercest bulls. Bulls like Jack Daniels Happy Hour, Hammer, Kid Rock, Sling Blade, and, of course, the great Little Yellow Jacket. Like missiles, they were loaded into the chutes while the broadcasters on the Outdoor Life Network (OLN)—the cable station that broadcasts every BFTS event except for the eight televised by NBC—set the stage for the championship round. They had 15 minutes to fill while the dirt guy—who was responsible for finding and trucking in 3 million pounds of dirt for every BFTS event—operated a Peterbilt skiploader and smoothed out the surface in front of the chutes. The leveled dirt would provide better footing for the bulls and a softer landing for the riders—and, as usual, there would be teeth-rattling, bone-jarring landings during the championship round.

That night it was Rob Bell, a 26-year-old Canadian, who got the chance to ride Little Yellow Jacket. A slim chance. Four seconds into the ride, Little Yellow Jacket sent Bell flipping over his massive head. Bell's chin clipped the bull's left horn, opening a gash that required three stitches. He had no one to blame but himself and the PBR's computer, which randomly matched the riders and bulls.

Six weeks removed from the finals, where he'd won a $20,000 bonus as the PBR's 2003 Bull of the Year, Little Yellow Jacket looked as ferocious as ever. And that night in Jacksonville, he and his four-legged friends dominated. Two other riders suffered chin gashes that required stitches before Mike Lee, wearing his signature helmet, boarded Kid

Rock, 2003 runner-up as Bull of the Year. With a small cross dangling from the zipper of his vest, Lee made his hand wrap, pounded his left fist closed, and nodded for the chute gate.

As Kid Rock lurched out, the spur on Lee's left boot got caught in the rails. The force of the lunging bull yanked Lee's foot loose as he tumbled off the bull. But the ride wasn't over. Lee was hung up; with his hand still caught in the rope and the bull still bucking, Lee tried to stay on his feet. Kid Rock jerked him up and down off the ground like a mad puppeteer.

The force finally pulled Lee's hand free and nearly pulled his riding shoulder out of its socket. He squeezed his eyes closed and grimaced while his arm hung limp.

Because he'd failed to get out of the chute cleanly, Lee would get a reride option—an opportunity to ride another bull, also awarded when the judges determined a bull performed so poorly that the rider didn't have a fair chance to post a high score. Lee looked in greater need of medical attention than another bull ride. Still clutching his arm and 10 feet from the exit gate, Lee turned around and twirled his right index finger. Then he nodded at an official.

Yes, he was taking the reride later in the round. After all, this was the same guy whose scar on the right side of his head was a reminder that he'd come back from emergency brain surgery 3 months sooner than the doctor had predicted he would.

Next up, Jody Newberry, the 2003 Rookie of the Year, on Moody Blues, who on average bucked off 65 percent in 4.5 seconds. Like clockwork, 4 seconds into the ride, Newberry was slipping off the right side of the bull.

"Hustle, Jody! Hustle!" riders behind the chutes shouted.

As Moody Blues spun to his right, Newberry straightened up. He held on until the 8-second buzzer sounded and with his 10th qualified ride in the last 11 attempts showed why he was considered the hottest rider on tour. His 89-point score was just shy of the coveted 90-point club, the mark of excellence, but enough to move Newberry into the lead with the highest cumulative score on two bulls.

Sling Blade, Baby Cakes, Night Life, and Blueberry Wine made quick work of the next four riders, and back into the chutes climbed Lee. This time he settled onto Bullet Proof, a bull ridden six times in 10 attempts and the same bull Lee had ridden at the 2003 finals for 89 points. He nodded for the gate, and Bullet Proof blew into the open space. The bull took two jumps, turned to the right, and Lee was done.

Unable to hang on to the rope with his injured arm, he tumbled to the dirt. The crowd applauded his effort, then braced for the final ride. One man stood between Newberry and the victory—well, for precisely 4.7 seconds he did. That's how long it took Silver Select to buck off Brian Wooley and secure a winner's check of $32,490 for Newberry. The riders finishing between second and 10th won a combined $47,000, while the rest of the 35 went home empty-handed—save a one-night appearance fee of $200, barely enough to cover hotel, travel, and food expenses, even when piling in four to a truck and four to a room and eating fast food.

Life in the PBR was a far cry from life in the Professional Golfers Association Tour, where the top 125 pros got free rental cars and free accommodations, and the top 50 money winners during the 2003 season earned no less than $1.3 million each. During the 2003 PBR season, Shivers earned $1.2 million—with his million-dollar bonus to be paid out $100,000 a year for 10 years. Every other rider in the top 10 made no less than $112,000. But no rider 30th or lower on the money list made more than $54,000; and Steven Shelley, 50th on the list, earned just $20,847.19.

Top rookies in the National Football League and the National Basketball Association got millions of dollars before they even suited up. And those were guaranteed salaries. In bull riding, there are no guarantees—other than pain.

After being presented an oversize winner's check in Jacksonville, Newberry looked like he'd just made a hole in one. "I tell you what. I surely wasn't planning on winning this one," Newberry said with a loopy smile during a TV interview. "I didn't even get my hair cut or nothing before I got out here. I'm not presentable right now. But I'm going to go home and get my hair cut and come back ready to win another one."

Facing a $500 fine from the PBR if they skipped the postevent auto-
graph session, Newberry and the other able-bodied riders returned to
the arena. A PBR employee waited with a boxful of Sharpies and
checked the riders' names off a list as they took their pens and headed
into the arena, where 1,000 fans waited for a chance to get up close and
personal with their favorites. Hedeman and the other PBR executives
understood the value of giving fans a chance to connect with the
riders—something that would've been impossible in the NFL, NBA,
and Major League Baseball.

The riders circled the arena, signing cowboy hats, programs, ticket
stubs, and anything fans asked them to autograph. They also posed for
pictures and waited for the regular propositions.

"Where are you going after this?" a comely groupie once asked rider
Cody Whitney.

"To my hotel room," Whitney said.

"Can I come?"

"I don't know. I'll have to call my wife and see."

But it was mostly a wholesome sight—until later, when at darkened
bars or hotel rooms, buckle bunnies asked riders to sign their breasts.
On the rodeo circuit, it was a tradition that allowed riders to get into
the groupies' shirts before the groupies got into the riders' pants.

As the autograph session came to an end that night, the riders
headed back to the locker room to gather their equipment. Several
grabbed bottles of Bud Light from tubs that were loaded with beer before every event, while others grabbed bottled water. It was clear the
riders were heading in separate directions, some back to the hotel for
the night and others to the designated after-event party bar—something the PBR typically held at a country-and-western bar and advertised to fans as a chance to get autographs and mingle with the riders.

Back at the hotel, riders Cory Melton, Ross Coleman, and J. W. Hart
drank beer in the lobby while waiting for Hedeman, who, as usual, had
the use of a limousine. Beer in hand, Hedeman returned, and the riders
fell in line behind him and piled into the black stretch limo. Talk turned
to beer drinking and bar fights and women—like some of the women
who scurried into the bathroom at the 8 Seconds bar to fix their lipstick

and hike up their halter tops as midnight and the black stretch limo approached.

Inside the bar a small crowd formed around a mechanical bull. Cowboy hat pulled low, the rider bobbed, rocked, and whirled in rhythm with the machine. Suddenly someone blurted out, "It's a girl."

Indeed it was. A girl named Candace Middleton. Twenty-one, trim, and cowboy-tough pretty.

One jerk too many, and off the mechanical bull she went, her cowboy hat falling off and her long red hair tumbling out. She walked away looking proud. She drove dump trucks 6 days a week for a living but dreamed about riding bulls. No woman had ever competed at a PBR event, and most of the world's top riders found the notion of a woman riding bulls against men laughable. Women did ride bulls in organized competitions for small prize money, but they were required to stay on for only 6 seconds and had the option of holding their bull ropes with both hands.

Riding one-handed, Candace said, she became the first woman to ride a bull at the 8 Seconds bar. In another part of the bar, patrons who signed a waiver could try to ride real bulls. But tonight, healing from a calf injury, Candace rode only the mechanical bull. Earlier, she'd gone to the BFTS event at Veterans Memorial Arena to watch the world's best riders and hoped to get some advice during the postevent autograph session.

"Don't do it," one rider told her. "It's too dangerous. . . . Quit."

"That's one thing I won't do," responded Candace.

Later, in the dim lights of the loud bar, other women showed similar determination as Candace—not to ride a bull but to climb atop the riders. Riders guzzled free beer, leaned against the bar, and waited for the buckle bunnies to approach. Approach they did, as if pulled by magnetic force. The riders surveyed the pickings and searched for one they could take to the hotel for the night.

About 90 minutes later, Ross Coleman and Cory Melton—tall, strapping riders and two of the buckle bunnies' favorites—stood behind two young, shapely blondes. The pawing began. Earlier that night, a stranger had asked one of the women if her breasts were real. She looked offended and determined to prove they were. So there, in plain view of dozens of bar patrons, she lowered her top and pulled out her right breast, and the man gave a squeeze.

"They're real, all right," he said, grinning.

When 8 Seconds closed down for the night and Hedeman led the way back to the limo, he did so with three fewer riders. Coleman and Melton had left with the two blondes determined to join them.

The good news for the bull riders going home alone was that they'd survived the night unscathed. Shortly before closing time, outside the bar, tempers had flared. Someone had pulled a butterfly knife. Bouncers tackled the man. Someone had punched the man's wife. All hell had broken loose before the cops arrived. The limo driver recounted the details, and the riders looked disappointed they'd missed the action.

Pulling up at the hotel at two-thirty in the morning, they staggered out of the limo. Two riders went in search of more beer. The others went in search of their rooms.

Three hours later, still pitch dark outside, it was quiet enough inside the hotel lobby to hear a cow pie drop. The ding of the elevator broke the silence.

Out staggered the first bull rider.

Another ding. Another rider.

Another ding. Another rider.

Another ding. Another rider.

Hungover bull riders filtered into the hotel lobby with most of the sober riders still in bed.

Out of the elevator came J. W. Hart. His initials stood for John Wesley, but some of the announcers fibbed, telling the crowd they stood for John Wayne. That morning in Jacksonville, J. W. Hart looked like John Wayne after a weeklong stagecoach ride. Red circles rimmed his glassy eyes. But when someone mentioned they were surprised to see him up so early, Hart grinned.

"We're cowboys," said Hart, known as the Iron Man because he'd ridden in 197 events before a torn groin muscle in 2003 ended his streak. "That's the way we do it. Just takes some conditioning. Like running a marathon."

A marathon. Perfect. Each of the 27 regular-season events would serve as roughly 1 mile on the marathon-like race to the finals starting October 22 in Las Vegas. The opening leg of the race would be grueling, with Jacksonville the first of 19 consecutive weekends of Built Ford Tough Series events.

Hart dumped the last of his bags into the trunk of a taxi and climbed into the backseat with two other riders. Not far behind were the others. The morning was young, and so was the season. But the riders had planes to catch and dreams to chase, and so off they went in rental cars, shuttles, and taxis, one weekend event down and 26 more to go before the finals, with the $1 million bonus and gold buckle waiting to be claimed.

The marathon had begun.

CONCESSIONS	
Italian sausage	$5
Jumbo hot dog	$4.50
Nachos grande	$7

Alas, no deep-fried Twinkies. "That would be an idea, though," mused Myra Rivette, administrative assistant for concessions.

STANDINGS

1	Jody Newberry	520.5 points	6	Craig Sasse	252 points
2	Dan Henricks	453.5 points	7	Cody Hart	252 points
3	Dave Samsel	419.5 points	8	Gilbert Carrillo	201.5 points
4	Brian Wooley	314 points	9	Mike Lee	166 points
5	Jason Bennett	314 points	10	Cody Whitney	135.5 points

THREE

HEADS & TAILS

Corey Navarre fished a quarter out of his pocket. He looked at Lee Akin.

"Heads the bed, tails the couch," Navarre said.

It was past midnight, about 2 hours after the first night of competition ended at the PBR's third stop, a 2-day event in northwest Louisiana. An hour-long Bible study group had just broken up, and Navarre and Akin were ready for bed. Best friends, travel partners, and former rodeo team-mates at Southwestern Oklahoma State, they stood out on the bull riding circuit. Navarre is white and Akin is black, one of the few black riders who'd reached the Built Ford Tough Series.

In keeping with rodeo tradition, they were sharing a

room with two other riders. But for Navarre, Akin, and others treading below the top-10 money winners, sharing a hotel room was more than tradition. It was a way to make ends meet. Riders often slept two to a bed, but the hotel room at the Horseshoe Casino, where the PBR riders were staying, featured an unexpected luxury: beds *and* couches. The coin flip would determine who slept where.

Navarre flipped the quarter into the air, caught it in his right palm, and slapped it on his left wrist.

Heads.

"You're on the couch," Navarre said.

"What?" howled Akin. "You said 'heads the bed'—not that you'd get the bed."

Navarre rolled his eyes.

"Heads, I'm in the bed. Tails, I'm on the couch."

Navarre reflipped the coin, caught it in his palm, and slapped it on his wrist. Heads again.

Akin eyed the quarter as if it might be a two-headed trick coin. Navarre turned it over, revealing tails on the other side. "Satisfied?" he asked.

Akin frowned. Forget the quarter. He was still trying to make heads or tails out of what had happened to his career. Six months earlier he'd been on the cover of the PBR's monthly magazine, *Pro BullRider,* with his photo next to a headline that trumpeted "A Rising Star." At 29 years old, with his high cheekbones, caramel-colored skin, and fashion model looks, he seemed destined for magazine covers.

He graduated from Southwestern Oklahoma State in 2002 with a degree in biology but never seriously considered a career outside of bull riding. After spending several years competing in the PRCA, he turned his attention to the PBR. With a thunderclap, he arrived on the BFTS in 2002, with top-10 finishes in six of his first seven events and $50,000 in winnings.

But an elbow injury sidelined him for 7 weeks, and a knee injury kept him out an additional 8 weeks. His body healed, but his confidence crumbled. Akin proceeded to fall off 18 of his next 20 bulls; and in July, hoping to regain his form at small-time bull riding events, he climbed aboard about 30 more bulls and could count on one hand the number he'd successfully ridden.

Tuff Hedeman added insult to injury. During a PBR telecast, he noted that Akin had a degree in biology and suggested Akin put away his riding gear, put on a white lab coat, and get back to dissecting frogs. Akin felt the world was dissecting him.

He developed his love for rodeo while he was growing up in Hemet, California, at the knee of his mother, DeBoraha. She rode horses and competed in barrel racing and in 1990 became the first black woman to compete in the 20-year history of the International Professional Rodeo Association Finals. In yet another family breakthrough, in 2002 Akin became the only black rider on the PBR's top circuit. Featured in *Savoy* magazine, he was touted by some as the next great black rodeo star. But he wouldn't be the first.

That honor belonged to Bill Pickett, the oldest of 13 children and the son of a former slave. It was at the turn of the 20th century when Pickett invented a rodeo event called bulldogging, better known as steer wrestling. Frustration was the mother of his invention.

The story, according to writer Paul Harwitz, goes like this: In 1903, on a ranch in Rockdale, Texas, a longhorn steer refused to enter a corral. The animal kept scattering the herd, and Pickett lost his patience. Aboard his horse, Pickett rode alongside the steer, jumped off, and wrestled the steer to the ground. The animal kept resisting, so Pickett bit the steer on the lower lip and slammed it to the dirt.

Other black stars followed. Myrtis Dightman, considered the Jackie Robinson of rodeo, broke the color line but never could break through for a world championship. He once asked his white friend and fellow rider Freckles Brown what it would take to win the world championship. "Keep riding like you've been riding—and turn white," Brown replied. With white judges awarding the scores, Dightman had no chance. But he played an important role in breaking the barrier in the 1970s when he met a short and skinny kid from Watts, site of the 1965 riots in Los Angeles County.

Charlie Sampson was his name. Introduced to horses at a young age, Sampson wanted to be a champion bull rider, and he knew Dightman could help. Dightman, by then retired, agreed to tutor Sampson; and in 1982 the kid from Watts became the first black cowboy to win a world bull riding championship. Lee Akin dreamed about becoming the second.

Though prejudice no longer seemed a serious obstacle, Akin occasionally confronted it. Like the incident in Mississippi in 2000. After a rodeo, Akin remembered, he returned to his hotel room before heading to a bar where he was supposed to meet fellow riders.

"When I walked in, it was like a movie: The whole place just stopped and looked at me," Akin told a reporter from the *Florida Times-Union*. "I asked what the cover charge was or if there was a cover charge to a lady near the front door, and the lady just looked at me. Some guy takes me outside and asks me if I saw the sign. There were a bunch of signs, so I asked which one. He pointed to a sign that said, 'This is a private club. We have the right to refuse service,' and goes, 'I think you know what that means.' I asked him if there was a place I could shoot pool, and he said, 'Not around here there ain't,' and just walked away."

At the start of the 2004 season, however, Akin knew the bulls and his self-confidence, not prejudice, were the chief obstacles to his winning the championship. Even his good nights were bittersweet. At the PBR's second stop, Akin made the championship round. Then he drew Little Yellow Jacket, who launched Akin over his horns and kicked him in the head. Akin, frustrated by a string of bad luck and bad rides, grumbled, "I feel like if I didn't wear my seat belt, I'd fall out of my truck."

THE SOFT STRUMMING OF A GUITAR and a stack of Bibles greeted people filtering into CenturyTel Center. Open to the public, the so-called Cowboy Church service attracted about 300 PBR fans, who clustered in one section of the arena. The men removed their cowboy hats when Todd Pierce, a bareback-rider-turned-pastor, stood before them. These were no ordinary fans.

Wearing their PBR T-shirts and PBR jackets, many of them had gathered at a Holiday Inn the day before as if they were attending a family reunion. There was the self-proclaimed Texas Rowdy Bunch, a six-pack of Texans who put a large "Rowdy Bunch" sticker on the side of their van. There was Larry Seamans, who escaped the pressures of work by attending bull ridings and liked to say, "If the PBR don't get your fire going, your wood is wet." Then there were Bill and Peggy Duvall, who wore matching blue and yellow PBR jackets. No fans were more devout than the Duvalls.

The retired couple from West Virginia had known nothing about bull riding when they were flipping through the TV channels in 1995 and came across a PBR event, punctuated by the rapid-fire Texas twang of Donnie Gay, then the PBR's lead commentator. Gay cracked up the Duvalls with his signature lines—"A shot in the shorts," he quipped after a bull hooked his horns into a rider's backside, and "His bell's ringing and nobody's home," he boomed after a rider got dumped on his head and wobbled to his feet. The Duvalls decided they just had to see this in person.

Hooked after attending their first live event, they started going to about half of the PBR's regular-season bull ridings and attended each year's finals in Las Vegas. Bill Duvall, a lanky, white-haired man who looked younger than his age of 73, made his fortune in the automotive and truck service industry. Now he and his auburn-haired wife of 71 spent a small fortune on their annual PBR travels. They bought the PBR's most expensive tickets at $100 apiece, stayed at the PBR headquarter hotels, and occasionally treated the bull riders to steak dinners.

The Duvalls knew all the riders, some well enough that Bill Duvall drank beer with a few—up until 2 hours before the bull riding began. Of course, that was a few years earlier, before the PBR, growing protective of its image, cracked down on such behavior.

Accustomed to socializing with the wealthy, the Duvalls enjoyed the down-home people they met on the PBR tour. There were plenty of them gathered in the Holiday Inn lobby in Bossier City in anticipation of the PBR's third stop of the 2004 season. Many of those fans attended the next day's church service, held more than 8 hours before the first bull would burst out of the chutes on the second night of competition. Some of the riders were still sleeping off hangovers. But

10 of them—including Akin and Navarre—were up and at the arena to praise God.

So was Adriano Moraes.

Suspicion that he'd retired from bull riding had ended the previous week in Worcester, Massachusetts, at the second event of the season. Moraes, absent from the season opener after missing his flight from Brazil, rode all three of his bulls in Worcester and won his first BFTS victory since April 2002.

About 15 minutes into Cowboy Church in Bossier City, Pierce handed the microphone to Moraes, who told the crowd he was there to talk about the best year of his life and the worst season of his career—which were one and the same.

He was stocky, with thick arms and thick legs, and bright eyes that projected warmth. Frowning on the use of profanity in public, Moraes might shout, "Holy macaroni!" Or compliment a bull by calling him a "tough son of a buck." Or substitute "pain in the brain" for "pain in the ass." He turned down offers of $50,000 and up to endorse companies that sold liquor or tobacco, because he didn't want to influence kids to drink or smoke. With his good looks and gregarious personality, he charmed the fans and prompted exchanges like this:

Young girl: "Adriano!"

Moraes: "What??!!"

Young girl: "Our babysitter likes you!"

That Saturday morning, Moraes was at Cowboy Church to share a personal testimony about his abrupt descent only 2 years after winning his second PBR championship. Moraes's undeniable gift for bull riding vanished during the 2003 season, when Tuff Hedeman declared on TV that it was time for the Brazilian to quit. Desperate, Moraes poured all of his energy into preparing for an event in Nashville in June 2003. He started working out, lost 13 pounds, and focused with laserlike intensity. Moraes told his wife, Flavia, that Nashville would be his breakout event and was so convinced that he took her and his three sons with him so they could all enjoy his long-awaited triumph. They witnessed something else.

During the 2-day event, Moraes bucked off both of his bulls; and after the final night of competition, the family went straight back to the hotel room. With the boys sleeping in a bed next to them, Adriano Moraes and his wife wept.

"It's over," Adriano remembers saying. "My career is over."

"It's not over, Adriano," Flavia soothed him.

She was a devout Catholic and, since they'd met 14 years earlier, had urged Adriano to get his priorities in order: God first, family second, then bull riding. But after he'd won the 2001 PBR championship, the order had shuffled. In fact, at times Adriano Moraes thought he was the god of bull riding. So when his career suddenly nose-dived, Moraes lost what defined him. If he was a loser in bull riding, he concluded, he was a loser in life.

But that night in Nashville, after months of ignoring his wife's advice, Moraes decided he had no choice but to let it all go—the pressure, the worry, the fear—to let go of bull riding as the source of his identity and remember he also was a husband, father, and son of God. The next morning, Moraes woke up and looked at his wife with the megawatt smile his family had not seen in months. Adriano and Flavia said nothing. They just smiled.

Over the next several weeks, Moraes's home life improved, and gradually so did his bull riding.

The week before the Horseshoe Louisiana Shootout in Bossier City, Moraes won at Worcester, signaling the Brazilian champion was back and a potential contender for the 2004 championship. Yet during his talk at the church service, he talked only about his tortuous 2003 season.

"I was living behind the shine of my gold buckles, not my spirituality," he said in his Brazilian accent. "If you don't have your faith, you're going to fail, like Adriano Moraes did."

When the church service ended, Navarre and Lee approached Moraes. They'd been sitting near the front row during the talk, spellbound. They told Moraes how much they appreciated his candor, and then the three men huddled in prayer. Hands resting on each other's shoulders, they formed a small circle and bowed their heads. Back at the hotel, other riders were praying Troy Dunn would go back to Australia.

INSTEAD OF "G'DAY, MATE," it was more like "Get lost, mate."

On the first night of the Horseshoe Louisiana Shootout, about an hour before the competition started, Justin McBride was in the locker room, recounting a recent hunting trip—"Killed a big, stupid buffalo with a bow and arrow"—when the legendary Australian walked in.

"Troy Dunn, what are you doing here?" asked B. J. Kramps, a Canadian rider, and without waiting for an answer added, "How long are you here for?"

Once again, before Dunn could answer, Kramps continued, "It must be really encouraging—you show up, and the first thing we ask you is when are you going to leave."

Dunn had sun-bleached brown hair and a tanned face that made him look younger than his 36 years. He was sturdily built at 5 feet 10 inches tall and 165 pounds and had the ethereal calm of Crocodile Dundee. Australia's answer to Moraes, he had won the 1998 PBR championship and more than $1 million on tour. His last full season had been in 1999; and in recent years, he'd become legendary for swooping in from Australia, winning bagfuls of money, and jetting back to his two ranches in Queensland. Back again for a stay of indeterminate length, Dunn said, "It'll be bloody good if I could win some cash."

From across the room, Jody Newberry watched Dunn as if he were in the presence of royalty. "Best bull rider that ever walked the face of the earth," Newberry declared. But now Dunn was among the oldest.

Of the riders who finished the 2003 season ranked in the top 10, the average age was 25, and only one was older than 30—Owen Washburn, 32, who had retired in 2001 before coming back the next season.

But on this night, Dunn wouldn't stay around long. In the first round at Bossier City, after a 79.5-point ride on Tuff Snuff, Dunn stiffened after his dismount and limped out of the arena. He'd aggravated a back injury so badly that he turned down a reride option, unheard of for someone as tough as Dunn. After a visit to the sports medicine room, he left the arena with a sleeve of anti-inflammatory pills and doubtful for the second day of competition—a reminder that bull riding was a young man's game.

FOUR HOURS AFTER THE COWBOY CHURCH Saturday morning, Corey Navarre returned to the near-empty CenturyTel Center and stood behind the chutes. He had muscled shoulders, a square jaw, and the intensity of a Secret Service agent. Behind the curtain of his serious face was an introspective 26-year-old. As he watched the bulls mill about their pens, he contemplated his past and future.

Growing up in Sulphur, Louisiana, Navarre cared little for team sports. He possessed the individualism often associated with the American cowboy and as a teenager got turned on to bull riding. He bought a used mechanical bull and practiced as often as time allowed, but nothing compared to riding the real thing, staring down fear as he climbed atop 1-ton bulls.

"It's man versus beast," he said. "It's not you and five other guys working as a team. It's just you, and you're responsible for your wins or your losses. The challenge, just being able to tame something that's untamable. The feeling of conquering something . . . "

His words drifting off, Navarre gazed at the bulls in the back pens.

"These guys are athletes as well," he said, nodding at the bulls. "They try just as hard to buck us off as we do to stay on them.

"When you get on a rank bull, it's like walking a tightrope. There's no room for mistakes. If you make a mistake, you're going to hit the ground."

After winning more than $175,000 in the PBR during the 2001 season, Navarre took home less than $13,000 the next season; and his 40th-place finish and $45,000 in winnings in 2003 marked only modest improvement. Part of his struggles stemmed from injuries that included a crushed cheek and fractured eye socket, which led to his wearing a helmet, and a blown-out knee that required reconstructive surgery. But even with a clean bill of health as he entered 2004, the first two events of the season offered no sign of a turnaround. Navarre bucked off his only bull at the season opener and rode one of two bulls the next week.

Later that night at the CenturyTel Arena, during the second round of the Horseshoe Louisiana Shootout, Navarre settled atop Lancaster's. When the chute gate opened, the bull lurched hard to the left, then whipped back to the right. Despite his strained riding arm, Navarre looked steadier than the quick-moving bull did. Lancaster's worked into a flat, low spin to the right; and Navarre could have exchanged his riding helmet for a blindfold and still made the 8-second buzzer. He earned only 82.5 points for the ride and that, coupled with his 85.5-point ride on Slingshot the night before, secured him a spot in the championship round. Not that anybody in the sellout crowd of 12,000 was thinking about Navarre. Next up was Louisiana's pride, Chris Shivers.

Before the chute gate even opened, Toe Mash reared up and rocked Shivers. Riders behind the chute reached across Shivers's chest and back to steady him. But Shivers looked unfazed. When he called for the gate, Toe Mash bucked into the open and kicked up his hindquarters as if attempting to do a handstand. But he bucked rhythmically, almost languidly; and Shivers rode effortlessly, spicing the ride by whipping his free hand hard and high in the air. Dismounting to cheers, he earned 86 points and moved into the overall lead.

It was time for the championship round, time to load up the rankest of bulls, time for another look at Little Yellow Jacket, who made rider Spud Whitman look more like Sputnik. Little Yellow Jacket launched the 32-year-old Kansan into orbit before he came crashing back to earth.

Riding eighth in the round, Navarre climbed atop Wild Bill and stayed in rhythm as the bull spun left before a late turn-back to the right. His score: 90 points! Instead of rejoining the riders behind the chutes, Navarre ran toward the locker room with seven riders left, including the crowd favorite. Wild cheers greeted Shivers as he boarded Tahonta, unridden in nine attempts. The chute gate opened, and the bull reared as if in slow motion, then dropped his front end with the force of an anvil. Shivers tumbled off and hit the dirt headfirst. Hands pressed against his forehead, he squeezed his eyes closed in pain and slowly left the arena.

Navarre still had a chance at victory, but there was no sign of him. The next four riders bucked off, leaving one last rider, Brian "Pee Wee" Herman, and one last bull, Pandora's Box. Navarre hustled back behind the chutes and explained he had to get something in the locker room. With that, he popped a false front tooth into his mouth and sheepishly explained he'd lost it not from a bull wreck but from tripping over the family dog. He wanted a full set of teeth just in case he had to do the postevent TV interview.

Almost as soon as Pandora's Box left the chute, he threw Herman to the ground, a vicious buck-off that suggested Little Yellow Jacket might have serious competition for the Bull of the Year award. But the night's competition was over, with Navarre winning his first PBR event since 2001.

Moraes had matched Navarre's 90-point score while becoming only the second rider in the PBR to cover Kid Rock. But Navarre was the only rider to have stayed on all three of his bulls and, by virtue of his top cumulative score, won the event and a check for $27,132.

Later, heading to the locker room after doing his TV interview with a full set of teeth and signing autographs, Navarre sorted through his equipment and his mixed feelings. He was thrilled with his victory but felt badly for his travel partner, Akin, who had bucked off both of his bulls. It led to the awkward situation in bull riding where winners went home with losers.

Carrying his duffel bag packed with equipment over his shoulder, Navarre walked through a phalanx of riders who pounded him on the back in congratulations. He left the building with a smile. And so did Moraes.

With his third-place finish, Moraes moved into first place in the overall standings. As only the Brazilian would say, "Holy macaroni!"

CONCESSIONS

Catfish basket with fries	$6
Funnel cake	$4
Strawberry daiquiri or margarita	$7 small, $9 large

Deep-fried Twinkies. "No," said Chuck Walter, director of food services for CenturyTel Center, "we haven't gone that route yet."

STANDINGS

1	Adriano Moraes	1,354 points	6	Corey Navarre	760 points
2	Jody Newberry	908.5 points	7	Brian Herman	744.5 points
3	Mike Lee	879 points	8	Cody Hart	700 points
4	Reuben Geleynse	823 points	9	Mike White	694 points
5	Jason Bennett	803.5 points	10	B. J. Kramps	690.5 points

FOUR

RIDE AT YOUR
OWN RISK

GREENSBORO, NORTH CAROLINA
SATURDAY & SUNDAY, JANUARY 24 & 25, 2004

In the front yard of a wooden house set back off a two-lane highway in Archdale, North Carolina, two young boys squealed as they rode a metal bucking barrel. One boy pushed and pulled while the other sat atop the barrel and gripped a rope as if riding a real bull. But both of the boys grew quiet when Jerome Davis emerged from the front door of the house.

Davis eased his wheelchair down a wooden ramp and rolled across a dirt yard toward the passenger side of a truck. A friend opened the door and moved aside as Davis's wife, Tiffany, positioned herself between the wheelchair and the truck. Bending over, she wrapped one arm around Davis's legs, the other around his torso, and lifted his 5-foot-11-inch, 165-pound body into the front seat. The boys, who'd been playing on the bucking barrel, and their parents got into another car. They all were headed for the Greensboro Coliseum and for Tiffany and Jerome Davis, the most bittersweet weekend of the year—the PBR's Jerome Davis Challenge.

At the end of the introductions that night in the darkened Greensboro Coliseum, the spotlight turned away from the leading riders and shone near the center gate, illuminating a cowboy in a wheelchair. Before the PA announcer could finish his speech about grit and courage and heroism, the cheering fans rose to their feet. They knew who it was.

Jerome Davis used to ride at the event named in his honor. Now, at age 31, he was raising bulls. Confined to a wheelchair, he was a stark reminder of the sport's inherent dangers and a symbol of perseverance. Davis's crooked grin and soft brown eyes belied his determination.

In 1995, Davis took on all comers in the PRCA and beat them all, becoming the first bull rider from North Carolina and the first from east of the Mississippi River to win a world championship. No one was prouder than his mother, Pam. But as she stood in Greensboro Coliseum, with her son in his wheelchair and under the spotlight, she was terrified by the prospect of one of Jerome's bulls paralyzing another rider. Jerome was aware of the irony of a paralyzed rider breeding potentially killer bulls, but he avoided talking about it. During the PBR's 2-day event named in his honor, however, he would have no choice.

In the first round of competition at the fifth stop of the season, Jody Newberry, looking for his 16th successful ride in the last 19 attempts, pinned his long legs against Blue Jack. Deep into the ride, Newberry fell off the right side, and Blue Jack's hooves came down like teeth from a pitchfork. The hooves plunged and, like an act from God, only grazed the outside of Newberry's legs as they sunk into the dirt. Rolling away as bullfighter Dennis Johnson came in for the save, Newberry scrambled to his feet and then checked the clock: 7.4 seconds. A fraction of a second had separated him from a qualified ride, but a fraction of space had saved him from serious injury.

Aboard Moonshine, McBride made his suicide wrap and nodded for the gate. The bull bucked to the left, spinning like a top, while McBride, his free hand locked at a 90-degree angle, stayed in perfect position—that is, until the buzzer sounded. Dismounting to the right, McBride landed on his knees, and his head whipped forward. The force sent dirt spraying, but McBride was grinning when he reached his feet and saw he'd earned 85.5 points for the ride. Later in the round, Mike Lee shot out of the gates on Dough Boy, and the bull stretched him like a rubber band. Back and forth Lee snapped, pliable enough to make the buzzer and score 83.5 points. Next up, Adriano Moraes on Black Hawk. The bull lunged out right, reversed directions, and worked into a tight spin. Moraes's free hand chopped down like a tomahawk with every buck, and his right spur pounded the bull. As if that didn't show enough control, Moraes dismounted with a quick spin to the right and landed on his feet.

The crowd had witnessed some of the best rides of the season. When the first night of competition ended, however, the most sought-after autograph was Jerome Davis's. Fans pressed forward, leaning over the arena railing and holding out cowboy hats, posters, T-shirts, and programs for him to sign. A friend collected the items and set them atop a clipboard on Davis's lap.

With only partial use of his hands, Davis awkwardly gripped a felt-tip pen between his stiffened fingers and carefully scrawled his name on each item. "Smile, Jerome," urged camera-toting fans, and each time he flashed that crooked grin.

His life had changed forever on March 14, 1998. On that day, entering the Tuff Hedeman Championship Challenge in Fort Worth, Texas, Davis led the PBR standings and in the first round had drawn Knock 'em Out John. Davis knew what to expect from the bull notorious for jerking back its head. Sure enough, seven jumps into the ride, Knock 'em Out John jerked back his head. But the power of the bull laid waste all precautions.

Davis's head slammed against the bull's head. The blow knocked Davis unconscious. He landed on the dirt headfirst.

Tiffany rushed behind the chutes as paramedics carried Davis out on a stretcher; and Tater Porter, a fellow rider, tried to calm her by saying it looked like Davis would be okay. He was wrong. X-rays showed Davis had severed his spinal cord and snapped two vertebrae, which left him paralyzed from the chest down.

When Tiffany told Jerome the doctors said he would never walk again, he wanted to hear it for himself. "I don't want to say never," Jerome Davis remembers the doctor telling him. "I'll give you a 1 percent chance."

"That's all I need," Davis replied.

There was a reason no one east of the Mississippi River had won a world bull riding championship before Davis did. Most kids in North Carolina grew up dreaming of wearing the powder blue basketball uniform of the Tar Heels or getting behind the wheel of a stock car, not wearing cowboy boots with spurs or getting on top of a bull.

Though Davis's family grew up riding horses, most of what he learned about rodeo came from watching the sport on TV. In 1991, competing in bareback, saddle bronc, and bull riding as a high school senior, he finished runner-up for the all-around title at the national high school finals. He drew scholarship offers from the top rodeo programs in the country and settled on Odessa Junior College in Texas, where as a freshman he won the 1992 national collegiate bull riding championship. Just 3 days later, he entered a pro bull riding event in Reno and drew Orange Pop, a bull he knew nothing about—and a bull he'd never forget. Orange Pop slung Davis over its head, crushed his rib cage, broke his collarbone, and punctured his lung. When Davis's mother arrived at the hospital in Reno, she found her son hooked up to tubes. *Let this be the final bull ride,* she thought to herself; yet when she spoke to her son, something else came out of her mouth.

"Jerome, I don't know what your plans are," she remembers saying. "But I'm going to tell you this: It's going to take more than any Orange Pop to keep you down."

It wasn't long before Jerome Davis returned to bull riding.

With the PBR still in its infancy, he and other top bull riders focused on the PRCA. He finished fifth in the world in 1993 and third in '94, and in '95 won it all—the world championship and the gold buckle. As the PBR's purses and stature grew, he turned his attention to the upstart tour and early in the 1998 season emerged as a top contender for the title. Knock 'em Out John ended those hopes and presented Davis with new challenges.

Seven months after he returned home from the hospital, Tiffany and three friends lifted him onto the specially made saddle so he could ride his horse around his property. With Jerome on the wide leather saddle with the high back, his mother blinked back tears as her son slowly rode across a pasture. A month later Davis called his family with surprise news: He and Tiffany, then his longtime girlfriend, had eloped and gotten married. For the newlyweds, no wedding vow rang truer than "for better or for worse."

FEW THINGS ARE AS DIFFICULT AS RIDING A BULL. One of them is for a bull rider to find affordable health insurance. At the time of the accident, Davis had no personal insurance, nothing but the $20,000 policy the PBR carries for each rider at every event. By the end of the first night in the hospital, Davis's insurance benefits had run out. Like other paralyzed riders, he leaned on the rodeo community to bail him out. The PBR, fellow riders, and a few prominent NASCAR drivers helped raise almost $500,000; yet ultimately Davis's medical bills approached $1 million.

One day the Archdale sheriff knocked on Davis's front door and handed Davis a letter. It was a warning. Unless the hospital bills were paid, the letter explained, the Davises' home and assets could be seized.

The couple hired a lawyer. Negotiations began.

The hospital agreed to take roughly $500,000. Thanks to the fundraising, that meant Jerome still had money left from his past winnings. He used some of the money to start a new career raising bulls, but his immediate challenge was getting through the day. In the mornings he struggled to the edge of the bed, gritted his teeth, and, emitting small grunts, wheeled himself into the shower. There he sat under steaming water that loosened his muscles.

As the months passed, Davis stunned his family by what he'd learned to do, such as operate a tractor with handheld gears that allowed him to mow the grass and bale hay on his grandfather's old 120-acre dairy farm, on which Jerome and Tiffany lived. He also oversaw the upkeep of 150 cows, started a bull-breeding program, and helped design a rodeo arena built on the farm.

In addition to the Jerome Davis Challenge—in which Davis had a financial stake—the PBR gave him an event on the Challenger Tour, the PBR's minor league circuit, to be held in Davis's new arena. The inaugural event drew many of the PBR's star riders, who came to honor Davis; and before the first-day competition began, a semitruck pulled up to that wooden house off the two-lane highway in Archdale. Two men unloaded four boxes and a huge platform. Riders and family members wondered what it was. But Jerome Davis knew.

It was a set of handrails he'd ordered, the apparatus he planned to use to learn how to walk again. J. W. Hart and Justin McBride helped set up the handrails; and the next day, with Tiffany steadying her husband and his friend Rob Smets locking his knees, Davis grabbed the handrails and stood with assistance for the first time since his accident. He was willing to try anything in his quest to walk again and once sought information on a faith healer who worked with paraplegics.

Oftentimes, Jerome invited young riders to his ranch to test his bulls. Sitting in the far end of the arena in his wheelchair, he studied the animals as they bucked, and he offered the young riders advice. On Sunday nights, when friends passed the farmhouse and saw the den light on, they knew Davis was there, watching the televised PBR events. In his wheelchair, he'd sway side to side as if riding the bulls himself.

The PBR prize money had skyrocketed since Davis's accident; and in June 2003, he watched the special NBC-televised event during which Shivers rode Little Yellow Jacket for a shot at $1 million. "I wonder how a paralyzed man could ride," he joked at the time. "For a million dollars, I'd love to figure out how."

ON THAT COLD AND SNOWY WEEKEND of the 2004 Jerome Davis Challenge, Greensboro officials blamed the icy roads for dozens of accidents. That wasn't counting the wrecks at the Jerome Davis Challenge.

From his pens in Archdale to the Greensboro Coliseum, Davis hauled a string of his most fearsome bulls, including Wicked Charlie. On day 2 of the event, Cody Hart, a thick 25-year-old who'd won the 1999 PBR championship, drew the bull. Davis was eager to see the matchup. With a front-row view, Davis watched as the chute gate opened and Hart and Wicked Charlie burst out.

The ride lasted 5 seconds.

As Hart hit the ground, the bull rope wrapped around his boot and jerked him underneath Wicked Charlie. Down came the bull's hooves. The first one landed on Hart's right knee; the next crushed Hart's stomach.

Unhooked, Hart ran for the side fence, reached for the top rail, and slumped to the ground. He motioned for help, and the sports medicine team rushed out. The crowd watched in silence.

For 3 long minutes, the trainers and orthopedic surgeon huddled around Hart. The most spectacular wrecks scared the fans. But wrecks like these, resulting in internal injuries, could be far worse. Finally, with assistance, Hart rose to his feet and left the arena.

NBC's cameras were rolling. A national audience was waiting. The show went on.

While fans might have been worried about Hart, they were puzzled with Chris Shivers. After falling off Vegas on day 1, Shivers bucked off Peacemaker on day 2, marking the fifth straight time he'd failed to stay on a bull for 8 seconds.

On his way to the 2003 title, Shivers had ridden 55.7 percent of his bulls. But this season, in 14 attempts, he was riding 35.7 percent and had gotten bucked off each of the three times he'd made the championship round. Already quiet, Shivers grew even more reticent as his slump deepened and the whispers started.

What's wrong with Shivers? Is he hurt? Is he distracted? Is he too content after winning the $1 million to give his best? There were more questions than answers as the Jerome Davis Challenge headed into the championship round.

Little Yellow Jacket continued his rampage, tossing Craig Sasse to the ground and posting the high mark among all 15 short-go bulls. Bo Howdy, with Moraes aboard, bucked as if on a trampoline. Moraes just soared with the bull and scored 86 points on his ninth qualified ride in 11 attempts that season. But Reuben Geleynse, a soft-spoken Canadian, had taken the overall lead with an 86.5-point ride on Coyote; and the competition came down to two more riders: Brent Vincent of Sulphur, Louisiana, and McBride.

Neon Nights, with McBride aboard, lurched out of the chute and then bucked back in. Catching a back hoof on the gates, the bull unhooked himself with another buck and sent McBride to the ground. But the judges ruled McBride had gotten fouled and awarded him a reride. In position to snatch the victory with a qualified score on Shock and Awe, Vincent experienced awe and shock. He slapped the bull with his free hand a fraction of a second before the buzzer sounded. Then came McBride's reride on massive Cheylo. There was no need to pull out the scale to see the bull weighed close to 2,000 pounds, and McBride needed to ride him for 85 points to win the event.

For all Cheylo's strength, he couldn't buck fast enough to shed McBride. Nor could McBride look flashy enough to wow the judges. He earned 84.5 points, matching Geleynse's three-round total of 255.5 points for a share of the victory, and in the overall standings moved past Lee and into second place behind Moraes.

After the event ended, Jerome Davis signed autographs for a half hour before steering his wheelchair out of the arena. Near the exit, he intersected paths with Cody Hart, who on Davis's bull, Wicked Charlie, had suffered a bruised sternum, a cracked rib, torn ligaments in his right knee, and a pulled hamstring.

"You all right?" Davis asked.

"Yeah. But if he'd stepped anywhere else than where he did, he probably would have killed me."

"How you feel?"

"Like shit," Hart said. "Twenty-one hundred pounds is a lot of weight on you."

CONCESSIONS

Chicken tenders with fries	$6
Giant roast beef sandwich	$5
Nachos with cheese, salsa, and hot peppers	$4

Deep-fried Twinkies? Don't even think about it. Said Zia Torabian, assistant food and beverage manager at Greensboro Coliseum: "We have enough fried food."

STANDINGS

1	Adriano Moraes	2,071 points	6	Luke Snyder	1,165.5 points
2	Justin McBride	1,927 points	7	Jody Newberry	1,162 points
3	Reuben Geleynse	1,582 points	8	Jason Bennett	1,158 points
4	Mike White	1,562 points	9	Dan Henricks	1,096.5 points
5	Mike Lee	1,518.5 points	10	B. J. Kramps	1,040.5 points

FIVE

DOWN GOES
THE CHAMP

⬤

ATLANTA, GEORGIA
SATURDAY, FEBRUARY 7, 2004

Like the snap of a broken shoulder blade, the news rever-
berated all the way from south Florida. Less than 24 hours
earlier, at the PBR's seventh stop, a bull named Hot Rod
Harry had bucked off Chris Shivers in Tampa, Florida, and
turned him into arena carpet. The impact of the stomping
bull broke Shivers's right shoulder blade, an injury that
would require surgery. Since he'd need 8 weeks of rehabilitation anyway, he opted for an additional surgery to take

care of a nagging hip problem. All in all, he suddenly was facing a 5-month recuperation period.

If there was such a thing as a good time to get stomped by a bull and break a shoulder blade, this was it. The time off gave Shivers a chance to rest and refuel. But it also virtually ended his chances that season of winning an unprecedented third title. Someone else's quest looked in jeopardy, too.

Saturday night in Atlanta, Adriano Moraes limped into the Georgia Dome for the eighth stop on the PBR tour. His powerful build and cheerful disposition belied his physical condition. Moraes was in serious pain. Several of his fingers tingled and occasionally went numb, the result of arthritis and nerve damage in his arms. His "good" arm, the right one, was misshapen from where he'd torn his triceps—and he wore a heavy brace on his left elbow, which was destabilized by ligament and nerve damage. He also competed with torn ligaments and torn cartilage in his right knee.

Tandy Freeman, the PBR's orthopedic surgeon, had recommended surgery for the knee and left elbow. But Moraes declined, and Freeman understood why: Time recuperating meant time away from bull riding; and at 33 years old, Moraes knew his window of opportunity for winning a third PBR championship was closing. So as the 2004 season approached, he decided to ride in pain—and it only got worse.

In the championship round of the Tampa Bay Open, while dismounting a bull, Moraes sprained his left knee. Freeman listed him as questionable for the Atlanta Classic at the Georgia Dome, yet there was no question Moraes would ride if he was physically able. For one, contenders were gaining ground. In Tampa, Justin McBride earned his second victory in 4 weeks and moved past Mike Lee.

When Moraes arrived at the Georgia Dome, he headed straight for the sports medicine room and propped himself onto an examination table. Freeman walked over and looked at the rider's swollen left knee, peeled open a sealed package, and attached a syringe to an 18-gauge needle. Inserting the needle into the side of Moraes's left knee, Freeman pulled back the syringe as it filled up with bloody fluid. After Freeman drained 60 cubic centimeters of fluid, Moraes eased himself off the table, pronounced himself fit to ride, and hobbled toward the locker room like an old man. In fact, he looked creakier than the rider they called "Grandpa."

At 5 feet 5 inches and 145 pounds, Gary "Grandpa" Richard, one of the few black riders to have reached the top rung of the PBR, appeared as fit and trim as any other rider on tour. His full head of black hair was free of gray. But the creases around his mouth, deepening on his dark, weathered face when he smiled, gave away his age. Once, they called him the Houston Solution, referring to his hometown of Houston, Texas. But in recent years, they started calling him "Grandpa"—partly because he had three grandchildren and partly because at 41 he was the oldest rider on tour. Too old, some declared in April 2003.

That year, in a matter of three days, Richard not only lost his spot on tour, but also a $20,000-a-year maintenance job with the Houston school system, which helped him support his six children and grand-children. Many suspected it was the last time Richard would compete on the PBR's top tier. Richard's father hoped it was the last time his son would compete, period. He worried that Gary's skills were deteriorating with age and made him vulnerable to a catastrophic injury.

But before the 2004 season, Gary had arthroscopic surgery on his right knee. He was pain-free for the first time in years. And now here he was, sitting in front of his locker in the Georgia Dome and back among the PBR's top 45 riders. He looked around the room.

"This is the best of the best," he said. "When you're here, you're at the top of your game."

Dressing in a far corner of the room, Richard got ready next to Brian Wooley, a rider from Texas who was nearly 20 years younger than "Grandpa." But as if to dispel any stereotypes, Richard said, "I feel like I'm 21 years old again. Like Tony the Tiger. That's how I feel, grrrreat!"

Yet he made concessions to age. Spraying his right leg with Tuff-Skin, he wrapped adhesive tape from the top of his thigh to the bottom of his calf. Despite the off-season knee surgery, he still was competing without the posterior cruciate ligament he'd torn years ago. Changing into his riding gear, Richard found himself amidst the banter and camaraderie of the locker room, where riders swarmed a Copenhagen rep passing out free cans of snuff.

Then Richard found out he'd drawn a first-round bull named Land Shark, a dangerous head-slinger. "Yuck," he said before heading to the pens to size up the bull. About an hour later, during introductions, Richard sized up the crowd—20,000 strong.

Scheduled to ride second, he climbed into the chutes and settled on his bull. The bull looked more like Drunken Catfish than Land Shark. He took three weak jumps, dropped to his knees, and toppled over on his right side. Unhurt, Gary rose to his feet knowing he had an automatic reride—awarded to a rider when the judges determine a bull has performed below par. But a below-par performance was unlikely from Richard's reride bull, Ninja.

In 12 attempts, only six riders had ridden Ninja for 8 seconds, with those six scoring an average of 88 points. If Richard matched that average score, he'd be all but guaranteed a spot in the championship round. Midway through the first round, blinking nervously, Richard settled atop Ninja. He tightened the rope. "Go," he said, and the chute swung open.

One jump. Two jumps. Three jumps. Four jumps and . . .

Off fell Richard, hitting the dirt 3.3 seconds shy of the buzzer. He retrieved his bull rope and headed back to the locker room muttering, "I overrode him."

Standing in front of his locker, Richard tossed his riding glove, bull rope, vest, and chaps into a heap. He stared at the equipment.

"Dadgummit," he said. "Kind of bull you need. Just overrode him. I knew better."

Richard had blown a chance to pick up good money. But the man who ran the PBR wasn't about to blow his chance to secure some valuable publicity.

Randy Bernard, the PBR's CEO and ultimate schmoozer, spent much of the night chatting up Rudy Martzke, the sports TV columnist for *USA Today,* who along with his wife took in the show from front-row seats, compliments of the PBR. Bernard made sure to introduce Martzke to his good friend Bernie Taupin, the famous songwriter who'd written many of Elton John's lyrics. He also introduced Martzke to Moraes. Hook Martzke on the sport, Bernard thought, and maybe the PBR would get some pub in *USA Today.* Martzke looked like he was loving it, and what wasn't to love?

In the championship round, Ross Coleman rode Cripple Creek Slick Willy for 91 points and took the lead. Cauy Hudson of Elm Creek, Nebraska, was in second, two points back; and Mike Lee was in third, 3.5 points behind Coleman. It was a familiar and bittersweet spot for Lee. In all seven of the season's events, he'd been in the money, and three times in the top five. But he'd failed to win an event. Some riders said Lee's effortless style had cost him points, while others said he simply hadn't drawn the right bulls for a victory. But Lee's father, Dennis, and Moraes noticed something else. Both had watched Lee closely, and the young rider was getting ahead of the bulls. He was anticipating with uncanny skill but reacting too quickly to the bulls' moves. It was a sign of phenomenal ability but also a sign of impatience and inexperience. While Lee had quicker reflexes and more agility than Moraes, the Brazilian drew on the wisdom of a 15-year riding career in knowing how to stay in rhythm with the bull's speed and when to react. If a rider got too far behind the bull's pace, he slipped into the bull's power zone. If he got too far ahead, he moved into empty space and tumbled off the bull.

Rating a bull, Dennis Lee called it. By any name, it was one of the hardest things to master.

That night in Atlanta, during the championship round of the 1-night event, Moraes climbed aboard Slider, unridden in 18 attempts. Moraes needed at least 88 points that night in Atlanta to overtake Coleman. He settled into position and pushed down on the front of his black cowboy hat while Slider wriggled in the chutes.

"It's not going to work," Moraes silently told the bull. "It doesn't matter how much pressure you put on me. You're not going to scare me. I got you. This is your last day as an unridden bull. You're going to get conquered today."

Moraes called for the gate. When it opened, Slider took two jumps and turned hard to the left—the exact point where he'd thrown off most of the previous 18 riders. The motion rocked Moraes to the right, but he recentered himself and continued his silent talk with Slider.

"You stupid bull, you're not going to put me onto the ground today. I'm stronger than you are."

Whirling and bucking, Slider launched himself high enough for a man to limbo underneath him. But Moraes spurred the bull with his right foot and kept spurring until the buzzer sounded.

Moraes dismounted, triumphant. In came the score: 91 points!

Moraes had done it again, overtaking Coleman by 1.5 points and capturing his second victory of the season. When the event ended, someone handed him a cell phone. On the other end of the line was a PBR employee, back at the headquarters in Colorado Springs, waiting to write a story about the Atlanta Classic.

"Guess who won again!" Moraes crowed.

Walking by as Moraes savored the details of his victory as he relayed them by phone, Canadian rider Reuben Geleynse said, "He's going to be hard to beat."

But as Moraes limped back into the sports medicine room, where trainers wrapped ice around his left knee, a question begged to be asked: Could the body of a man who would turn 34 in April hold up during the PBR's 10-month marathon?

Later that night Moraes limped into the Marriott's restaurant with a small wall separating the dining area and the bar. He sat down at a table with Freeman and three other people and ordered chicken strips, fries, and a glass of wine. On the other side of the wall, McBride, Coleman, and a handful of others drank beer and whiskey. Moraes and McBride, one and two in the standings, acknowledged each other with a friendly wave. But neither showed any intention of joining the other.

Between bites, Moraes talked about his love for bull riding and about how in Brazil he'd once won a half dozen cars and finally got around to selling them when the bank called to say his account was overdrawn. These days his bank accounts were in better shape, his having amassed $86,000 in winnings over the past 7 weeks to go along with the more than $1 million he'd earned during his career. But it wasn't just about the money and the $1 million bonus, Moraes said. That's not the sole reason he endured the pain and risked serious injury. It was about his goal to be considered the best bull rider—in the history of the sport.

For Moraes to be considered the undisputed best would require that he win an unprecedented third PBR championship—the one he was suddenly favored to win even with 19 events left before the finals in Las Vegas.

CONCESSIONS	
Cuban sandwich	$9.25
Grilled Reuben sandwich	$8.50
Shrimp po'boy	$9.50
Smoked turkey wrap	$9
Sautéed chicken or sausage pasta	$9.75

"Deep-fried Twinkies," said Tony Grant, club-level concessions manager for the Georgia Dome. "Haven't heard of that. Not yet."

STANDINGS

1	Adriano Moraes	3,098 points	6	Reuben Geleynse	1,666 points
2	Justin McBride	2,446 points	7	Dan Henricks	1,565.5 points
3	Mike Lee	2,426.5 points	8	Dave Samsel	1,383 points
4	Mike White	2,202.5 points	9	Brian Herman	1,357.5 points
5	Jody Newberry	1,756 points	10	Troy Dunn	1,184.5 points

SIX

TWO IS THE
UGLIEST NUMBER

★

Anaheim, California
Saturday & Sunday, February 14 & 15, 2004

Cowboy hats, cowboy boots, spaghetti-strap tops. On the PBR tour, it could be hard to distinguish one crowd from the next, but Anaheim had its own flavor—a taste of Hollywood. Bo Derek watched the action from a catwalk over the chutes while fans watched Derek in her snug jeans and fringed brown suede jacket. The other celebrity guests were Jeff Probst, host of the TV show *Survivor*, and Tommy Lasorda, former manager of the Los Angeles Dodgers.

Randy Bernard, the PBR's CEO, made sure the PA

announcer called attention to the celebrity guests—just as he'd make sure to remind sponsors about the thousands of fans the tour had drawn that night to Arrowhead Pond. Out to prove the PBR had more than regional appeal, Bernard had taken the show to places like New York City, Philadelphia, and Anaheim. Bright lights and big cities meant potentially more money from sponsors, and Bernard tried to cash in on the glitz by parading out Derek, Lasorda, and Probst.

Derek and Probst seemed content to watch from a distance, but Lasorda wanted to meet some of the riders. Before the first-round action began, Bernard pulled aside Justin McBride. "Justin, I want you to meet Tommy Lasorda," Bernard said. "Tommy, this is Justin McBride, our reserve world champion."

The pudgy, white-haired man needed no introduction. McBride knew all about Lasorda, who had guided the Dodgers to four National League pennants and two World Series championships. But McBride figured Lasorda didn't know a damn thing about him. Which was beside the point.

Within seconds of their meeting, Lasorda launched into a profane pep talk, urging McBride to shed the label of reserve world champion, designated by his "back number"—the number that corresponds with a rider's finish the previous season and the number that stays on the back of his riding vest until the end of the following season. For 10 months, a rider has to wear that number. And there was no number McBride despised more than the two on his back.

With his Dodgers having lost the World Series twice, Lasorda knew McBride's frustration. "When I see you next year," he barked, "I don't want to see that goddamn two on your back. I want to see number one."

McBride shook Lasorda's hand and marched toward the chutes.

At 5 feet 8 inches tall and 140 pounds, McBride relied on his athleticism and balance. Some riders pull their bull ropes so tight, it appears they're trying to strangle the bulls. McBride kept his so loose that he looked like he was getting ready to ride a merry-go-round.

His father had ridden bulls. So had his grandfather, who had been killed in the ring when a bull punctured his lung. Even McBride's mother, Lori, had ridden a few bulls. So Justin felt it was something he not only wanted to do but had been born to do.

He rode his first bull when he was only 2½ years old. It was a red and white mutant that weighed about 100 pounds. McBride's father, Jim, lifted Justin onto the bull, gave him a mini bull rope, and set the two loose on the front yard grass as family members watched the spectacle.

"Good God, they died laughing," Jim McBride said. "He'd just ride the hair off that bull."

GROWING UP IN MULLEN, NEBRASKA (population 492), McBride gained attention as a bareback rider. But he dreamed of winning the world bull riding championship. He taped posters of the star riders like Hedeman, Jim "Razor" Sharp, and Ted Nuce onto his bedroom wall and watched his heroes every year during the televised National Finals Rodeo (NFR)—rodeo's equivalent of the Super Bowl. Boasting that he could ride better than some of the pros, McBride headed outside, flipped on the headlights of the family truck, and rode a metal bucking barrel hanging between two trees.

As a high school senior, he won the 1997 national high school bare-back championship and landed a rodeo scholarship to the University of Nevada, Las Vegas (UNLV). Though McBride competed in bareback riding during his freshman year of college, he emerged as one of the team's top bull riders and a world-class cutup. One day, McBride and his rodeo teammates were lounging in their physical education class while the rest of the students were going through gymnastic exercises. The instructor, fed up with the cowboys, wondered aloud if any of them had the ability to perform the exercises. With that, McBride went into a handstand, circled the gym mat, and popped back onto his feet. His teammates howled, and McBride flashed a shit-eating grin.

That year in Las Vegas, he developed a taste for Jack Daniel's, and casino blackjack, and a willingness to bet on his talent. The big gamble came after his freshman year. Bored with school, McBride dropped out, bought his PBR card, and hit the minor-league circuit. At an event in Fresno, California, McBride got knocked unconscious. At an event in Weatherford, Oklahoma, he got kicked in the side of the head and needed a dozen stitches to close the gash. He went broke within a few months and headed to Fort Collins, Colorado, where he moved in with a pal from Mullen, got a job working at a gravel pit, and crushed rock 8 hours a day for about $7.50 an hour.

By January 1999, having saved up just enough money to get to a minor-league PBR event in Knoxville, Tennessee, McBride bet on himself again. He finished third, won $4,000, and that day thought to himself, *Wow, I'm not going back to the gravel pit.* Instead he went to Bakersfield, California, where he finished fourth at another minor-league event and, thanks to another $10,000 in winnings, cracked the PBR's top 45. From there it was on to Odessa, Texas, and his first big-league bull riding event, where he rode Panhandle Slim and Holly-wood—two of the PBR's most ferocious bulls—won the event, and pocketed a check for $25,747. The little fart stick was on his way.

Earning almost $90,000 that year, McBride followed up by raking in more than $145,000 in 2000 and finishing ninth in the overall standings. Late in the 2001 season, he was in contention for the championship along with two veteran star riders—Moraes and Ty Murray. But his hopes for the championship ended in a bar fight, when McBride punched somebody in the face and broke his own right hand, the one he used to grip his bull rope.

He finished third that season and in 2002 finished fifth. Having won more than $500,000, McBride enjoyed the money but desperately wanted to win a championship. His single-minded obsession with being number one stood in stark contrast to the wonderment of two new arrivals on the BFTS.

THE PHOTOGRAPHER FOCUSED HIS LENS, then lowered the camera.

"You might want to take out the chew," he said.

Rookies.

Paul Gavin reached into his mouth with his index finger and scooped out the plug of Copenhagen, deposited it into a Styrofoam cup, straightened his shoulders, and smiled for his official PBR photo.

Gavin, a clean-cut 21-year-old from Monmouth, Illinois, looked like he should've been chewing bubble gum instead of tobacco. He was among more than 200 riders who had started the year in the minor leagues and the first of two rookies to make it to the big leagues of bull riding.

Eight events into the season, the PBR made its first cut, dropping the BFTS's bottom-ranked five riders and calling up the five top-ranked riders from the minor leagues. Occasionally the new group of riders included a rookie. This time it included two. Waiting to take his photo was James White, a 28-year-old black rider from Houston and an understudy of Gary "Grandpa" Richard who was now thinking less about the PBR's glamour than what he'd have to do to stay there. The call-up guaranteed him a spot in the next four events, but White still had to pay his own way. To buy his plane ticket to Anaheim, he had had to clear out his bank account. Some of the riders wanted money. White *needed* it. As with every PBR event, there were a few ways to cash in: Riders finishing in the top eight of every preliminary round and in the top eight of the championship round earned checks from a pool of $7,800 per round, and the riders with the 10 best cumulative scores at the end of the event earned checks from a pool of more than $50,000, with $24,500 going to the event winner. That was in addition to several bonuses, starting with the Mossy Oak Shootout—a chance for the first-round leader to ride a bull for a minimum of $5,000, with the money rolling over like a lottery jackpot every time a rider failed to cash in and increasing up to $100,000. But there were no guaranteed payouts on the BFTS other than the riders' 2-day event appearance fee of $400, of which the PBR withheld $146 to cover every rider's $20,000 insurance policy at each event.

In the first round, White rode Matrix for 86.5 points, which was tied for the seventh-best score of the round and earned him a check for $195. But he'd need more than that to comfortably afford to stay on tour. So that next night, he arrived with a look of intense focus. So did rider B. J. Kramps.

Kramps, the Canadian wise guy, kept the jokes to a minimum. Kramps had fallen off six of his last seven bulls, and that day he'd drawn Double Bogey, who in the first round had bucked off veteran rider

Gilbert Carrillo. All day, Kramps replayed the ride in his head and visualized what he'd have to do to stay on the bull. It was a practice unique to bull riding: spending hours, sometimes days, thinking about a ride that optimally would last 8 seconds and oftentimes less.

The hours of mental preparation paid off. Kramps made the buzzer; but while the judges were totaling their scores, he was still on the bull. Though he'd visualized the ride perfectly, he'd forgotten to plan the last step: the dismount. In general, the technique is straightforward: For right-handed riders, yank the tail of the bull rope, freeing the riding hand; bail out to the right; fall onto hands and knees; speed-crawl before standing and running for safety. For left-handed riders like Kramps, it was the same technique, only in the opposite direction. When the 8-second buzzer sounded on Kramps's ride that night, he slipped off the right side of Double Bogey and got hung up.

Kramps tried to get to his feet and shake loose, but to no avail. The agitated bull picked up speed, and Kramps bounced across the dirt like tin cans tied to the back of a newlywed's car.

Todd Pierce, bareback-rider-turned-pastor, was standing on the outside of the chutes, preparing to help Mike Lee tighten his bull rope, when Double Bogey and the bouncing Canadian rider sped past. As if mistaking the bull for a purse snatcher, Pierce jumped off the chutes and lunged. He missed the bull and hit the dirt. He scrambled back onto his feet, chased Double Bogey into the corner, and leapt on the bull's head. A wise move? Uh-uh. But it did slow down the bull long enough for bullfighter Greg Crabtree to snatch the tail of Kramps's rope and unhook him.

But Double Bogey was within goring distance of all three men, and Kramps was facedown in the dirt. Pierce covered Kramps with his own body as the bull leapt over the men and ran for the center gate and into the exit alley. A muffled voice stunned Pierce.

"Uh, I'm okay, Todd."

It was Kramps, in his signature deadpan, smothered under the pastor.

"Oh, sorry, B.J."

Kramps had suffered only a mild concussion, and Pierce suffered only a moderate tongue-lashing from the pissed-off bullfighters. It was their job to save the riders, they told Pierce, not the pastor's. Tied for 16th after two rounds, Kramps just missed qualifying for the championship round. So did Adriano Moraes, missing the short-go for only the third time in eight events. Just as surprising as who failed to qualify was someone who did qualify—James White. While fellow rookie Paul Gavin got bucked off both of his bulls in Anaheim, White followed up his first-round ride on Matrix with an 85.5-point ride on Geronimo, leaving him matched up with Ugly in the championship round. It was Ugly, all right. White hung on for 5 seconds before getting thrown off. Standing up and dusting himself off, he left the arena unsure if he'd made enough money to get to the next week's event in St. Louis. But while White was hoping for a few hundred dollars, others were dreaming of the $1 million.

With Lasorda watching and a chance to gain ground on Moraes, McBride boarded Hot Water Dip. The buzzer never sounded so cruel, coming ⁴⁄₁₀ second after McBride fell off the bull. It was exactly the type of ride that could keep him forever Justin McBridesmaid.

But Mike Lee seized the opportunity with his third straight top-five finish, which moved him past McBride and back into second place in the standings.

Greg Potter, a veteran Australian rider, won the Anaheim Open and collected a check for $29,245. But he smiled no more than James White, who finished 10th in his first BFTS performance and earned $625—a paltry sum compared with Potter's haul, but enough money to keep the dream alive. Twelve hours later, Randy Bernard was dealing with a nightmare.

That season, eight PBR events were scheduled to be broadcast on NBC, and Bernard considered none bigger than the tape-delayed coverage of the Anaheim Open. The telecast would follow NBC's live coverage of the Daytona 500 and provide an opportunity for the PBR to tap into a huge national audience and convert NASCAR fans into bull riding fans. "We feel that the two audiences are compatible," Jon Miller, NBC's senior vice president for sports programming said in advance of bull riding's big day. "And we are thrilled to showcase a hot young sport like the PBR." Bernard had touted the scheduled telecast as "one more stepping-stone toward increasing exposure for PBR athletes."

But inclement weather made the Daytona 500 and its scheduled finish time as unpredictable as a bull ride. Rain delayed the race, which forced NBC to slash its 90-minute PBR telecast to about 20 minutes. Furious hard-core bull riding fans bombarded the PBR with e-mails and phone calls. The strategic placement of a bull riding broadcast behind NASCAR's biggest race meant nothing to the PBR faithful, especially in light of NBC's truncated coverage of the Anaheim Open. Bernard posted an apology on the PBR Web site and, with the fumes of the Daytona 500 debacle in the air, understood more than ever that the tour's loyal fans cared about just one race—the race for $1 million and the prized gold buckle.

CONCESSIONS

Carved turkey, roast beef, or pastrami sandwich, with chips	$8
Frozen margarita	$12
Bananas Foster	$6.50
Cherries jubilee	$6.50

So why no deep-fried Twinkies? "We don't have that many fryers," said Ruben Crane, general manager for the food and beverage supplier at Arrowhead Pond. "We need them for french fries."

STANDINGS

1	Adriano Moraes	3,235.5 points	6	Jody Newberry	1,841.5 points
2	Mike Lee	2,971 points	7	Reuben Geleynse	1,750.5 points
3	Justin McBride	2,815.5 points	8	Ross Coleman	1,740.5 points
4	Mike White	2,202.5 points	9	Troy Dunn	1,725 points
5	Brian Herman	1,877 points	10	Greg Potter	1,608.5 points

SEVEN

REVENGE OF THE
BULLFIGHTER

INDIANAPOLIS, INDIANA
SATURDAY, MARCH 6, 2004

With revenge on his mind, Rob Smets blew past the animal-rights protester outside the RCA Dome. The woman wore a bull mask and a sandwich board that on the front read "Rodeo Making Sport of Cruelty" and on the back "Abuse Should Not Amuse." Handing out pamphlets, she decried bull riding as mistreatment of the animals. If only the protester had followed Smets to the Outdoor Life Network's TV truck, she would've seen it was guys like him and his fellow bullfighters who were suffering most of the cruelty and abuse.

The three bullfighters that worked every BFTS event

wore snug jerseys, shorts, and cleated shoes and stood outside the chutes, ready to intervene if a bull tried to trample or hook a fallen rider. Fans used to call them rodeo clowns back when they wore face paint, baggy pants, and overalls, which was like seeing a member of the Secret Service wearing a big red nose and a water-squirting flower on his lapel. All bullfighters used to be rodeo clowns, responsible for entertaining the crowd and protecting the riders. But the self-respecting, modern bullfighter uniforms are as serious as the new job description: bull rider bodyguards. Gags are left up to the barrelmen and the latter-day rodeo clowns who still wear face paint and the funny-looking attire.

Guardian angels, in-arena announcer Brandon Bates called the PBR's bullfighters. Smets, a stocky 44-year-old, was the oldest in the business and one of the best. He had short brown hair and a square jaw that looked like it belonged to a boxer. Built like a Division II linebacker, Smets occasionally went after bulls as if they were running backs and he were Dick Butkus. He talked trash to the bulls as if they understood his insults and taunts. But now, in Indianapolis and inside the TV truck, Smets grimaced as he watched a replay of the previous week's encounter between him and a black bull named Sniper. There it was: the first round of the Philadelphia Invitational at Wachovia Spectrum, Andre Moraes on Sniper, everything running like clockwork, until Moraes got bucked off and hit the dirt. The next moment belonged to Smets and the two other bullfighters—Dennis Johnson and Greg Crabtree. Smets took charge, moving in and distracting the bull as Moraes scrambled to safety. Textbook move. So far, flawless. But impulse took over. Smets wanted more.

He wanted to show the crowd what he could do. He wanted a shot at the bull, one-on-one. He moved in on Sniper.

Waving him on, Smets tried to dodge the charging bull, got scooped by its horns, and flipped end over end and onto the dirt. Quickly on his feet, Smets again waved on the bull, and Sniper came back. This time the bull pitchforked Smets's backside and launched him face-first into the dirt.

Undeterred, Smets waved the bull forward one more time. Sniper caught him from behind yet again and tossed him into the air. Gravity slammed Smets to the dirt.

"Flipped him like a cheese omelet," cracked Justin McKee, one of the OLN commentators.

Smets scrambled to his feet and moved toward Sniper before Cody Lambert, vice president and livestock director for the PBR, stifled his own laughter long enough to tell Smets to give it up. On horseback, the cowboy known as the "pickup man," on standby to lasso uncooperative bulls, saved Smets further embarrassment. He roped Sniper by the horns and led him out the center gate while Smets punched the protective barrel always kept in the arena.

The bull had made him look like a rookie: Smets feinting right when he should have feinted left, rushing in when he should have held back, and going back for more when he should have quit.

Now, a week later in Indianapolis, Smets boiled over while watching the replay in OLN's truck. "That bull and I are going at it tonight," he fumed, "and this time he's mine."

An hour before introductions, Smets got dressed in his work uniform alongside Dennis Johnson and Greg Crabtree, two of the PBR's other regular bullfighters, and regaled his junior colleagues with stories. Like the time in Salt Lake City when Smets took a bull horn in the ass. Right between the cheeks.

"How far up there?" asked Crabtree.

"Four and a half inches," Smets said. "Straight to the sphincter muscle."

"Smets hasn't had a loud fart since," cracked Flint Rasmussen.

While Smets and the other two bullfighters went after the bulls, Rasmussen went after the laughs. Rasmussen, known as a barrelman because of the steel barrel he and his counterparts used to protect themselves, got his laughs with style—moonwalking across dirt like the King of Pop, kicking and jumping like a cheerleader, and jigging to the song "Cotton-Eyed Joe." Stylish moves were of no interest to Smets. As introductions drew near, not even Rasmussen could get the grizzled bullfighter to laugh.

Smets pulled on his uniform top, wrapped his ankles with adhesive tape, and strapped on a hockey girdle.

Poking his head into the dressing room, Tommy Joe Lucia, the PBR's chief production officer, looked at Smets. "Is it going to happen tonight?"

"Yes," Smets said firmly and continued to get ready. On went the bicycle shorts, the thick cotton shorts, and the cleated shoes. He leaned against a locker and stretched his calves, working out the kinks, aches, and pains accumulated over his 26-year career. Then he made a final stop in the sports medicine room, where a trainer rubbed heating balm on the back of Smets's permanently stiff neck. On his way out, Smets swallowed five Advils and broke into a jog.

The crowd was waiting. So was Sniper.

IN THE OLD DAYS, the bullfighters' main job was to produce laughs. That was before Melvin "Wick" Peth arrived on the rodeo scene in 1955. By Peth's own admission, when it came to being a rodeo clown, he had a major shortcoming. "I was a piss-poor clown," he said.

Instead of giving up on rodeo, Peth gave up the gags. But a funny thing happened: Peth helped redefine the job of a rodeo clown, giving birth to the modern-day bullfighter.

Focusing on protecting the riders and showcasing the art of bull protection, he went after the bulls like they were opponents. He rushed them, dodged them, taunted them, and did it with unsurpassed skill. Then along came a kid whom Peth branded a "young punk."

The kid was Rob Smets, then 18 and a hell-raiser from California.

Riding bulls in high school, Smets had a big heart and a bigger mouth. He was an average rider and remembers the day he was sitting on a fence during a high school rodeo and popping off to the bullfighters. "If you think it's so easy," they shot back, "why don't you try it?"

Why not, thought Smets, who hopped into the ring.

Instead of riding bulls, Smets found he was a natural at fighting them. He displayed the necessary quickness, instincts, and courage. And though his father encouraged him to learn a craft, Smets decided to pursue a career as a bullfighter.

A 6-inch scar ran down the back of his neck, which he'd broken twice. The first time was in 1992, when he fractured vertebrae C4 to C6, the same injury that former Detroit Lions football player Mike Utley suffered in a game and that left him in a wheelchair. Four years later Smets broke the C1 vertebra in his upper neck, the same injury that paralyzed actor Christopher Reeve during an equestrian accident. By contrast, the injuries left Smets with little more than a permanently stiff neck. But he knew he'd been lucky. For that reason, he swore off freestyle bullfighting—where the men go one-on-one with a bull for 40 to 70 seconds and for which, while competing on the Wrangler Bull-fight Tour, Smets had won five world championships—and promised his wife he'd focus on rider protection.

But impulse ruled Smets, who continued to engage in bouts like the one with Sniper. And when he lost, he always vowed revenge. His chance in Indianapolis came in the second section of bull riders that night.

With B. J. Kramps riding Sniper, the bull took a few sluggish jumps before the 8-second buzzer sounded. It was as if Sniper had saved his fury for Smets; instead of heading for the out gate, the bull lingered in the arena.

Chugging forward, Smets circled in front of the bull and slapped him on the snout. Round one to the bullfighter.

Sniper sauntered toward the center of the ring. Smets positioned himself behind the barrel and prepared to climb on top. Those who had seen Smets compete in freestyle competitions knew what was coming when Sniper charged. Smets would either leap over the bull or walk down the animal's back. The move would establish dominance—the bullfighter's equivalent of a knockout.

But as Smets propped a foot on the barrel, the pickup man on horseback sailed his rope into the air and lassoed Sniper by the horns. Just like that, the showdown ended. Later, Smets learned that Cody Lambert had hollered at the pickup man to get Sniper out of the ring before Smets got run over yet again, which naturally ticked off Smets.

While Sniper was led out of the arena, Smets trotted over to the chutes and, still panting, grinned while explaining to Tandy Freeman, the PBR's orthopedic surgeon, how he'd outsmarted the bull. Freeman rolled his eyes. The "war" had proven to be no more than a skirmish.

In truth, the fans were more interested in the battle between Adriano Moraes, Justin McBride, and Mike Lee. Though less than a third of the way into the season, Moraes was threatening to turn the race for the championship into a rout.

Two weeks earlier at the St. Louis Open and the PBR's 10th stop of the season, Moraes had ridden Spotted Jacket for 90 points in the championship round for his third victory of the season. He finished third the next week at Philadelphia, giving him a big lead over Justin McBride and Mike Lee as he arrived at the RCA Dome for the Indianapolis Invitational, the 12th stop of the season.

In baseball, the magic number for a hitter is .300. Manage hits in three out of every 10 at-bats, and the player has had a good year. In the PBR, the magic number is 50 percent. Make the 8-second buzzer on every other bull, and a rider has had a good year. By those standards, Moraes was on pace for an unfathomable year. He arrived in Indianapolis having successfully ridden 21 of 25 bulls, for a staggering rate of 84 percent. In the PBR's past four seasons, only Ty Murray, the seven-time all-around world champion and two-time bull riding world champion, had successfully ridden more than 70 percent of his bulls over the course of a season. Moraes's impressive string in 2004 included scores on three of the tour's baddest bulls—Mossy Oak Mudslinger, Kid Rock, and Western Wishes—and six rides for 90 points or more.

In the first round at Indianapolis, Moraes drew X Rated. Out of the chute, the bull feinted left and staggered back to the right. Moraes was not fooled. Maintaining his spot in the pocket, Moraes looked in command on his way to the 8-second buzzer, whereupon he dismounted, landed on his feet, and gave the bull a quick Clint Eastwood stare. The judges awarded him 86 points for the ride. Then it was McBride's turn.

The bull was Mohegan Sun, bucking for only the second time on the PBR. Out of the chute, he spun hard to the right and completed four revolutions before reversing direction. McBride stayed centered, the 8-second buzzer sounded, and in came the score: 88 points. During the

1-night competition, McBride and Moraes headed into the championship round one-two in that night's standings.

In that final round, with Moraes on a quick spinner named Western Wishes, the bull whirled to the left. In control, Moraes spurred with his right foot on his way to 91.5 points—the top score of the night—and the seventh time in eight tries that Moraes had ridden his bull in the championship round. The only way Moraes could lose was if McBride stayed on Mossy Oak Mudslinger, among the PBR's rankest bulls, and scored 89 points.

Moraes made a point to watch every ride, like a disciplined baseball player preparing for future at-bats and watching every pitch. But as McBride settled onto Mossy Oak Mudslinger, who had bucked off McBride in the last round of the 2003 finals, Moraes climbed down the metal deck behind the chutes and walked toward the locker room.

An OLN reporter dispatched someone to stop him. If McBride bucked off or scored less than 89 points, the reporter needed Moraes for the postevent TV interview.

Moraes stopped. He looked irritated and brusquely predicted McBride would ride the bull and score at least 90 points. But there was nothing predictable about Mossy Oak Mudslinger's trip.

Out of the chute, the bull departed from his regular pattern and spun to the right. Then he spun back to the left. No matter. He couldn't shake off McBride before the 8-second buzzer.

In came the judges' scores: 91.5 points! McBride had triumphed.

Cupping his hand, Moraes shouted, "Go, Justin," and then marched toward the locker room. He still had a commanding lead in the standings, but McBride won $57,363, moved back in front of Lee, and shattered Moraes's aura of invincibility. Of course, the riders weren't the only ones battling it out.

So were the bulls.

That night in Indianapolis, in the championship round, Little Yellow Jacket bucked off Lee in impressive fashion. Yet the judges awarded the highest scores to another bull—Crossfire Hurricane, who dumped rider Bryan Richardson. With the cowboys determining Bull of the Year by a vote at the end of the regular season, the judges' scores served as a potential guide—not the ultimate measuring stick. The random draw meant one bull might face better riders over the course of a season. So the riders judged them not only on the number of consecutive buck-offs but also on how good the bulls looked when throwing riders. Riders liked to know that even the greatest bull could on occasion be conquered and that, when he was, the ride produced high scores. A qualified score on Little Yellow Jacket, for instance, was virtually guaranteed to be 90 points or higher. But the scores from Indianapolis for the two-time reigning Bull of the Year made him no shoo-in for a third straight championship.

But even after the event, the only bull on Smets's mind was Sniper. Back in the dressing room, Smets's cell phone rang. It was Carla, knowing her husband had ignored her advice to avoid a rematch with Sniper.

"I got him," Smets boasted. "I waited on the fake." As the conversation continued, disappointment crept across Smets's face. "I didn't do enough," he said, subdued. "I didn't get enough out of that bull." But that had no effect on Smets's ultimate goal. Measuring himself against Peth, he wanted to be remembered as the greatest bullfighter. Peth had retired at 54. Smets vowed to continue until he was 55, which would require 11 more years in the business—by which time Sniper and countless other bulls with which Smets had tangled would be long since retired.

CONCESSIONS	
Pork barbecue sandwich	$4.50
Rib tips	$4.50
Philly cheesesteak sandwich	$4.50

No deep-fried Twinkies? "Why would we serve those?" asked Gael Doar, spokesperson for the concessionaire. "Sounds awful."

STANDINGS

1	Adriano Moraes	4,865 points	6	Dave Samsel	2,248.5 points
2	Justin McBride	3,473 points	7	Jody Newberry	2,227 points
3	Mike Lee	3,088 points	8	Greg Potter	2,191.5 points
4	Ross Coleman	2,748 points	9	Dan Henricks	2,079 points
5	Mike White	2,319.5 points	10	Reuben Geleynse	2,047 points

EIGHT

THE FORT WORTH MASSACRE

Fort Worth, Texas
Saturday & Sunday, March 13 & 14, 2004

The bull rider lay sprawled on the arena dirt like a wet bag of cement.

The four-man sports medicine team, followed by paramedics, rushed in. But for Ross Johnson, it looked like it might be too late.

Behind the chutes, a PBR official pressed a cell phone against her ear. "He's not moving," she said, the color draining from her face. Standing nearby, rider James White placed his cowboy hat over his chest, bowed his head, and whispered, "God, please help him."

One moment Johnson had been atop the bull named Panda, trying to ride out the 1,700-pound storm. The next moment he was bouncing across the dirt and under the thrashing bull. As Johnson fell off Panda, his right spur had caught the bull rope, sucking him under the bull. Now Panda's stomping hooves came down like metal pistons, pounding Johnson on his back, his shoulder, his neck, and the side of his skull.

Blood oozed from his head onto the dirt.

"Ross! Ross! Ross!"

Bolting from her seat in the stands, Abby Johnson screamed for her husband, her shrieks piercing the hushed arena. Ross Johnson's father and stepmother tried to calm her, but it was hard to stay calm as the crowd of about 5,000 inside the Will Rogers Memorial Center watched in stunned silence.

By the time Johnson's spur came loose and the bullfighters separated him from the bull, he lay motionless and directly in front of the open center gate through which the bulls exited. Panda circled back.

Bullfighter Rob Smets, kneeling beside Johnson, peered over his shoulder at the approaching bull. A week earlier at Indianapolis, Smets was consumed with exacting revenge on Sniper, but now his only thought was saving Johnson—and he knew he had but one option.

Smets draped his body over Johnson's and prepared to take the blow. Panda charged forward. Smets closed his eyes and covered his head. He heard the beating hooves.

Mercifully, the bull passed behind him and through the center gate. Out rushed the orthopedic surgeon, the athletic trainers, and the paramedics. As they hurried into the arena, they were certain of only one thing: Johnson was either unconscious or dead.

It wouldn't have been the first death on the PBR tour. In 2000, at an event in Albuquerque, New Mexico, Promiseland tossed Canadian rider Glen Keeley and stomped on Keeley's chest. Doctors performed emergency surgery, but their efforts were unsuccessful. Keeley, 30 years old, became the first rider to die from injuries suffered during PBR competition and joined the long list of riders who'd died in the arena. The list included well-known professional riders such as Lane Frost, the 1987 PRCA champion, who died in 1989; Ronnie Rossen, who died in 1991;

and Brent Thurman, who died in 1994. Although the number of amateur riders killed is unknown, during a 3-month stretch in 1993 three riders died at amateur bull ridings in Canada.

But that night in Fort Worth, as paramedics strapped Johnson onto a flat board, lifted him onto a gurney, and wheeled him out of the arena, not one rider withdrew from the event, the 13th BFTS stop of the 2004 season. Officially it was the Tuff Hedeman Championship Challenge. But even before Johnson's wreck, the PBR's medical staff was calling it the "Fort Worth Massacre," a reference to the 2003 stop in Fort Worth, which had been a bloody mess.

Nine riders had been injured so severely that they couldn't compete the next week, and three of them ended up in the hospital. At one point, the line of riders needing treatment extended outside the sports medicine room. The fans here expected as much.

This was no Jacksonville, Atlanta, or Anaheim, where Western wear was more fashion statement than part of the culture. This was "Cowtown," and the locals took the nickname for Fort Worth as a compliment. What else would you call a city whose minor-league hockey team went by the nickname Brahmas?

The main attraction was the old Stockyards, where cattle drivers used to stop for a visit at the saloon or the bordello, sell their cows at the slaughterhouse, or resume their cattle drives. For the tourists, twice a day they drove longhorn steer down Exchange Street, the animals' hooves clop-clopping against the cobblestone as they made their lazy saunter. Things got rowdier when the locals squeezed into the coliseum and started downing $3 beers and $4 Jack and Cokes. No padded club seats or luxury boxes there. Just old-fashioned hard-back chairs, rickety steel rails, and the aroma of history.

Built in 1936 by the Works Progress Administration—part of President Franklin Delano Roosevelt's New Deal program to create jobs and economic relief for those suffering through the Great Depression—the yellow brick building with the 200-foot tower between the two entrances stood proud and dignified but as weathered as an old rodeo cowboy.

When Fort Worth rodeo fans heard of a good bull riding, they came in droves. They wanted thrilling rides and horrifying wrecks. They were sure to see both at the "Fort Worth Massacre."

THE RASH OF INJURIES WAS EASY TO EXPLAIN. Every year Hedeman assembled the country's rankest bulls, the kind of bulls he'd loved to ride during his own storied career. The ranker the bull, the more dangerous and the tougher to ride. But the ranker the bull, the better the chance for a high score—the kind of scores one needed to win an event and a world championship. And no one had wanted to win more than Tuff Hedeman.

Having grown up in the working-class section of El Paso, Texas, he was born Richard Hedeman and was the youngest of seven children and a snot-nosed runt. When he was 5 years old, a neighbor accidentally slammed Hedeman's hand in the door of his pickup truck. He never screamed or cried.

"Tough nut," the man said.

It was Tuff that stuck.

As a young bull rider, he was far from the most talented. Other riders joked about his pigeon-toed walk, his Coke-bottle glasses, and his stained teeth. But what he lacked in ability or style, he compensated for by living up to his nickname.

Studying the likes of Cody Lambert, Hedeman transformed himself into a promising rider; and as a high school senior in 1981, he landed a scholarship at Sul Ross State University in Alpine, Texas. But the scholarship barely kept him above the poverty line. He was so broke he couldn't pay to have his cowboy shirts starched for competitions like the rest of his teammates did. He did have a car, though it was a miracle it still ran. It was a 1964 Buick Electra given to him as a high school graduation gift.

"I was poor as you could get," recalled Hedeman, who, in joking about his financial status, quipped, "I couldn't even pay attention."

To make ends meet, he worked part-time for a local rancher and earned $50 for the sunup-to-sundown shift. He occasionally borrowed money from teammates and friends and persuaded the college rodeo secretary to let him pay his entry fees after the event. Which meant he *had* to win.

When his teammates were blowing off practice, he was at the arena, riding bulls. When his teammates were sleeping in, he was at the arena, riding bulls. A bad bull ride infuriated him—even if it was a teammate who got bucked off.

"You gotta really want it," Ed Vickers remembers Hedeman barking at him when the two rode together at Sul Ross. "If you don't want it, you might as well quit."

When Sul Ross made the 1982 National Collegiate Finals, Cody Lambert won the all-around championship with the highest individual point total from all events, and his brother, Chuck, finished all-around runner-up. Hedeman competed in saddle bronc riding, steer wrestling, team roping, and bull riding. In the final round, he rode the standout bull Elmer, and Sul Ross won the national championship. Then Hedeman turned pro and attacked the circuit like a starving man would attack a buffet. It took him less than 2 years to qualify for his first NFR, and he showed up in Las Vegas a changed man.

The Coke-bottle glasses were gone, replaced by contacts; the rumpled cowboy shirts were gone, replaced by starched new ones; and the stained yellow teeth were gone, replaced by capped teeth and a gleaming white smile. The girls began to notice Hedeman, and so did the world's best riders.

Traveling the country from one rodeo to the next, Hedeman rode in the same car with Frost and Lambert—more bull riding talent than anyone had ever seen in one vehicle. Invariably, one of the three won the bull riding event, and Hedeman's bank account and reputation continued to grow.

Trading in another clunker, he bought a used Cadillac. A few years later, he and fellow rider Jim Sharp bought a 310 Cessna twin-engine plane. Hedeman found himself riding in bull riding's fast lane.

Whether on a bull, in a rental car, or at the blackjack table, he loved to gamble. He drove rental cars over medians and on top of sidewalks. Once, at the state fairgrounds in Red Bluff, California, he and fellow rider Ted Nuce steered their rental cars onto a horse-racing track and pressed hard on the accelerator, dirt kicking up behind the cars as they raced around it. Another time in northern California, with six riders packed into a rental car, Hedeman sped down a mountain. Vickers screamed for Hedeman to let him out of the car.

Hedeman just drove faster.

Qualifying for the NFR and the PBR finals almost every year, he became a fixture in Las Vegas and the casinos. He liked to bet on horses and professional sports, but his game of choice was blackjack—high-stakes blackjack. Friends saw him win and lose more than $20,000 at a sitting. When he won, he was among the most likable customers, tipping the dealers. When he lost, he could turn as nasty as a 2,000-pound bull, ripping up cards and cursing the dealers.

But by his midtwenties, Hedeman had beaten the long odds, the little snot-nosed runt having grown into a sturdy 5-foot-11-inch, 175-pound frame and a full-fledged rodeo star. Yet he still wasn't the sport's most popular rider. That distinction belonged to Lane Frost, Hedeman's best friend.

Frost had a lanky frame, tousled brown hair, and an undeniable charm. He might not have been the best bull rider ever—Hedeman and Sharp won more championships—but he was one of the few competitors to acknowledge the fans. He did it like no one else, with a two-handed wave after his rides.

After rodeos, Frost not only signed autographs for all who requested them but also stopped and chatted with the fans as if they were personal friends. Hedeman and Lambert threatened to leave Frost behind. But they never did, in part because they knew Frost truly appreciated the fans.

On July 30, 1989, the day of the championship round at the Cheyenne Frontier Days, the sky was gray, the arena was muddy, and the grandstands were packed. Heading into the short-go, Frost was in second place and drew a bull named Takin' Care of Business. He rode the bull until the 8-second buzzer, let go of the bull rope, and rolled off the bull's hindquarters. The bull pivoted and circled behind Frost. The attack took less than 10 seconds.

Frost tried to scramble away, but his boots stuck in the ankle-deep mud, and the bull drove into Frost's back and knocked him to the ground. Frost curled up into a ball. But the bull drove his right horn into Frost's left side. When the bullfighters finally waved away the bull, Frost got to his feet and motioned for help.

Then he collapsed.

Soon after arriving at Memorial Hospital late that afternoon, Lane Frost was pronounced dead.

At his funeral, 1,200 people squeezed into the pews at the First Baptist Church in Atoka, Oklahoma. Others packed into church classrooms to watch the service on TV monitors; and when there was no room left, the others gathered on the church's front lawn. The *Daily Oklahoman* newspaper estimated that 3,500 people attended, this outpouring for the same rider who earlier in his career remarked that it "would be neat" if someone ever asked for his autograph.

Four months after Frost died in the bullring in 1989, Hedeman, with thoughts of his best friend on his mind, won his second world bull riding championship. He also named his first son Robert Lane. Five years later, New Line Cinema released *Eight Seconds*, a movie about Frost's life starring Luke Perry, with Hedeman and Lambert two other featured characters. Though not a huge commercial or critical success, the film struck a chord with Frost's legion of fans and remains the most-watched bull riding film ever.

With Frost gone, Hedeman became the sport's number one ambassador. After each of the Bullnanza events in Guthrie, organizers held an open-bar party on the third floor of the arena. Riders beat a hasty retreat to the party as soon as the event ended, leaving but one rider in the arena.

"Pig," they shouted out from the third-floor balcony.

Fans knew him as Tuff, but his friends called him Pig. "Because he's a pig," Jim Sharp once explained.

"Pig!"

Hedeman waved them off. Signing autographs and posing for pictures, he worked the line of fans until every request was obliged. Once, with Hedeman still signing autographs, A. G. Meyers, who handled promotions for the Bullnanza events, shouted for the arena workers to cut off the lights. Hedeman shouted back. "Tell A.G. to send me a bill, because we're not cutting off the lights," he said, refusing to leave until every autograph had been signed.

The lights stayed on.

Hedeman wasn't warm and cuddly like Frost and never would be. But the fans admired him—not just because he'd won the PRCA world championship in 1986, 1989, and 1991 and the PBR championship in 1995 but also because the son of a bitch rode every rank bull out there. In fact, Hedeman and one of the toughest bulls in rodeo history squared off in one of the most memorable rides ever.

LAS VEGAS, 1995. Hedeman already had clinched the PBR championship, but no one left the building. The crowd waited for Hedeman's highly anticipated final ride: Tuff versus Bodacious.

Bodacious had his own agent and promoter, and the bull had spawned an empire of videotapes, merchandise, even apparel. He'd been featured in *Penthouse* and *GQ*, and although his birth certificate said "J31," everyone in the world of rodeo knew him as Bodacious. They also knew him as the world's baddest of badasses—an ornery cream-colored, cowboy-eviscerating bull. Before the last round of the 1995 PBR finals, riders had boarded the bull 135 times during his 4 years of competition, and only six of them had stayed on for the required 8 seconds. Six! Ninety-five percent of them failed—mere mortals playing a fool's game atop a 2,000-pound beast.

Among those six men who had succeeded in riding Bodacious was Hedeman. And in the final round of the 1995 finals, the two got reacquainted. Hedeman climbed into the chute and settled onto the bull. He pulled his bull rope tight and called for the gate, and out they soared.

On his third jump, Bodacious jerked back his head. The force drove Hedeman forward. His face smashed against the bull's head. Twisting sideways, bouncing off the bull's back, Hedeman crashed to the dirt.

He got back on his feet without assistance and left the arena with blood pouring from his disfigured face. The gold-buckle ceremony would have to wait; Hedeman was on his way to the hospital.

Doctors performed more than 10 hours of reconstructive facial surgery. For weeks, with his jaw wired shut, Hedeman ate his meals through a straw. He lost more than 20 pounds. But 6 weeks after the wreck, Hedeman showed up at the NFR. He showed up looking thin, tired, and weak but carrying his equipment bag. He was there to compete.

In the eighth round, Hedeman checked the draw. His worst nightmare. He'd drawn Bodacious. Hedeman, without his neck brace, returned to the arena.

With other riders standing behind the chutes, he climbed atop the bull that had ravaged his face. When the gate opened, Hedeman held on to the back of the chute and let the bull go out solo. As Bodacious ran off, Hedeman tipped his hat toward the bull.

On his next trip, Bodacious knocked out yet another rider. His owner, Sammy Andrews, immediately retired the 7-year-old champion bull.

A year after Hedeman's wreck, bones still jutted out from Hedeman's face. He underwent another reconstructive surgery and never looked quite the same as he had before the wreck, even with six titanium plates holding his face together. But he was the same old Tuff—gambling, abusing rental cars, and riding bulls—until 1998, when a neck injury forced him to retire.

He settled into a house in Morgan Mill, Texas, with his wife, Tracy, and their two young boys and prepared for life after bull riding. Drawn to the spotlight, he took a job as a TV commentator for PBR broadcasts and remained the most marketable bull rider in rodeo—and one of the best paid.

His job as PBR president, which required that he attend every BFTS stop and sign autographs, paid him more than $100,000 a year. His TV gig paid him about $100,000. He took in tens of thousands of dollars more from endorsement deals with Bud Light and a handful of other companies, not to mention his annual bull riding event in Fort Worth and a BFTS event in Bossier City that he copromoted with the PBR and Ron Pack, Hedeman's close friend and business adviser.

To many of the young PBR riders, Hedeman was a hero and an after-hours ringleader. At 41, he was trim, with a full head of light brown hair and bangs framing his handsome face. He liked to join the other riders at the after-event parties and proved to be a loyal supporter of his highest-paying corporate sponsor—Bud Light. He held the beer bottles with the same ease and frequency that he'd held a bull rope.

After a welcome dinner held the night before the Tuff Hedeman Championship Challenge began, he ushered the men onto a chartered bus. It was loaded with liquor and strippers. The 30-minute bus ride ended at New Orleans Nights, an upscale gentlemen's club in Fort Worth. Clutching a stack of $20 bills, he worked the strip club like a master of ceremonies, peeling the twenties off his stack and buying lap dances for his guests. Maybe it was the main reason riders annually voted the Tuff Hedeman Championship Challenge the PBR's best event. Or maybe it was the ferocious bulls.

TEN MINUTES AFTER JOHNSON WAS TAKEN OUT OF THE ARENA, an announcement came over the PA system: "Ladies and gentlemen, we have an update on Ross Johnson. The doctor asked him where he was, and he replied, 'Fort Worth.'"

Ross Johnson was alive! Cheers filled the arena. But the 24-year-old rider from Alvord, Texas, wasn't out of danger. His eyes fluttered as he lay still on an examination table inside the sports medicine room. Tears streamed down Abby Johnson's face as she gently stroked her husband's stomach. "You're a tough son of a gun," said Johnson's father, Bobby.

Tandy Freeman, who directed the medical team for the PBR, hovered over Johnson where three padded examination tables were sardined. Balding at age 46, Freeman had an impassive face and exuded a calm that put the riders at ease. "The first rule when you're in an emergency situation: Check your own pulse," Freeman liked to say. His own pulse was reptilian.

He had the same drawl as many of the riders, plus the requisite boots, jeans, and Western shirt that completed the cowboy look. But he was tall, with a slight paunch, and ill equipped to ride a bull. He never had.

An orthopedic surgeon based in Dallas, he had built his practice rebuilding shoulders, elbows, legs, knees, and ankles hit by bulls. At each of the PBR's 29 weekend events, Freeman and his staff of trainers— Rich Blyn, Peter Wang, and Tony Marek—brought four trunks filled with medical supplies, enough to run a small emergency room. At the events, if Freeman wasn't in the sports medicine room, he could be found sitting on the corner of the chutes, holding a Styrofoam cup of coffee and waiting for the inevitable. One in every 15 bull rides resulted in a new injury requiring some form of treatment. As Freeman once said, "It's not *if* you'll get hurt, but when and how bad."

That line became the mantra of the PBR.

Competing with pain or injuries was more than a badge of honor for the riders. It was the only way to get paid. There were no guaranteed checks other than a modest appearance fee. And that provided incentive to ride with a broken rib, a separated shoulder, or a partially collapsed lung—all of which Freeman had seen.

Bull riding was a brutal sport, and the 2004 season had been no exception. Twelve events into the season, Freeman and his staff had treated riders for the following injuries: broken cheekbone, broken eye socket, broken collarbone, broken shoulder blade, torn groin muscle, two broken ribs, four lacerated chins, 15 concussions, and too many strains, bumps, and bruises to count. Over the course of the season, they expected to go through more than 2,000 pounds of ice to reduce swelling; 425 cases of tape to wrap knees, hands, wrists, ankles, and fingers; and 150 syringes. HealthSouth and the PBR paid the $250,000 cost, which included salaries for the three trainers. Other than getting reimbursed for travel expenses, Freeman worked pro bono.

Once upon a time, there was no sports medicine room, no orthopedic surgeon, and no athletic trainers. Riders had been lucky to have an ambulance on hand. In those days riders treated their own injuries with a handful of aspirin, a 12-pack of beer, and occasionally something stronger—phenylbutazone, commonly known as bute, an anti-inflammatory drug given to injured horses. Over the counter, under the counter, the riders would take what they could get. They distrusted most doctors, especially the ones who advised them to give up bull riding. That, thought the riders, was like someone telling the doctor to give up medicine. So they stuck with the aspirin and beer as their primary form of treatment. But that began to change in the late 1970s.

Walt Garrison, then a fullback with the Dallas Cowboys, started putting on rodeos; and J. Pat Evans, team doctor for the Cowboys, came along to treat injured contestants. Evans was a beefy man with short-cropped hair, and what the riders liked about him most was that he never suggested they quit. The goal, Evans told the rodeo cowboys, was to get them healed and back competing as quickly as possible. A rider with a broken foot gave Evans a chance to prove his point. He built a cast with a spur lodged in the back.

Wearing a cowboy boot on his good foot and the cast with a spur on his broken foot, the rider returned to action.

Eventually Evans started directing a full-time orthopedic staff for rodeo events, and the PBR wanted its own. Freeman joined the tour as its on-site doctor in 1995, and wherever the PBR tour went, he and his staff followed. More astonishing than the number of injuries bull riders suffered was the number of times a rider walked away from a wreck relatively unscathed. But that March night in Fort Worth, Johnson's wreck marked the first time that season a rider had to be carried out of the arena on a stretcher. Instead of sending Johnson to the hospital, Freeman kept him at the arena for observation. For one, he thought Johnson would get more attention in the PBR sports medicine room than he would in the local emergency room. Two, Freeman worried about the expense.

To treat someone with a concussion, emergency room doctors routinely ordered a CAT scan and MRI; and by the time the riders were discharged, the cost approached $5,000. At PBR events, the rider carried $20,000 in insurance. But with a $500 deductible and the rider responsible for 20 percent of medical expenses, a $5,000 bill would leave the rider responsible for $1,500—a huge burden for riders scratching out a living.

But 30 minutes after the wreck, Johnson's condition worsened. He no longer knew where he was. His brain had begun to swell. On Freeman's orders, Johnson was moved back onto the stretcher and taken to the hospital.

BACK INSIDE THE ARENA during first-round action Saturday night, Jody Newberry had taken the lead with a 90-point ride on Jack Daniels Happy Hour. But when the first round of competition ended Saturday night, most people's thoughts were with Johnson—just as they were when the bull riding resumed Sunday afternoon. The final round of competition began with no sign of the fallen rider.

Midway through second-round action, a cowboy entered the arena and wrapped Rob Smets in a bear hug. "I love you, man," he whispered into Smets's ear. "I don't know how to thank you."

It was Ross Johnson. Smets hugged him back.

Then Johnson joined the riders behind the chutes, and one by one they filed by to shake his hand and welcome him back. "How you feeling?" asked Owen Washburn.

"Hurting from the top of my head to the bottom of my toes," he said with a grin.

Hedeman walked up and gave Johnson a hug. "Man, I didn't know if I'd ever see you again," Hedeman said. "Glad to see you standing here."

Johnson had emerged from the wreck with nothing more than a concussion, six staples on the side of his head, and a very sore tongue. Riding without a mouthpiece, he had clamped down on his tongue, which had left a blackish purple bruise across the pink flesh. As Johnson mingled with the riders, the PA announcer called the crowd's attention to the back of the chutes, and Johnson raised his right hand to acknowledge the cheering crowd.

Later, during second-round action, Mike Lee climbed aboard Mesquite Heat, unridden in nine attempts. Out of the chute, the bull reared back, twisting its body like a spastic worm, and then did it again. Then he reared back even farther, the bull's body rising straight up and down. Legs slipping off the side of the bull, Lee looked like he was trying to hold on to a rocket. Somehow he managed to hold on for the full 8 seconds before falling off the bull.

"Mike Lee," Justin McKee exclaimed during the OLN telecast, "how he did that I have no idea!"

The judges posted their scores: 92.5 points! Though the score fell short of the highest in PBR history—96.5, achieved by only Bubba Dunn and Chris Shivers, Shivers having done it twice—the 92.5 was the highest score yet that season. The ride showed why PBR insiders considered Lee, still 2 months away from his 21st birthday, the best young rider on tour and contender for the 2004 championship. But the day in Fort Worth belonged to the bulls.

They dominated the second round and the short-go that followed, bucking off all 15 riders in the championship round. And with Little Yellow Jacket tossing Reuben Geleynse and Hotel California throwing Tony Mendes, the two bulls validated their chances at Bull of the Year honors. Mike Collins, a 25-year-old rider from Adair, Oklahoma, and one of only two riders to ride two bulls during the 2-day event, got bucked off Blueberry Wine on the last ride of the day. But with the cumulative point lead, he won the event by default. Lee finished third, Moraes finished 19th, and Justin McBride finished 22nd; and the hobbling riders headed back to the sports medicine room.

As the room eventually thinned out, melting ice bags, unraveled ace bandages, and wrapped, bloody surgical scissors remained the testament to the mini massacre. In addition to Johnson, the official injured list included a dislocated leg tendon to Gilbert Carrillo; a concussion and sprained neck to Brendon Clark; an aggravated shoulder injury to Dave Samsel; and a concussion and dislocated right shoulder to Craig Sasse. "All in all, not bad," Freeman said. "Only had to send one rider to the hospital."

That rider perched himself on top of a padded examination table for final inspection. Freeman looked at the 4-inch bruise stretching from Johnson's Adam's apple to under his left ear. He checked the gash on the right side of Johnson's head. Then he looked directly into Johnson's eyes.

"You need to be wearing a helmet," Freeman said. Getting treatment at the adjacent table, rider Brendon Clark caught Johnson's attention and arched his eyebrows. The look said it all: *Wear a helmet? Don't even think about it, Ross.*

"There's another one that needs to be wearing a helmet," Freeman said, nodding at Clark. "Don't listen to him, Ross. The helmet will protect you against injuries. And that means you'll be riding longer."

Freeman cited the success of protective vests as proof. Cody Lambert had invented the vests after Frost's fatal injury. And when vests became mandatory equipment in the mid-1990s, the incidence of serious chest and abdominal injuries dropped tenfold, according to Freeman, who anticipated the same reduction in head injuries if helmets were mandatory. But of the top 45 ranked riders entering the 2004 season, only nine wore a protective mask or helmet, and Freeman had grown resigned to the other riders' reluctance. Furthermore, the PBR had expressed no plan to make helmets mandatory.

Freeman handed Johnson a pouch of six Vicodins. "Take them as needed," he said.

Back in the locker room, Clark considered the advice Freeman gave to countless riders about wearing a helmet. "Maybe we should wear helmets," he said. "But we're cowboys, and I think we ought to be wearing cowboy hats."

A week later Ross Johnson showed up for competition with nothing more than a cowboy hat to protect his head.

CONCESSIONS	
Grilled hamburger	**$3.50**
Popcorn	**$3.50**
Cocktail with choice of whiskey, scotch, bourbon, or vodka	**$5.25**

Unless it goes down easy with a mixed drink, they don't have it—and that includes deep-fried Twinkies.

STANDINGS

1	Adriano Moraes	4,951 points	6	Mike White	2,319.5 points
2	Justin McBride	3,557 points	7	Greg Potter	2,319 points
3	Mike Lee	3,520.5 points	8	Dave Samsel	2,248.5 points
4	Ross Coleman	2,748 points	9	Reuben Geleynse	2,210.5 points
5	Jody Newberry	2,627 points	10	Dan Henricks	2,079 points

NINE

WANNABES, WASHUPS & DREAMERS

THIBODAUX, LOUISIANA
SATURDAY & SUNDAY, MARCH 27 & 28, 2004

The license plates told it all. Georgia. Florida. North Carolina. Texas. Wisconsin. The cars and trucks pulling into the parking lot outside the Thibodaux Civic Center carried bull riders from across the South and beyond to this Humps N' Horns event, the bottom rung of the PBR's two-tiered minor-league system.

While the tour's top 45 riders competed before sellout

crowds in cities like Atlanta, Nashville, and Philadelphia, the road to the Built Ford Tough Series wound through towns like Jasper, Texas; Las Cruces, New Mexico; Afton, Wyoming; and this week, Thibodaux, Louisiana, a Cajun-spiced outpost about 70 miles west of New Orleans. The locals served up jambalaya, boudin, and boiled crawfish in a place where Bayou Lafourche, murky waters infested with alligators, cut through the heart of town. Not that the dangerous reptiles kept those living in Thibodaux from paddling down the bayou during annual races in their pirogues, canoes made from hollowed-out tree trunks. Some in this town of 14,431 still speak Cajun French.

In all, 78 riders—among the 656 card-carrying members of the PBR in 2004—showed up to compete for about $13,000 in prize money at the Bud Light Humps N' Horns. There were no stars in the mix of riders, who included aging veterans, frustrated wannabes, and peach-fuzzed newcomers like Eathan Graves. Emerging from a camper with Texas plates, Graves wore a cowboy hat about two sizes too big for his tiny head and appeared at least a year away from needing a razor. He looked like he'd crumple in the face of a stiff breeze, much less in the face of a raging bull. According to his California driver's license, he was 18, but he looked barely old enough to drive. At 5 feet 8 and 115 pounds, he was among the frailest riders in Thibodaux, if not all of professional rodeo.

For months he'd eagerly waited for the day he'd turn 18, the minimum age to be eligible for PBR competition. It didn't matter if you had never been on a bull before, as long as you had $345 for the permit. Similar to baseball's minor-league system, the PBR-sanctioned Humps N' Horns and US Smokeless Tobacco Company Challenger Tour events serve as a feeder system, giving riders a chance to break into the top-45 money earners and qualify for the BFTS. To start, Graves and other new riders had to buy a permit, which made them eligible for non-BFTS events, with most spots available on the Humps N' Horns tour—the lowest tier of the PBR's minor leagues. The next step was to earn $2,500 in PBR winnings, which qualified a rider to upgrade his status from permit holder to cardholder and increased his chances of securing spots at Challenger Tour events, where the bulls were ranker, the purses larger, and the chances of amassing enough money to crack the top 45 infinitely better.

The road to the majors could be long and expensive. Graves's journey had begun in January 2004. When he and three buddies piled into a truck, he hit the road and the minor-league circuit. The truck was not only their transportation but also their home. At night the four young men squeezed into the truck camper and slept on makeshift beds made of foam and futons.

As they drove from event to event, Graves kept in his daily planner a neat record of his performances at each event. The handwritten entries showed stops in Macon, Georgia; Tallahassee, Florida; Tucson; Knoxville, Tennessee; Columbia, South Carolina; North Charleston, South Carolina; Beaumont, Texas; Abilene, Texas; Hidalgo, Texas; and Laredo, Texas. The entries also showed a total winnings of $1,500 and that Graves had successfully ridden 48 percent of his bulls. And inside that daily planner, he also kept a fake million-dollar bill—a reminder of his ultimate goal: to win the coveted PBR championship and end-of-the-year bonus.

Graves never considered college rodeo as an option, even though 134 schools—mostly small 4-year colleges and junior colleges—offered scholarships. As the PBR's popularity and prize money had grown, so had the number of riders bypassing college and heading straight for the pros. To hear the riders' broken grammar and habitual use of "ain't," one might have assumed there was little going on beneath those cowboy hats. But they knew how to negotiate life on the road—finding cheap hotels, cheap food, and, in some cases, cheap women—and when interlopers entered their world, they detected bullshit with the unerring accuracy of a bomb-sniffing dog. A deep understanding of Chaucer and Tolstoy, a grasp of quantum physics, or a command of Middle Eastern politics was irrelevant on the PBR tour. Winning the national college bull riding championship was no guarantee of PBR success, either. Of the nine riders who'd won the past 10 college bull riding championships, only one, Corey Navarre, had made a steady living on the PBR. Not even Will Farrell, who won the college bull riding championship in '99 and '02, had made it in the PBR.

Chris Shivers, who had won the PBR title in 2000 and 2003, had never set foot on a college campus. Nor had Cody Hart, who won it in 1999, or Adriano Moraes, who won in 1994 and 2001. Of the PBR's first 10 champions, only Tuff Hedeman, Michael Gaffney, and Owen Washburn—all older than 30—had competed in college rodeo.

By midafternoon Saturday in Thibodaux, the riders began inching forward in a line that snaked outside a small office inside the Thibodaux Civic Center to pay their $155 entry fee. There were no entry fees at the BFTS, where the purses were almost seven times as big as they were at Humps N' Horns events—not counting BFTS bonuses, which sometimes reached $100,000 a ride.

Matt Merritt was a chipper 22-year-old barrelman from North Carolina. Accompanied by his new fiancée, he took his floppy shoes, face paint, and bagful of gags on the road 45 to 50 weekends a year, typically making $1,000 for a 2-day event. He'd seen the PBR's star barrelman, Flint Rasmussen, leave sellout crowds doubled over in laughter. So he figured his only shot at becoming the PBR's star clown was if Rasmussen retired or got freight-trained by a bull.

While Merritt lugged his gear into the Civic Center, Troy Kibodeaux, an aspiring stock contractor who hauled his prize bull Chocolate Chip 4½ hours from his home in Sulphur, Louisiana, drove into the parking lot. This was the first bull riding event for Chocolate Chip and Kibodeaux, who only recently had started breeding bulls and explained, "One bull got good, and so I called the Big Man."

The "Big Man" was Jerry Nelson, who stood 6 feet 6 inches and weighed over 300 pounds. He wore his shock of white hair pulled back, and his unruly white beard was almost long enough for him to pass as an aging member of ZZ Top. He looked as big and imposing as some of the bulls, and these were some serious bulls. Nelson had made his fortune in oil equipment sales before deciding to sink a few million dollars into the bull-breeding business. In just 10 years, he'd built one of the largest cattle holdings in the United States and one of the rankest strings of bulls in rodeo, including a promising 4-year-old named Just a Dream.

"Little Yellow Jacket can't pack the son of a bitch's water," Nelson said. "When we bucked the son of a bitch in Houston, you could have driven a Peterbilt underneath him."

While Nelson occasionally sent his top bulls to the PBR, he used his second- and third-string buckers while copromoting and producing the Bud Light Humps N' Horns. It was here that Nelson was in his element, away from the bright lights and the politics of the PBR, and trying to make a buck in shit-kicking towns like Thibodaux. But Nelson didn't produce on the cheap. To provide commentary at the Thibodaux event, he hired Donnie Gay, the eight-time bull riding champion who also did commentary for PRCA events televised on ESPN and had once served as the lead commentator for PBR telecasts. Gay was short, stocky, and opinionated. Though he remained a celebrity in the world of rodeo, he looked at home inside the dimly lit Thibodaux Civic Center (capacity 3,858), with the scoreboard that belonged in a high school gym circa 1970.

About an hour before the competition began, Gay inspected the audio system. He was looking for the microphone he was supposed to use. "Which mic?" he asked.

"The one with the broken handle," someone replied.

A microphone with a broken handle in an aging building. Figured. But Gay smiled and said, "I'll go anywhere for the right money."

Another reason Gay had come to Thibodaux was to watch Kendall Galmiche, a promising 18-year-old rider from Carriere, Mississippi, who had turned down an offer to play baseball for Mississippi State to pursue a career in bull riding. Gay liked what he'd seen while coaching Galmiche. But not all the riders here were as bright eyed or promising as Galmiche. Bloodshot and bleary eyes were a testament to the late nights and long drives on a quest that for some began to look like a cruel mirage. The BFTS felt a million miles away, or at least as far as Thibodaux was from that weekend's BFTS event in Fresno, California, at the 15,000-seat Save Mart Center. But like a narcotic, bull riding kept luring back riders like Jacob "Spook" Wiggins, a 29-year-old Texan with close-cropped black hair and a mischievous grin. If not one of the sport's best riders, Wiggins was one of its best storytellers.

He kept up a running chatter and talked about drunken orgies, nights in jail, punching out his best friend, driving 24 hours to the next rodeo, the time a bull gored him in the nuts and doctors needed 54 stitches to sew them back together, and on and on. "I'm jinxed with injuries," he said. "Every year I start to make the finals, I get killed off."

Then there was Robby Shriver, a blond-haired, upbeat 27-year-old from Screven, Georgia, who spoke with a mixture of conviction and desperation. He'd upgraded to cardholder status 2 years ago, but after a slump was competing mostly in Humps N' Horns events. "Everything I have right now, I'm putting into this sport," he said, "and, God willing, I will make the PBR finals this year. . . . I need to win tonight."

It was a 2-night competition, with half of the 78 riders competing Saturday and the other half competing Sunday. Each rider got one bull, and the eight riders with the top scores advanced to the championship round. The eight riders with the highest cumulative scores earned checks from the purse of $13,000. Graves and his buddies helped set up the event Saturday but wouldn't compete until Sunday.

Saturday night, Gay got a look at his promising pupil, and he liked what he saw in the first round when Galmiche rode a bull named Snoopy for 84 points. Waving him over, Gay offered some advice and encouragement as Galmiche prepared for the championship round.

But his short-go ride lasted only a few seconds, with Galmiche getting bucked off and landing awkwardly. He limped out of the arena and soon was strapped to a stretcher and headed to the hospital. Glancing at Galmiche being carried to an ambulance, Gay never missed a beat, keeping up a steady banter as, one by one, the bulls carrying riders came bucking out of the chutes. It was a reminder of the cold-natured business: rider down, show goes on.

Shriver got bucked off Slim to None—the bull's name corresponding with Shriver's chances of making the 2004 PBR finals. Then there was Tater Porter, who'd won almost $650,000 during his 9-year career with the PBR before injuries relegated him to the minors. At 33, he found himself competing with riders 10 years his junior. Standing in the comically named VIP room—with its thin supply of cheese squares, vegetables, water, and beer—Porter looked around at some of the young upstarts and said, "I'm wanting my old job back, and you see these 18-

year-olds champing at the bit to get your job. So you better stay one step ahead." That night Porter scored an 82 on Killin' Time, enough to suggest a comeback was in the making but not enough to win any money in Thibodaux. Jared Farley, an 18-year-old from Australia, emerged as the first-night leader, with an 88-point ride. Unsure if the score would hold up for even a check, Farley bolted town and headed for the next bull riding event.

Sunday morning, Jerry Nelson, his wife, Beverly, and Gay met for breakfast at the Ramada Inn. Between bites of eggs, bacon, and grits, they talked about the PBR and the state of bull riding. Nelson grumbled that the PBR was shying away from some of the ranker bulls, such as his own Satan's Twin. This coming from the man who owned Knock 'em Out John when the bull knocked out Jerome Davis in a wreck that left the rider paralyzed from the chest down.

Nelson also questioned the motivation of some of the riders on the minor-league circuit. "Chasing dreams?" he harrumphed. "They're chasing the girls."

Gay moaned about how little the new riders knew about the sport, adding, "Justin McBride don't know if bulls sleep on the ground or roost in the trees." He also lamented the young riders buying their cards and going straight to the PBR-sponsored events, saying, "That's like buying your kid a motorcycle or a machine gun and not giving him proper instruction and hoping he comes home okay."

Ignoring the dangers, many of the young riders were lured onto the minor-league circuit when they heard stories about riders like Luke Snyder.

STYLISH SIDEBURNS AND A CHERUBIC FACE gave the brown-haired, brown-eyed Snyder the look of a boy-band heartthrob. But he proved to be more than a pretty face. The kid named Luke from Raymore, Missouri, looked destined for stardom before he was old enough to drive.

He finished runner-up at the International Youth Finals at age 16. Before he even turned pro, he had an agent and three endorsement

93

deals. At 16, he finished runner-up at the International Youth Bull Riding Finals. But in 2001, his rookie season on the PBR, nobody could've guessed how fast and far he'd rise.

Snyder finished third at his first Challenger Tour event and won another Challenger Tour event 3 days later. Just like that, he was on his way to the BFTS. But not alone.

His parents, Michael and Susan, accompanied their son as he blazed through his rookie season, finishing fourth at the Tuff Hedeman Championship Challenge and consistently finishing in the top 10. Snyder qualified for the 2001 PBR finals and hit the jackpot in Las Vegas, winning the finals event championship. One of only two riders to ride all five of his bulls, he left Vegas as Rookie of the Year and with year-end winnings totaling almost $350,000.

As soon as he got home to Missouri, he bought a $40,000 Cadillac Escalade equipped with 20-inch chrome rims. He blasted gangsta rap out of the industrial-strength speakers and looked like the PBR's bling-bling solution in appealing to the young MTV crowd coveted by Madison Avenue marketeers.

His climb fueled fantasies of more than a few young riders bent on instant success. But the idea of instant success was folly, because they knew only part of Snyder's story.

His bull riding career started on the living room couch. As a kid, Snyder tied a rope around the cushions, rode his own imaginary bulls, and instructed friends to conduct the postride "TV interviews." He was preparing for fame, and his parents encouraged him. When Luke turned 8, Michael and Susan drove him across the country to youth rodeos, and the buzz began. Snyder's parents paid for private lessons with Gary Leffew, a onetime world champion known as the guru of bull riding coaches. As Luke's talent grew, so did his obsession with the PBR.

At age 16, he called the PBR headquarters and asked about the possibility of doctoring his birth certificate. He couldn't bear waiting until he turned 18, the minimum age for a rider to compete in a PBR-sanctioned event. Patience was not Snyder's virtue.

His parents pulled him out of high school after his junior year and put more than 50,000 miles on their camper, taking Luke from one rodeo to the next while they homeschooled him during his senior year. Then in moved agent Mark Nestlen and companies eager to attach themselves to bull riding's next "big thing." His rookie year only whetted the appetites of those looking for a fresh face in bull riding.

Deciding Luke was old enough to take care of himself during his second PBR season, Snyder's parents and Luke found new, unofficial chaperones—Ross Coleman, Justin McBride, and Cory Rasch, then three of the tour's most notorious hell-raisers. During a get-together at a bull owner's house, while Snyder was talking on his cell phone, Rasch shoved him into the pool. Snyder went bonkers. The cell phone was soaked and broken.

"Just put it in the oven," Rasch suggested.

Snyder had a better idea. He walked into the bull owner's kitchen and put his cell phone in the microwave. Thirty seconds later, the microwave blew up, the perfect metaphor for what loomed.

He won his first regular-season BFTS event in 2002 but dropped from seventh to 16th in the final standings while earning less than half of the $350,000 he had taken home as a rookie. In 2003, he finished no higher than second at any event and finished 17th in the overall standings, earning $104,159. The rising star was sinking.

Midway through the 2004 season, Snyder went 10 straight events without earning a check and during one stretch got bucked off nine bulls in a row. This was the part of Snyder's story that young aspiring pros didn't know—or ignored. Getting to the PBR was hard enough. The partying lifestyle made staying there just as hard.

While Snyder was trying to get back on track in Fresno, California, the minor-leaguers were trying to make their fantasies come alive in the dank Thibodaux Civic Center.

THE MINOR-LEAGUE CIRCUIT WAS A MONEY PIT FOR MOST, but it also was a breeding ground for future standouts. In 2004, 33 Humps N' Horns events and the 49 Challenger Tour events provided an outlet for riders like Eathan Graves. Sunday in Thibodaux, he got the chance to compete against some of the best riders in the world.

James Pierce, the event's copromoter, had arranged to bring in Justin McBride and three other BFTS regulars—Ross Johnson, Brian Wooley, and Willis Trosclair. On Friday and Saturday, they'd competed in Fresno at the PBR's 15th BFTS stop of the season. At six o'clock Sunday morning, McBride and company boarded a plane for New Orleans, where a limo was waiting to take them to Thibodaux.

Shortly before the scheduled afternoon start Sunday at the Bud Light Humps N' Horns, the black stretch limo pulled into the parking lot, and out they stepped—McBride, Wooley, Trosclair, and Johnson, who just 2 weeks earlier had survived the scariest wreck of his life. "It's just great to be here in Chicago," he joked.

When McBride swaggered into the dressing room, the loud chatter died. Even Wiggins, with his storyteller's gift of gab, went silent. They were in the presence of a bull riding star.

Outside the locker room, looking for his name on the draw sheet, Graves broke into a smile and pointed to the list. "Justin McBride," he said.

More than awestruck, Graves looked excited about his chance to ride against the PBR's 2003 reserve world champion, because after the limo pulled off and after the special introduction for the PBR guys, McBride would have to stay on one of Nelson's bulls for 8 seconds—just like Graves and all the other riders.

McBride and the other PBR riders were competing as a favor to Pierce, but they were looking to do no favors for the likes of Graves. So maybe it was jet lag. Or overconfidence. Or the bulls. But the PBR guys went down like rookies, McBride and the three others all getting bucked off in the first round.

Graves, yet to ride, was settling on top of his first-round bull. Gay poked fun at Graves's nonexistent butt, and the kid promptly rode his ass off. Like a toy sailboat bobbing atop crashing waves, he stayed afloat on Rapid Rat, electrified the small crowd, and advanced to the championship round with a score of 86.

Riding last in the championship round, Graves had a chance to win his first event. But four jumps into the ride, he got bucked off, which relegated him to second place behind Jared Farley, whose 88-point score from Saturday night held up for the victory. He'd already left for his next event, so he would be receiving the check by mail.

After changing clothes, Graves headed to Nelson's cramped office. "Eathan, you want some money?" Nelson's wife said.

"I'd love it."

She handed him his second-place check of $2,740.40, and he asked where he might be able to cash it. Someone suggested he deposit it in his checking account. "Don't have one," said Graves, who produced a $1,100 uncashed check he'd won 2 weeks earlier.

With the payday in Thibodaux, Graves learned, he had qualified to upgrade his status to cardholder, which would help secure spots at the Challenger Tour events and move him one step closer to the BFTS and the 2004 finals. Beaming, he walked into the parking lot, pulled out his cell phone, and called home.

"Hey, Dad. Good. How are you? I won second. They bucked me off in the short-go, but I was only a couple of jumps from winning. I won 2,700 bucks."

Across the parking lot, Troy Kibodeaux paced in front of his truck. He was killing time—or it was killing him.

He'd poked his head inside Nelson's temporary office twice and found it crowded, so he returned to the parking lot and waited for the right moment. He wanted to know if Nelson was interested in buying Chocolate Chip, still in the pen outside the arena. Fact is, Kibodeaux hoped to leave Chocolate Chip with Nelson and drive home with $2,500 for his bull. He felt good after watching Pancho Flores ride the bull for an 83.5 and sixth place.

"I'm just getting started—getting started at the bottom, where some people have to start," Kibodeaux said. "Jerry gives a small man a chance to get in with the big guys."

With dusk setting in, Kibodeaux walked back inside the arena to Nelson's office. He leaned against the doorjamb and waited for the Big Man to initiate the conversation. Looking up from a stack of papers, Nelson saw the aspiring stock contractor.

"Bring him to New Iberia—we've got another bull riding over there April 16—and let me look at him again," Nelson said. "Holler at me in 2 weeks."

Kibodeaux nodded. "Thank you, Jerry," he said, collecting a $100 check, standard payment for each time a bull bucked at a Humps N' Horns event.

Minutes later Kibodeaux backed up his truck to the pen, loaded up Chocolate Chip, and began the 4½-hour drive home with $2,400 less than he'd hoped to have—but still with a bull and a chance.

CONCESSIONS

Crab cake with crawfish	$6
Tea cookies	$1
Hamburger	$2.50
Hot dog	$2

In Thibodaux, they seemed willing to fry everything *but* Twinkies.

STANDINGS

1	Adriano Moraes	5,930.5 points	6	Greg Potter	2,994 points
2	Mike Lee	4,687.5 points	7	Mike White	2,604 points
3	Justin McBride	4,469 points	8	Reuben Geleynse	2,458 points
4	Jody Newberry	3,278 points	9	Mike Collins	2,362 points
5	Ross Coleman	3,177.5 points	10	Brendon Clark	2,350 points

TEN

PROTECTING
THE BULLS

⭐

KANSAS CITY, MISSOURI
SATURDAY & SUNDAY, JUNE 12 & 13, 2004

Randy Bernard stepped out of the locker room at Kemper Arena when a PBR official came running down the hall. "We're introducing, and there's not a cowboy out there."

Bernard looked frantic. "What were they thinking?" he fumed. "It's not even seven o'clock."

Go-go-go!

Fast as they could, the riders tromped down the hall toward the darkened arena, most heading for the alleyway. During competition, the alleyway serves as the exit for the bulls. But during introductions it serves as the entryway for most of the riders. First one in was Corey Navarre and . . . WHAM.

Facedown in the dirt, Navarre looked up and saw the loose bull that had just run him over. While Navarre was helped to the sports medicine clinic, the other cowboys scrambled into the arena. About 30 minutes later, walking gingerly, Navarre arrived behind the chutes. The collision with the bull had sprained Navarre's right knee and broken one of his ribs. He was out for the night—and hacked off about a pre-event riders' meeting, which in turn had led to his frantic run to the arena.

"Stupid," Navarre said, referring to the meeting's subject matter. "Stuff we all know."

But it was no ordinary meeting—it had been triggered by angry bull owners.

When it comes to bull riding, it's the riders, not the bulls, who suffer most of the injuries. So for years promoters took precautions to protect the riders, such as requiring the bulls' horns to be shaved until the ends were flat and no larger in circumference than a half-dollar coin. But now the stock contractors wanted more protection for their bulls, especially the prize ones worth $50,000 and up.

Primarily, the owners were concerned about riders who were pulling their bull ropes too tight and lingering in the chutes too long. Or with the ropes wrapped around the bull's girth and directly behind his front legs, lingering just long enough to "soak" the bull—rodeo vernacular meaning to cut off a bull's circulation, sap his strength, and thereby reduce his bucking power. Riders under the most intense scrutiny were Ednei Caminhas, Moraes, and the other Brazilians, a group notorious for pulling tight ropes and fidgeting in the chutes. For more than 2 years, Robbie Herrington, a prominent bull owner, had stewed about the practice, and Herrington had clout.

Most stock contractors, such as H. D. Page, stayed silent, worrying the issue would prompt animal-rights groups like People for the Ethical Treatment of Animals (PETA) to cause trouble. But Herrington wasn't afraid of trouble, and his beef went back to an incident in June 2002.

At the 2002 event in Louisville, Kentucky, Caminhas had been in the chute on Herrington's bull Dillinger, the PBR's Bull of the Year in 2000 and 2001, a bull that had cost Herrington $50,000. As Caminhas shifted into position, with riders already having helped pull and tighten his rope, the bull dropped to his forelegs. Rising up, he dropped again. A bullfighter waved something in Dillinger's face, trying to get the bull back on his feet, and Dillinger kicked his left hind leg through the chute slat and yanked it back out. Though Caminhas finally nodded for the gate and rode the bull, it would be Dillinger's last ride.

X-rays showed the bull had broken the hock in his left hind leg.

"It's time to do something," Herrington barked at the back judge that day.

"I've already fined him," Herrington remembers the judge saying, to which Herrington replied: "Make him get off."

Convinced Caminhas was "soaking" the bulls, Herrington called the PBR office and asked for every one of Caminhas's scores from the 2002 season. He sorted the data in a spreadsheet and found that Caminhas had scored an average of three fewer points than other riders on the same bulls. The implication: The bulls were underperforming with Caminhas on board because the Brazilian was cutting off their air supply while taking an excessive amount of time in the chutes. Herrington took the numbers to the 2002 finals in Las Vegas as evidence. But no action was taken as Caminhas went on to win the 2002 championship.

In April 2004, at the Ty Murray Invitational in Albuquerque, New Mexico, Herrington exchanged heated words with Moraes after Herrington's bull Coyote Ugly looked uncharacteristically sluggish during Moraes's 81.5-point ride. "The little bull, he couldn't take it," Moraes said.

"No shit," replied Herrington, claiming that Moraes had sat on the bull for 4½ minutes before leaving the chute. "Let's see if you can take it. Let's weigh you down for about 10 minutes and see what you can do. Goddang it, Adriano, you can ride the bull without doing all that."

The issue at last boiled over after the PBR's May 15 and 16 Pennzoil Invitational in Springdale, Arkansas, and the PBR's 20th BFTS event of the season. Moraes drew Hotel California, previously unridden and co-owned by Tom Teague and Dillon and H. D. Page. Though he rode the bull for 89 points, Hotel California looked sluggish during the ride and as he left the arena. When the Pages returned to their ranch in Ardmore, Oklahoma, they unloaded Hotel California from the hauling truck, and Dillon Page noticed a large lump shaped like a banana on the side of the bull.

Within days the lump doubled in size, and a veterinarian determined it was a hematoma and said it likely had resulted from the pressure of the bull rope during its last ride. The bull, until then contending for Bull of the Year, would be out of competition for 8 to 10 weeks. News of the injury infuriated Herrington.

Weeks earlier Dr. James Hall, a veterinarian whom Herrington and two other prominent contractors used, had urged Herrington to address the issue with the PBR. Herrington suggested Hall write a letter. Following Hotel California's injury, Herrington e-mailed his veterinarian's letter to the PBR headquarters.

"I wish to decry a practice allowed within PBR that I feel is both cruel and unfair," the letter began. "I am a practicing veterinarian, familiar with animal restraint in the old and new mode, and I believe that the 'deep cutting' of the bull rope into the heart girth is paralyzing and painful.

"Please find the enclosed, the textbook description of 'casting,' by which grown bulls can be lain down and held. This is also cruel to ask these bulls to expand and 'buck into' these unyielding pressures. If we just want to ride the 'nearly' unrideable bulls, then how much better would it be to allow a tranquilizer to be given to 'disadvantage' the bull in a more humane form. . . .

"I believe it is time to legislate fairness, to the secondary heroes of our sport, our bulls."

Within an hour of getting the e-mail, Bernard called Herrington, who asked Bernard to take the matter to the PBR board of directors. Herrington wanted the Brazilian-style ropes banned.

Most riders agreed that the main advantage of the Brazilian ropes was this: Unlike an American-style rope, the Brazilian rope is pulled from the opposite side of a rider's hand—with the tail coming up the left side for a right-handed rider and up the right side for a left-handed rider. So when a rider using a Brazilian rope slipped to the outside of a bull, the rope naturally pulled him back toward the middle. But some stock contractors speculated there was another advantage: Brazilian ropes could be pulled tighter.

The week before the Kansas City Classic, the PBR board met by teleconference. Of the allegedly guilty riders, one board member suggested, "Send the bastards back to Brazil." Cooler heads prevailed.

Cody Lambert, vice president of the PBR's board of directors and livestock director, rejected the idea that a Brazilian-style rope could be pulled tighter than an American-style rope. He also pointed out that Brazilians weren't the only riders taking too much time in the chute.

Cody Custer, the PBR back judge who had been sitting on the chutes during Moraes's ride on Hotel California, said he didn't think the rope had been pulled too tight. Moreover, he pointed out, Brazilians weren't the only ones using Brazilian-style ropes. Impressed by the Brazilians' success, American riders—such as Wiley Petersen, Ross Johnson, Gilbert Carrillo, and Adam Carrillo—traded in their American-style ropes for the Brazilian style. Furthermore, the PBR had no rules against any style of rope and had only general rules about how long a rider could take in the chute before starting his ride. Yet the board's response was unanimous: Something had to be done.

It went beyond animal rights. The stock contractors supplied the PBR with the country's best bulls, and they wanted their investment protected, because the value of the bulls and the cost of business were skyrocketing.

IT USED TO BE SO SIMPLE. Contractor goes to a sale barn. Rounds up 100 bulls. Pays by the pound just like the fast-food suppliers. Hopes for one or two buckers good enough for the rodeo. Takes the rejects back to the slaughterhouse. Those days are long gone. Bull breeding has gone high tech with such advances as artificial insemination, embryo flushing, and even cloning. A semen straw from Little Yellow Jacket sold for $500, a comparative bargain next to the $1,000 charged for a semen straw from Blueberry Wine.

"This thing is getting kind of crazy," said Gene Baker, a rancher and farmer in Anson, Texas.

Like he should talk. In 2001 Baker and Lyndal Hurst paid $100,000 for a retired bull named Houdini. Until then no one had paid more than $50,000 for a bull. Done bucking, Houdini stayed busy breeding some of the best crop of young bulls in the country. He was one of a kind until 2002. That year, in what is believed to be a first for the bull industry, Baker paid $20,000 to have Houdini cloned.

The scientific advances in bull breeding stemmed from a conversation between two friends—Bob Tallman, a famous rodeo announcer, and Sammy Andrews, a prominent stock contractor. It was 1992 in Las Vegas when they were bitching about breeders who advertised bulls by famous sires like Oscar or Red Rock, when in actuality the bulls came from some obscure sale barn. The uncertainty about a bull's lineage limited what most buyers were willing to pay for bulls. The only way to establish a credible market, thought Andrews, was to find a way to certify bloodlines. Then Tallman spoke the magic word: DNA.

Andrews knew nothing about it. Tallman knew plenty. Rodeo announcing was Tallman's calling, but animal science was his passion. In college he had studied artificial insemination, embryo transfer, and DNA. A fifth-generation cattleman, Tallman incorporated the science into his own bull-breeding program, started in 1972. Twenty years later, during his exchange with Andrews, Tallman thought, then uttered, "DNA"—the acronym for deoxyribonucleic acid, the blueprint for a genetic code. "Probably the smartest thing I ever said," he later remarked.

In 1996 Tallman and a business partner formed Buckers, Inc., which used DNA testing to certify a bull's bloodlines. They charged breeders to certify their bulls and list them with a registry, and the upstart company had the perfect way to drown out the skeptics: Bodacious.

Owned by Andrews, the bull ranked among the sport's most famous ever. In fact, riders grew to fear the bull so much, Andrews retired him in 1995. Now he wanted to breed him through this new program.

Every stock contractor in the business wanted a bull as rank as Bodacious—especially if they were certain the calf was a legitimate son. Tallman convinced Andrews that legitimacy required the use of DNA testing and a registry company like Buckers to keep records on all the certified bulls.

They hauled Bodacious to a semen collection agency in west Texas, called 13 prominent rodeo producers, and started collecting semen from those producers' top bulls, too. From 15 to 40, then to 100, the number of breeders using Buckers took off. Five years later the client list exceeded 600 bull owners. By 2003, the number of cattle registered at Buckers exceeded 11,000. In addition to a fee for registering each bull, Buckers got a percentage of any subsequent sale involving a bull registered with its company. The money came pouring in—even faster when Tallman conceived of another idea.

Looking for a way to attract more breeders and offer a way to show-case their bulls, Tallman set up futurities—bucking events for 2-, 3-, and 4-year-old bulls. Most times stock contractors couldn't tell if they had a decent bucker until the bull was 5. The futurities gave them a chance to assess the bulls' ability sooner, not to mention win some cash. Entry fees at the futurities generated first-place prize money upwards of $30,000.

Brilliant, thought Randy Bernard; and in 2003 the PBR bought out Tallman, renamed the company American Bucking Bull and recouped its investment by selling 19 shares of the new company for $25,000 apiece. Then the PBR created a buzz by offering a $100,000 first prize for the winner of a futurity for 4-year-olds the week of the 2004 finals in Las Vegas.

Sometimes stock contractors complained about politics within the PBR and took issue with the bulls selected by Lambert. But they had nowhere else to go to compete for the kind of money being offered: $280 every time a bull bucked in a preliminary round; $400 every time a bull bucked in the championship round; $750 for the top-rated bull at each event and $500 for the runner-up; $750 every time a bull combined with a rider for a score of 90 points or higher; and a handful of end-of-the-year bonuses, including $20,000 for the Bull of the Year. Not only that, but if an owner hauled more than 16 bulls to an event, he got $3.75 per mile. While the payoffs were high, so was the expense of doing business.

Each day a bull consumes up to 15 pounds of grain and nearly a bale of hay, costing about $80 a month. Then there's the transportation cost. Hauling 10 to 14 bulls to BFTS events requires a gooseneck rig that sells for up to $80,000. And if a bull owner plans to buck his bulls at BFTS events, they'd better be damn good. Of the thousands of bucking bulls across the country, only 15 are picked for the championship round at each BFTS event and another 55 to 85 bulls for the preliminary rounds. Over the 2004 regular season, there would be 27 championship rounds and 49 preliminary rounds.

As the PBR's popularity and prize money increased, so did the number of people shelling out money in search of bulls good enough to compete in the BFTS. Those higher costs spurred efforts to reduce the margin for error in bull breeding and prompted reliance on science and technology.

A few years earlier, Herrington had called the University of Southern California to see if there was interest in conducting experiments that would identify traits of a top-notch bucking bull. Armed with such information, stock contractors could take the guesswork out of breeding. But the information wouldn't come cheap. Southern Cal told Herrington it'd need $250,000 to conduct the study—with no money-back guarantee.

Then Herrington got a call from someone who offered to try it for free. Her name was Tina Rush, an avid PBR fan who was studying bovine genomics at St. Louis Community College of Florissant Valley in Missouri.

Dubbing her project "Rank Bulls Forever," Rush enlisted the help of one of her professors before getting in contact with Herrington through Teresa Underdown, an agent for riders. Before long Underdown was plucking hair strands from bulls and shipping them to Rush, who stored them in a freezer in the biotech lab at St. Louis Community College. The plan: Rush would use DNA testing on the hair strands to identify the leading characteristics of a rank bucking bull.

"The main hypothesis is there has to be some kind of genetic mutation or genetic alteration in bulls," she said. "Otherwise, all bulls would be rank."

Rodeo promoters could've really used such a program in the 1920s.

When rodeos first sprung up across the Southwest in the late 19th century, there was no such thing as bull riding. Bulls were bred strictly for beef production. Most of the rodeo events—calf roping, steer wrestling, and bareback riding—evolved from the skills cowboys needed to run a ranch. But at the turn of the century, with rodeo promoters looking for another marquee event, cowboys started riding steers, typically castrated before sexual maturity and as a result much tamer than the testosterone-charged bucking bulls. Then, around 1920, promoters upped the ante, holding their first bull riding events. Surely the sight of cowboys riding the 1-ton beasts would attract crowds. One problem: Many of the bulls didn't buck. Then promoters Ed McCarty and Verne Elliott introduced to rodeo a new breed of bull: crossbred Brahmas that originally had come from India and were known for their nasty streak and uncontrollable urge to buck. The sport was forever changed.

Every era had its superstar. Sharkey, who in 1913 during a 3-day competition in Salinas, California, threw 36 riders, none of them staying on the black bull for more than 3 seconds. Tarzan, the unridden bull from the 1930s that once tried to tear down the bars of the bucking chute before the gate could be opened. Jasbo, who earned his name when he plowed into the clown barrel belonging to Jasbo Fulkerson, knocked it over, and then tried to get inside the barrel with the terrified clown. Mighty Mike, who in the 1950s bucked every one of the star riders and killed a GI cowboy named Johnny Gravit when Gravit refused to let go of his bull rope and suffered fatal injuries while being dragged across the arena. Tornado, who in the 1960s bucked off 200 riders in a row before Freckles Brown finally conquered the bull. Oscar, the star of the 1970s that went unridden in his first 5 years of competition. Red Rock, a bull that in the 1980s went unridden in all of his 309 outs before Lane Frost rode him four times in a 1988 best-of-seven showdown with the bull. And who could forget Bodacious, a 1,850-

pound Charbray who dominated the '90s and sent Tuff Hedeman to the hospital for major reconstructive facial surgery. Yet for all the famous bulls of the past, veteran riders and stock contractors agreed that the sophisticated breeding programs of the 1990s had created more rank bulls than ever seen before. In fact, the joke in bull riding circles was that to keep up with the bulls, someone was going to have to start breeding riders.

Like the riders, the bulls are judged on every trip, with their ratings determined by the average score of the two judges, each allotted 25 points to rate the bull's performance. A bull that consistently scores between 23 and 25 will earn more than enough money to pay its feed and vet bills. But a bull regularly scoring 20 or below might be headed for the slaughterhouse, while scores in between that range will earn the label of a "user," middle-of-the-road bulls that help fill the pen. Most of the PBR bulls buck 26 weeks out of the year and travel thousands of miles to get to the BFTS spots, held in 20 states as far apart as Worcester, Massachusetts, and Anaheim, California.

Even with the scientific advances, some of the most successful stock contractors admitted they still depended on luck. How else to explain a crippled bucker in 1997 producing one of the PBR's great bulls? The crippled sire was known only by his branding number, "01." As a young bull, he'd shown extraordinary promise before breaking a leg. Eventually he was taken to the sale barn. But first, in spring 1996, Dillon Page and his son, H.D., the PBR's three-time reigning Stock Contractor of the Year, decided to use the crippled bull as a breeder. They set him out to pasture with about 50 fertile cows on the banks of the Washita River, where the Pages operate D&H Cattle Company on a 1,500-acre ranch. For the young bull known only as 01, it was 60 days of fornication.

The average gestation period for a cow is the same as a human's—approximately 40 weeks. So 9 months later, 01's offspring hit the ground—some 40 calves that weighed between 65 and 70 pounds. One of the newborn bulls was out of Miss Slinger and was born March 1, 1997. But like horses, for the purposes of tracking an animal's age, all cows and bulls born in the same calendar year share the same birth date, January 1.

Miss Slinger's newborn and the other calves continued to nurse on their mothers for 9 months, putting on more than 12 pounds per week and plumping up to between 500 and 600 pounds. Then Dillon and H. D. Page moved the bull calves into a 3-acre weaning trap, where they learned to feed on grain, hay, and grass and endure a little pain. With a yellow-hot electric brander, the Pages burned in the marking number— 790 for the son of Miss Slinger. Three weeks later, it was off to a wheat field, where the bull calves stayed from November to May before moving onto a pasture to eat Bermuda grass and keep bulking up.

With the bulls almost 2 years old, the Pages brought them to the arena. There, they wrapped a soft flank strap in front of each bull's hindquarters and strapped onto the bulls' backs a 60-pound, remote-controlled dummy. Released from the chute, the bulls bucked for 3 or 4 seconds, long enough for the Pages to assess the bulls' bucking abilities and quick enough to eject the dummies without hurting the bulls' confidence. Seriously. If a rider dominates a young bull or a dummy is kept on the bull's back too long, the Pages and other veteran stock contractors say, the bull might lose his confidence.

That fall day in 1999, no young bull bucked as fiercely as the son of Miss Slinger. Problem was, the dummy got hung up on him. The remote control jammed. Dillon and H. D. Page scrambled after the bull. The chase went on for 10 minutes before they cornered number 790 in the back pen. Worried they had spooked a promising bull, the Pages dispatched the son of Miss Slinger to the pasture with about 50 fertile cows. While the young bull mingled with the cows, the other 2-year-old bulls went through the Pages' standard training program.

For 3 weeks, in groups of 11, the bulls made daily runs into the arena and up to twice a week entered through the metal chutes. Confused, most of them herded in the back of the arena until they saw the Pages setting out food and water outside the exit gate. Lunchtime! When the Pages opened the center gate, the bulls came running. The goal was to teach the bull that inside the arena lurked danger, and outside the arena waited food, water, and a place to relax. That way, when the bulls bucked in competition, they'd hopefully head for the center gate and leave the arena as soon as a rider was thrown or dismounted.

But the son of Miss Slinger missed the training session, and the Pages hoped the young bull's time away from the arena would help him forget the trauma of his first bucking experience. After the bull turned 3, however, it was time to test him again. The Pages strapped on the dummy, wrapped the flank strap, and then opened the chute gate.

They watched in awe.

Number 790 bucked just as fiercely as he had a year earlier. The mishap of the hung-up dummy apparently had had no effect on his confidence. Now it was time to put a real cowboy on the brindled bull. So in the fall of 2000, H. D. Page hauled him to a PBR-sanctioned Challenger Tour event. H.D. returned home grinning, and Dillon knew what that meant: The Pages had themselves one helluva bull. They entered him in a bucking bull futurity for 4-year-olds when he was only 3, and the bull finished fourth. The next year, competing against bulls his age, 790 won the event and a first-prize check of $25,000. That year he went to the 2001 finals, and bull riding fans got their first look at a filled-out, 1,500-pound bull named Washita Mud Slinger.

It was an impressive sight. So impressive that apparel maker Mossy Oak offered the Pages $2,500 to $5,000 a year for naming rights, depending on how well the bull performed. The Pages accepted, and the bull became known as Mossy Oak Mudslinger. In the chutes, he stood straight and still. When the rider was ready, so was he. He was a favorite of most riders because, although Mossy Oak Mudslinger bucked off a high percentage of riders, those who managed to hang for 8 seconds regularly scored 90 points or higher.

Bucking bulls typically reach their peak at age 5; and in 2002, the 5-year-old Mossy Oak Mudslinger finished runner-up to Little Yellow Jacket as Bull of the Year. That year, Tom Teague, a multimillionaire businessman from North Carolina, paid the Pages $50,000 for a half interest in Mossy Oak Mudslinger. Yet for all of the bull's growing fame in PBR circles, the Pages noticed something was wrong.

The bull kept lifting a hind leg as if his back was hurting. They took him to the veterinarian. Two sets of x-rays showed no injury. They took him to a chiropractor, who claimed to have found the problem. But when the chiropractor was done with Mossy Oak Mudslinger, the Pages thought the bull looked even worse. They turned him out to pasture and gave him time to heal.

Easing back into action, Mossy Oak Mudslinger finished fourth in the Bull of the Year balloting in 2003 and by midseason 2004, at age 7, was in contention for the $20,000 bonus as Bull of the Year. It would likely be his best, if not last, shot at the award.

Few bulls buck as hard past age 7, and fewer still buck beyond the age of 10. Most bulls live until age 11 or 12, with the occasional bull living into his late teens. Once retired, many bulls head out to pasture as breeders, while the less fortunate head to the slaughterhouse.

The Pages took special pride in the bull bred from a crippled father—and cashed in. Between PBR earnings, semen sales at $400 a shot, and selling Mossy Oak Mudslinger's calves for up to $15,000 for a half interest, the bull had generated about $250,000—an excellent return considering Dillon Page estimated food for each bull cost $1,000 a year. And with Mossy Oak Mudslinger breeding at a healthy rate, the Pages estimated 20 to 30 percent of their bull calves ended up bucking on the BFTS. All but 5 percent of the others got sold for as much as $15,000 to stock contractors hauling bulls to smaller rodeos. But well-heeled investors weren't interested in those smaller rodeos. It was the quest for the next Super Bull that enticed newcomers like Cody King.

Financed by an older family friend he called "Dad," King spent more than $500,000 buying established bulls and assembling his own pen in 2004. He hired a chiropractor and a massage therapist for one of his stars, Slim Shady, who drank Gatorade and ate vitamin supplements at his home in Rio Medina, Texas, where King raised his bulls at Paradise Farms Rodeo Genetics.

With newcomers like King shelling out unprecedented money in search of a Super Bull, Herrington, lobbying on behalf of the other bull owners, demanded the PBR protect their investment against riders with razor-sharp spurs and bull ropes squeezed tight enough to cut off the bulls' circulation.

ROUGHLY 15 MINUTES BEFORE the scheduled seven o'clock introductions on the first night of the Kansas City Classic, the riders were called together for a rules meeting. Bernard, Custer, and Lambert stood before them. First, announced Lambert, there was a rule clarification. In the past, a rider could enlist the help of two people to pull the slack of his bull rope and pull it himself. The more people pulling, the tighter the bull rope could be wrapped around the animal's midsection. When three men pulled, the angry stock contractors alleged, the rope tightened to the point where bulls gasped for air—especially if the rider took too long in the chute. But from this day forward, Lambert said, if the rider pulled his rope, he counted as a third man and disqualified the ride. The rule clarification meant Moraes's controversial ride on Hotel California would have been disqualified, because he and two Brazilians had pulled his rope. Addressing the long waits in the chutes, Lambert told the riders to start their rides as soon as possible.

Furthermore, Lambert warned the riders about using sharp spurs. That issue had come to a head earlier in the year when Ednei Caminhas of Brazil, once suspended for 30 days for cutting a bull with his spurs, had left three gashes in King's prize bull Slim Shady. Before the second day of competition in Kansas City, the PBR conducted an unannounced spur check. About half a dozen riders were told to file down the points on the star-shaped rowels at the ends of the spurs, and Caminhas was told to change his spurs altogether.

The dulled rowels, required to be locked in place, are supposed to help a rider maintain his balance by giving him added grip with the feet. But the spurs are required to be so dull that they never cut the bull's skin, which the PBR says is seven times thicker than human skin.

In Kansas City, Moraes at first seemed unfazed by the closed-door rules meeting. He said he thought the real culprit was Caminhas. As for himself, Moraes said it'd simply be a matter of adjusting. Moraes's calm reaction to the rule clarification and to Herrington's fuming about his ride on Hotel California may have stemmed from the results of the past seven events.

After the Tuff Hedeman Championship Challenge, the PBR tour

bounced its way across the western half of the United States. Stop 14, Tacoma, Washington. Championship round. Mike Lee was in first and Adriano Moraes was in second, with only Justin McBride left to ride. Aboard McNasty, McBride turned in a 90.5-point ride, winning for the fourth time of the season as Lee yet again was denied his first victory of the year. Onward to Fresno, California, and stop number 15. Back from the dead came Owen Washburn, the 31-year-old former champion, who ended his season-long slump with a convincing victory. "It was getting lonely at the bottom," he said. Eastward ho!

Billings, Montana. Stop 16. Brian Herman, a 5-foot-3-inch Texan better known as "Pee Wee," landed headfirst in the dirt after his ride on Peacemaker in the championship round. He was still wobbling when he realized he'd won the event with the 87-point ride. "I honestly don't remember a thing," he said. And whoosh, it was off to Albuquerque, New Mexico, and stop 17. Another weekend, another pint-size winner. Mike White, a 5-foot-6 rider born in Louisiana and branded "Mighty Mike," won the event and moved into fifth place in the overall standings. Moraes had surrendered the spotlight but retained a significant points lead, thanks to a second-place finish in Albuquerque. The PBR tour ran back to its headquarters in Colorado Springs for stop 18.

Pikes Peak served as the jaw-dropping backdrop while a Brazilian climbed to the top of the heap. Not Moraes, but Caminhas, holding on for a wild 90-point ride on Mesquite Heat and the victory. Off to Nampa, Idaho, and stop 19, and off the charts went Michael Gaffney, a onetime world champ who at 34 looked to be in the twilight of his career. He drew Little Yellow Jacket in the championship round, and he rode the baddest bull in the PBR to the 8-second buzzer. In came the score: 96.5 points! Raucous cheers rattled the Idaho Center. Gaffney had just matched the highest score in PBR history. With all the excitement, Justin McBride's third-place finish went almost unnoticed—by everyone but Moraes. McBride pulled within 816.5 points of Moraes while moving almost 1,000 points ahead of Lee.

Gaffney's record-setting ride punctuated the end of the frenetic stretch, 19 consecutive weekends of BFTS events. Two-thirds of the way through the marathon, the riders could finally catch their breath—but not for long if they hoped to catch Moraes. He reasserted himself May 16 with a win in Springdale, Arkansas, his fourth victory of the year. Three weeks later he arrived in Kansas City for stop 22 of the PBR season with a 1,495-point lead over Justin McBride and a 2,325.5-point lead over Mike Lee. No other rider was within 3,000 points of the lead, and no rider could make up more than 900 points during any 2-day, regular-season event. And that would have required both an unprecedented perfect score on every bull and that Moraes fall off his bulls in the first two rounds.

In round one at the Kansas City Classic, fans inside Kemper Arena watched Moraes climb aboard White Line Fever and deliver an 84.5-point ride. But the next day, needing only a modest score to qualify for the championship round, Moraes got bucked off Uh Oh, a bull that had been ridden three out of five times. He joined the other riders behind the chutes.

Standing next to B. J. Kramps, Moraes watched Mike Lee ride Jack Daniels Happy Hour for 89.5 points—the highest score of the second round. "Nice ride," Moraes said, but added he would have scored it no higher than 82 points.

"Why?" Kramps asked. "Are you jealous he's going to steal your fame?"

Moraes turned red. His faced tightened.

"Are you serious?" he shouted three times.

The wisecracking Kramps realized he'd hit a nerve and then changed the subject. But Moraes, who'd finished out of the top 15 in the preliminary rounds, was still fuming while watching the championship round.

Heading into that final round, Lee, who had been a portrait of consistency with 10 top-10 finishes, found himself in position to win his first event of the season. Lee and Tony Mendes, a 26-year-old from Utah, were the only two riders to have covered their first two bulls, and Lee led Mendes in the cumulative scoring by 5½ points. Mendes got bucked off, and so did nine others, in the championship round before Lee climbed into the chutes. Dave Samsel of Kansas had survived a wild ride on Western Wishes for 91 points, edging past Lee by a mere

2½ points. To win, Lee simply had to hold on for 8 seconds. But the bull was the fearsome Slim Shady.

It ended with one last thud, Slim Shady slamming Lee to the dirt and denying him his first victory of the season. And it was worth noting that the event winner was Samsel, one of the American riders who earlier in the season had started using a Brazilian rope.

CONCESSIONS

Barbecue sandwich smothered with local sweet sauce	$5
Shredded-pork sandwich with fries	$6
Sheboygan bratwurst fresh grilled with sautéed onions and peppers	$5

In Kansas City, generally speaking, if you can't barbecue it, they don't serve it. So no deep-fried Twinkies.

STANDINGS

1	Adriano Moraes	7,948.5 points	6	Mike Collins	4,285 points
2	Justin McBride	6,354 points	7	Jody Newberry	4,244 points
3	Mike Lee	6,075.5 points	8	Brendon Clark	3,998 points
4	Mike White	4,541.5 points	9	Greg Potter	3,437 points
5	Ross Coleman	4,323 points	10	Brian Herman	3,326 points

ELEVEN

A CRY FOR HELP

Nashville, Tennessee
Friday & Saturday, June 25 & 26, 2004

The insults and punches were flying. There, in the middle of the melee breaking out in the Wildhorse Saloon, were Justin McBride and J. W. Hart. It all happened so fast.

One minute McBride, Hart, and the riders' girlfriends had been peacefully drinking beers at the site of the PBR's after-event party, near a strip of honky-tonks overflowing with patrons. The next minute they were in the middle of a brawl. It had started with the women—in particular a woman who had approached Hart and berated him for "doing me wrong." Hart said they didn't want any trouble; they just wanted to drink their beers. The woman turned to leave.

But as she walked away, McBride's girlfriend, Michelle

Beadle, let fly with some choice words. The woman whipped around and came back for Beadle. She didn't make it that far.

LeAnn Stilley, Hart's petite blond-haired girlfriend, rattled a few punches off the side of the woman's head and all hell broke loose. Fists swinging, bouncers tackling, beer bottles crashing to the floor. Greg Crabtree, one of the PBR's bullfighters, jumped into the melee as if trying to save the riders from Crossfire Hurricane. Hart, McBride, their girlfriends, and Crabtree got thrown out of the bar, but not before leaving their knuckle marks on a few people's faces.

The only guy who'd taken a worse pounding that night was rider Cory Melton. During first-round action at Bullnanza–Nashville, Happy Jack threw Melton to the dirt and knocked out the 22-year-old rider from Keithville, Louisiana. Shortly after Melton regained consciousness, he looked in the mirror and saw two chipped teeth.

"What month is it?" asked Tandy Freeman, testing Melton's post-concussion state.

"It's gotta be June or July, because I'm entered in a bunch of rodeos."

Pretty good, considering it was June 25 and some of the fully conscious riders probably didn't know what month it was. Freeman gave Melton a sleeve of painkillers, while Adriano Moraes and Justin McBride were feeling the pain of disappointment.

During the first round that night, Blondie bucked off McBride, and Moraes, taking a reride after scoring 73.5 points on Nip/Tuck, got bucked off Happy Ending. Since the rule clarification in Kansas City, it was the second time in three rides he'd failed to make the 8-second buzzer. "Oh, well," Moraes said when he saw McBride, "we're still number one and number two—even though we sucked."

McBride chuckled, and the two reminisced about McBride's trip to Brazil 3 years before, when he and Ross Coleman joined Moraes in Barretos for the largest annual rodeo in South America. McBride recalled the five security officers who escorted Moraes at every public appearance, the portable 30-foot likeness of Moraes that stood inside the arena, and the fans who wept when Moraes arrived. "He's like frickin' Elvis over there," McBride said.

They joked and talked about taking a future vacation together before realizing they were the last two riders in the arena. Moraes had planned it that way. On nights when he got bucked off, he hated to return to his hotel room, where he knew he would sit and brood over what he'd done wrong. Conversation provided temporary escape from the reflexive self-criticism. McBride typically washed down his own disappointment with whiskey and beer. With the arena virtually empty, the two riders left, Moraes heading back to the hotel and McBride and Beadle off to the Wildhorse Saloon and what would be one wild fight.

NIGHT 2. CHAMPIONSHIP ROUND. Face-plant. Pinwheel. Thud. Dirt-eating fall after dirt-eating fall. Fourteen riders climbed atop their championship-round bulls, and all 14 failed to make the buzzer.

Then it was Owen Washburn's turn. His equipment bag had gotten lost on the flight from his home in Nashville, forcing Washburn to borrow equipment from fellow riders. Using a bull rope that belonged to one guy, spurs that belonged to another, and someone else's chaps and mouth guard, he rode both of his bulls in the preliminary rounds and had the cumulative lead entering the short-go. But now he had to climb atop Little Yellow Jacket.

In their first meeting, at Portland, Oregon, in 2000, Washburn conquered the bull for an 87-point ride. But 4 years later, Little Yellow Jacket was a different bull—an eliminator. Washburn had learned as much that past April in Albuquerque, when he'd boarded the bull for the second time of his career and gotten overpowered. Now came the rubber match.

Out of the chute, the bull whirled left. Washburn leaned low and forward, surviving the hairpin turn. But when Little Yellow Jacket turned hard again to the left, Washburn went sailing off the bull to the right.

Bullfighters Rob Smets and Dennis Johnson darted in as Washburn scrambled to his feet, but no one was in further danger. Little Yellow Jacket struck his regal pose. Smets lazily tossed his cowboy hat at the bull, and the hat bounced off Little Yellow Jacket's muscled flanks and fell to the dirt. Never even flinching, the bull kept its eyes straight ahead,

(continued on page 119)

118

waited for the center gate to open, and sauntered down the alley to the back pens. Washburn still earned $55,406 for the victory, but Little Yellow Jacket earned yet more respect.

The event ended with a surprise runner-up: Allan Moraes, Adriano's younger brother. He was competing in his first BFTS, but it was a bittersweet night for Allan because of what had happened to his older brother. Getting bucked off Flabby Flan in the second round, Adriano Moraes landed awkwardly on his left leg, buckling his knee.

Despite the pain, Adriano Moraes was fuming, because he thought the bull had fouled him before getting out of the chute and he deserved a reride. He hobbled toward the sports medicine room, complaining about the judges—something he rarely did.

"No more Mr. Nice Guy," he barked.

Waiting on an examination table, Moraes assured Tandy Freeman that he was fine. Freeman would make his own diagnosis.

"Does this hurt?"

"No."

"How about here?"

"Ah!"

"Does this hurt?"

"Unh!"

The initial diagnosis: torn cartilage. If Moraes had surgery before aggravating the injury, he could recuperate in 2 weeks. Freeman recommended surgery the next week. Moraes shook his head. He was scheduled to fly to Brazil the next night and would catch up with his wife and three sons, who were there on vacation.

"I don't care if I have a broken leg," he said. "I haven't seen my wife and kids for 15 days. I'm going home."

Freeman shrugged as if to say, "Do what you want."

The next morning Moraes was sitting in the Nashville International Airport, waiting on his early-morning flight home to Keller, Texas, when Mike Lee, who had fallen off two of his three bulls that weekend, walked over and sat down. "I know why you fell off that bull last night," said Moraes, ever the teacher—or, in the eyes of some, ever the know-it-all. They talked about the ride before Lee changed the topic of conversation, bringing up the predominant culture of the PBR—the beer-drinking, bed-hopping lifestyle he so despised.

That weekend, Lee told Moraes, he'd shared a hotel room with two riders who had gone on the road without their Bibles—assuming they had Bibles at all. After the first night of riding, the riders brought buckle bunnies to the room. Before Lee knew it, the women were half-naked. Instead of leaving the room, Lee found himself staring at the women's exposed breasts and succumbing to lustful thoughts.

"I'm weak," Lee said. "I'm weak."

He had brown hair short enough on the sides to reveal his scar, but a little long on top. He rarely looked others in the eyes, with his own eyes often looking down at the ground. And his solid build contrasted with the weakness in the face of lust that Lee so lamented.

Outside a handful of devout Christians, he rarely talked to other riders. He protected his privacy the way a mother grizzly protects her young. And he used the Bible like some might use a road map and thought veering off course brought a man another step closer to hell.

After every ride, Lee dropped to one knee, bowed his head, and then raised his helmet heavenward. But it was his choice of celebrations after successful rides that prompted fellow riders to roll their eyes. Lee did a twirling pirouette, which he occasionally topped off by dropping into a split or gyrating his hips. Yet as soon as he left the arena dirt, he reverted to the PBR's most enigmatic recluse, often walking past fellow riders as if he'd never met them—or as if they didn't even exist.

Lee had played running back and fullback on the high school football team through the first half of his freshman year but started experiencing pain in his knees. Worried about how a knee injury might affect Mike's bull riding career, his father pulled him off the football team. And when Dennis Lee heard people were giving his son a hard time about leaving the team, he pulled his son out of school.

For the next 3½ years, under the vigil of his father, Mike Lee was homeschooled and focused on his riding career.

Years earlier, Dennis Lee had traded a lawn mower for a bucking machine, and Mike rode it so much, it was a wonder the bolts and screws hadn't fallen out. But he learned the finer points at the side of his father by riding the colts and broncos his father broke as a professional horse trainer.

Feel, read, and react, Dennis Lee told his son again and again.

"You have to rely on your heart and your spirit so you can feel the bull's spirit, vibration, and energy," Dennis Lee told him.

Mike, the youngest of three siblings, absorbed his father's every word. As instructed, he practiced his breathing, inhaling as the bull went up and exhaling as it came down. He practiced using the muscles of his stomach, hips, legs, and shoulders—the same muscles used to break a horse. He practiced positive visualization.

"All this stuff doesn't work without having your mind really quiet," his father told him. "You're riding basically with your heart and your spirit, because if your brain kicks in, then you can't find that feel."

Before every bull ride, Mike Lee tried to clear his head of all thought and emotion to the point where he had removed himself from the conscious world. The preride routine helped explain his zombielike state at BFTS events. Already a loner, Lee deliberately isolated himself even further when he prepared to ride his next bull.

In addition to internalizing his father's advice, Mike also inherited the man's obsessive work ethic. After competing in the Championship Bull Riding finals one year, he drove to Billy Bob's Texas, the legendary honky-tonk bar, so he could ride another bull for a cheap jackpot. Another time, during a steer-riding exhibition, event officials were about to release the last steer out of the gate because there were no more riders. Lee shouted for them to stop. In his sneakers, he ran over to the chutes, hopped on the steer, and, holding only a flank rope, rode the sucker halfway down the arena. At home, he lifted weights at least twice a week and sculpted his 5-foot-8, 165-pound frame. He also rode bulls at a nearby practice pen until he reached the verge of exhaustion.

Dennis Lee allowed his son to push himself, even though he admitted his own all-consuming work ethic had led to depression—and may have contributed to his divorce from Mike's mother, Teri. That didn't stop Mike from marrying young.

As the Bible instructed, Lee believed a man and woman must marry before consummating their relationship. That became more difficult after he met a shy, sweet blond-haired girl named Jamie, and the two began dating. Hormones raged, but Lee would not succumb. Believing lustful thoughts were just as sinful as the act of sin, he decided marriage was the only option. He was 19. Jamie was 17.

When Lee joined the PBR in 2001, riders found his behavior peculiar. While most of the riders fraternized in the locker room, Lee helped the PBR work crew set up for that night's show. When he felt comfortable enough, he talked about his plans to build a basement—just a basement—where he'd live with his wife until they could afford to build the rest of the house. Sometimes riders found Lee wandering the halls or camped out in the hotel lobby in the middle of the night. At home, it turned out, Jamie Lee found her husband unable to sleep and vacuuming the house at three o'clock in the morning.

When he first joined the PBR, Lee brought his own food to the events and, sharing hotel rooms with other riders, ignored their pleas for him to take his stinky sardines out of the room. He also ignored their pleas that he put on clothes, preferring to walk around the room naked.

But Cody Whitney, who once roomed with Lee, said Lee's most annoying habit was his urge to "slap box."

"Sometimes I like to get in a fight, get punched in the face two or three times," Whitney recalled Lee telling him. "It's good to get your butt whipped once in a while."

Despite Lee's marriage, the sexual temptations only multiplied. Scantily clad buckle bunnies were everywhere he looked—and Lee couldn't help but look. Just like he did that weekend in Nashville. "It's all about Bud Light and how many women you can sleep with," he told Moraes.

Usually, Lee confided his innermost and troubling thoughts to Todd Pierce, the young pastor employed by Pro Bull Rider Outreach, a non-profit organization that sponsored the Cowboy Church services and Bible studies at PBR events. But now Lee turned to the man he was chasing for the title.

For several weeks, Lee attended weekly prayer sessions that Moraes held at his house in Keller, Texas. Every time Moraes asked Lee to join him and his family for lunch, Lee declined. Then, one day near his home in Keller, Moraes was riding practice bulls at the same arena as Lee was.

Like most riders, Moraes rode no more than two or three bulls during a practice session. He shook his head in dismay after watching Lee ride his seventh bull. "Are you tired?" Moraes asked.

Lee nodded.

"You riding any more?"

Lee glanced over his shoulder. "Don't know," he said.

Moraes looked in the same direction. It was Dennis Lee, watching his son from behind the chutes.

"You're done," Moraes ordered. "That's enough."

Later, behind the chutes, Dennis Lee made eye contact with Moraes. "You talk too much, Adriano," he said.

"I know too much," Moraes shot back.

Moraes scoffed at the idea of a horse trainer like Dennis Lee trying to teach someone how to ride bulls and talked about how much better Lee would be if Moraes trained him. Moraes also was convinced that Lee's father was pushing his son too hard.

The way Dennis saw it, Mike pushed himself. That's also the way Clint Branger remembered it when Mike Lee attended one of Branger's bull riding schools in the mid-1990s. "He'd make a good ride and kind of lean back at the end and make the whistle and he'd be all upset at himself," said Branger, a retired rider who had been a star when the PBR began. "I was like, 'Hey, quit being so hard on yourself.' "

But as Lee's career progressed, it was hard to argue with the results. He finished 11th in 2002, his first full season on the PBR tour, then finished sixth in 2003 despite his having missed 3 months after the skull injury that left him with the zipperlike scar. For someone so young, Lee's consistency was astonishing.

Cody Custer, a former world champion, was so impressed that before the season started, he predicted Lee would win the 2004 championship. But Moraes predicted Lee would fail to win a championship until he distanced himself from Lee's father and became his own man.

That morning in the Nashville airport, Lee went on to tell Moraes that he'd called his wife, Jamie, and told her about the half-naked groupies in his hotel room. Moraes shook his head.

"*Never* tell your wife about seeing those things, because it only makes it worse," he said, adding that if Lee found himself in another awkward situation, he should call Moraes. "Anytime. Day or night. I'm always available."

As Lee walked off, Moraes rolled his eyes. He was less concerned with Lee than getting home in time to make his early-evening flight to Brazil. But he had yet to talk to his wife, Flavia, who served as his advisor and voice of reason.

The next day, instead of Adriano flying to Brazil, it was Flavia who was flying back to the United States. She accompanied Moraes 2 days later to Freeman's office in Dallas, where Adriano underwent knee surgery.

This wasn't just about his knee, and Flavia knew it. This was about a lead in the standings that could be wiped out by his aggravating the injured knee with only five events left until the finals in Las Vegas.

For Adriano Moraes, this was no time for risks.

CONCESSIONS	
Nachos with barbecued beef or barbecued chicken	$7.75
Chicken quesadilla	$7.75
Chicken tenders in a boat with french fries	$6.25

"I've heard of them," Sue Fullington, concessions manager at the Gaylord Entertainment Center, said of deep-fried Twinkies. "Why would you ruin a Twinkie by throwing it in a fryer?"

STANDINGS

1	Adriano Moraes	7,948.5 points	6	Mike Collins	4,285 points
2	Justin McBride	6,354 points	7	Jody Newberry	4,244 points
3	Mike Lee	6,205.5 points	8	Brendon Clark	3,998 points
4	Mike White	4,541.5 points	9	Owen Washburn	3,690 points
5	Ross Coleman	4,323 points	10	Greg Potter	3,437 points

TWELVE

DIRT ROAD TO PARADISE

CACHOEIRA PAULISTA, BRAZIL
WEDNESDAY–SUNDAY, JUNE 30–JULY 4, 2004

The black Fiat rattled down the narrow, bumpy dirt road, past the eucalyptus trees and the sugarcane fields, the grazing cattle and horses, and the loose dogs that gave chase. Kicking up dust, the car came to a stop at the base of paradise—a ceramic-tiled porch wrapped around a red ranch house that sat nestled in the valley of 1,000 acres of rolling hills, lush grass, and a panoramic view of the distant mountains. Out of the passenger's side of the Fiat climbed Adriano Moraes, who took a gimpy step on his left leg, thereby officially completing the 13-hour journey from his house in Keller, Texas, to his home in Brazil.

Down the driveway ran his 4-year-old son, Antonio. Moraes scooped up the boy and showered him with kisses. Next came 6-year-old Jeremias and, in the arms of Moraes's sister, 18-month-old Pedro. Moraes planted more kisses on his three sons and took in the sight of his ranch, dotted with banana, guava, and mango trees and home to wild parrots, roosters, horses, mules, and chickens. Alas, it also was home to termites. "A plague," Moraes grumbled about the insects, which left knee-high dirt mounds across his property.

He had built the four-bedroom ranch house, complete with a trophy room, maid's quarters, and guesthouse, from his career winnings of more than $2 million. It was unmistakably Adriano Moraes's house, with a huge portrait of himself hanging in the entryway of the guesthouse and his trophies prominently displayed on the shelves in his living room. Yet they lived modestly enough, with Flavia often wearing old T-shirts and sweatpants and Adriano wearing the jeans or Western shirts he got free from sponsors. Other than the ranch, his only major indulgence was a restored 1956 Chevrolet pickup truck for which he had paid about $30,000, leaving plenty of the money from his bull riding winnings in the bank.

Most of the country's riders competed with ragged equipment, hoping to make enough money to get from one rodeo to the next. There was no Brazilian-style PBR offering a $1 million bonus—or anything close to that bounty. Though the country had produced some great riders, none had made it as big in the United States as Moraes had. But unlike Pelé, the former soccer star and Brazil's most famous athlete, Moraes enjoyed a life of relative anonymity outside the rodeo circles. His ranch was about a 2½-hour drive north of São Paulo; and on that 5-mile dirt road leading up to it, Moraes sometimes stopped, grabbed a rock, and hurled it high into the palm trees, knocking loose acorn-size nuts. He chewed off the bittersweet skin and, if he had the right instrument, cracked open the nut and sucked out the meat. Here, in his home country, he also enjoyed cashew juice and his mother's homemade cheese and free-range chicken, which Elizabeth Moraes cooked on a wood-burning stove. There were no deep-fried Twinkies, but there was passion fruit, which Moraes ingested in multiple forms—passion fruit cocktail, passion fruit pie, and passion fruit ice cream.

Ah, home sweet home.

With knee surgery and recent struggles making Moraes look vulnerable for the first time of the 2004 season, he returned to his home base. The nearby Catholic community, Canção Nova, was his spiritual base, and Moraes said it was time to "recharge my batteries, because the spiritual world is much better than the material world." Yet that first night at the ranch promised to be a restless one.

Eyes flickering open and shut, Moraes kept checking his alarm clock. The minutes passed like hours. At five o'clock in the morning, he climbed out of bed, buttoned up his long-sleeved Western shirt, pulled on his jeans and cowboy boots, and headed for the stables. Halfway there, he stopped in front of the house where his parents lived, and across the lawn bounded his three dogs—Outlaw, the Catahoula leopard dog; Congo, the boxer; and Blue, the Australian cattle dog. Sufficiently slobbered on, Moraes continued his drive to the horse stables, where under the moonless sky he recognized the white face of his oldest son's horse. He rode it bareback into the pasture wet with morning dew and rounded up his 16 other horses. Then he saddled up 10 horses and fidgeted, pacing until his guests finished breakfast and joined him for the morning ride.

Wedged in a saddle labeled 2X—referring to the two PBR championships Moraes had won—he rode with purpose. It was time to tour the grounds and check on his cattle, and before long he found five ranch hands and a veterinarian trying to deliver a calf from a large incision in the side of a cow. Uncharacteristically subdued, Moraes watched. "He's going to die."

The veterinarian and ranch hands continued to wrestle with the calf, and Moraes moved on. Down a dirt track, up a steep hill, inside a wire fence, he led his entourage to the day's first chore: rounding up two dozen cows.

"Ho-ho-ho! Hey-hey-hey! Ah-ah-ah!"

Moraes and his father, Aparecido, a lifelong ranch manager with a small but muscular frame and a thick black mustache, hooted and yelped at the cattle. The cattle responded. Hooves pounded across the grass as the herd picked up speed.

Moving into position, Moraes and his father directed the herd; and the animals lumbered back through the wire fence, down the steep hill, and onto the dirt path.

"Ah-ah-ah, heh-heh-heh, hey-hey-hey."

Moraes and his father kept shouting, and the cows moved into the wooden holding pen as if they spoke the same language as the two men. There was much to do: wean and tag the calves, untag the cows, and separate the cattle into those Moraes would sell and those he would keep. These were the ranch chores that took Moraes's mind off his recent knee surgery and his recent slump on the PBR tour. Lost in the activity at the outset of a 10-day trip home, Moraes looked like a man at peace—until he heard the wailing of his 4-year-old son, Antonio. Standing outside the pens, Antonio burst into tears for no apparent reason. Moraes's voice dropped an octave, rose in volume, and in Portuguese he bellowed, "Stop crying, boy." Moraes picked up a rock and started to count.

"*Um, dois . . .* "

Before Moraes reached *três*, Antonio's sobs had halted.

"Americans coddle, but they don't correct," Moraes liked to say. It was easy to see where he had inherited his toughness and discipline. On the second day of their working the cattle, a spooked cow tried to jump out of the wooden chutes, and its left hoof caught Adriano Moraes's father on the head. The hoof left a muddy footprint on Aparecido's cowboy hat and dazed the 58-year-old man. He grabbed on to a wooden gate to keep from falling.

Sitting nearby, Flavia shouted for someone to bring water. Aparecido Moraes waved them off, looking more irritated than hurt, and motioned for Adriano to resume sending the cattle through the chutes.

Adriano chuckled. This was the same man who had ordered him as a little boy to wrestle calves—or else. The same man who for years had barely spoken a word to Adriano, the second-oldest of five children, other than to assign him daily chores. The same man who once—when Adriano had been sent home early from school—had scowled and slapped the boy in the face before Adriano could explain what had happened. But this also was the man who had softened over the years and found it easier to show affection to his grandchildren than to his own sons.

Adriano and Aparecido. In some ways, they were so much alike: hardworking and hardheaded. Whereas the father had struggled to control his temper, the son had struggled to control his mouth. "You should quit smoking, because you stink," Moraes remembered telling his father as a young boy.

For years Adriano had despised the man. Aparecido had driven Adriano to his first rodeos, but the two barely spoke. In fact, Aparecido didn't learn about his son's bull riding success until someone showed him an article in the newspaper. All those victories. All those buckles. And Moraes never heard a word of praise from his father. But over the years, he had learned how to forgive his father and had come to love him. When Adriano hired his father to run the 1,000-acre ranch, the two grew closer, even if their conversations rarely strayed from talk about the chores and developments on the ranch. At his house in Keller, Texas, Adriano sometimes missed his father so much he cried. For all the tension that had divided them years before, Aparecido had shaped the boy who had grown up to be one of the world's greatest bull riders.

April 20, 1970. On that day, Elizabeth Moraes felt the sharp jabs of labor pain. Aparecido set out on horseback to find the local midwife, but it took longer than expected. When they returned 3 hours later, Elizabeth was on the cold wooden floor with a baby boy between her legs and the boy covered in Elizabeth's star-patterned nightgown. For years Elizabeth Moraes joked that Adriano had become a star because as soon as he had entered the world, he was covered with them. But before the riches had come the rags.

Soon after he was born, Moraes's grandparents went broke and lost their land. The family set out on a journey that included one stop after another, with Aparecido finding jobs as a ranch manager to earn the bare necessities. Early on they lived in a house with dirt floors. At night, they could hear rats and snakes slithering through the corn kept in tubs against the house's thin walls.

In 1982, at age 12, Adriano Moraes saw his first amateur rodeo. With makeshift equipment, he began practicing at home on a bull named Rubber. He wanted to be cool, and to him the epitome of cool were those grizzled old rodeo cowboys riding bulls.

Three years later, when he saw his first professional rodeo, Moraes discovered something almost unimaginable: The riders got paid, with the best making almost $100,000 a year. Suddenly the idea of riding bulls beat the idea of scratching out a living as a ranch manager. He dropped out of school in the ninth grade and set out to become a pro bull rider with less-than-standard gear. Instead of a bull riding glove, Moraes used a motorcycle glove. Instead of a bull riding rope, he used a flank strap. He had no protective vest, no mouthpiece, and only one of his mother's thin nylon bags in which to carry his belongings.

At his third pro event, Moraes made the championship round, finished second, and won 10 times more money than he could have made in a month working as a ranch hand.

When Moraes's parents moved to another region of Brazil in 1988 because his father had found a better job, Adriano, then 18, stayed behind and continued working for the rodeo company and pursuing his riding career. He married a young woman, and they had a son, Victor; but the marriage lasted only 3 months. A year later he met his future wife.

It was a dusty bull ring in Matao, a town north of São Paulo. She was sitting in the stands. Moraes was standing in the arena. Moraes spotted the tall, slender young woman with shoulder-length brown hair and a pretty face, and he *had* to meet her. After the rodeo, Moraes hustled to his car, hit the gas, and pulled in front of the woman's car. Blocking her path, he climbed out of his car and walked over.

"Hi, I'm Adriano," he boomed.

She smiled bashfully. "I'm Flavia."

Less than a year later, they were married.

"I was at peace," he said. Then 21 and with Flavia at his side, Moraes emerged as one of the best bull riders in Brazil. Winning national championships in 1992 and 1993, he saw it was time to find a new mountain to climb. It required the couple to board a plane for the first time in their lives.

They flew to the United States in late 1992 to get a firsthand look at the vaunted American bull riders. Charlie Sampson, who had met Moraes 4 years earlier when Sampson was putting on a riding clinic in Brazil, was awaiting their arrival in Arizona. Moraes grew up watching American cartoons, so for his first American breakfast, Adriano ordered pancakes, just like ones the chipmunks on the cartoon "Chip 'n Dale" ate. For his first American dinner, he ordered a T-bone steak, just like the one the cat on "Tom and Jerry" used to eat. The Moraeses stayed with Sampson for 40 days, then drove to Keller, Texas, and moved into a cramped trailer with Troy Dunn, the Australian champion. With bull riders trudging into and out of the trailer at all hours of the night, Adriano and Flavia slept on a mattress on the living room floor and dodged cockroaches.

But it was worth it. For one, they'd seen the world's best bull riders compete at the NFR in Las Vegas, and later Adriano competed in a few open rodeos. He also did his first TV interview and, in broken English, declared, "If they let me ride, I can ride with these guys."

Enticed by a $60,000-a-year endorsement deal with a beef company, Moraes returned to the United States in 1994 and took the North American rodeo world by storm. He won the inaugural PBR championship, became only the third rider to cover all 10 of his bulls at the NFR, and won the prestigious Calgary Stampede. Six years later, with his English vastly improved and his riding skills as good as ever, he won the 2001 PBR championship and became the tour's first two-time champion. Now the third championship was within reach, but the season was taking a physical and emotional toll.

He needed time at Canção Nova, the Catholic community. It was here that Moraes tapped into spiritual strength—the strength he thought he needed to hold off McBride, Lee, and any surprise contenders down the season's homestretch.

During an evening service at a small chapel, Moraes knelt on the ground in prayer. But a few minutes later, he sat in the wooden chair and removed his left cowboy boot. The hard floor had aggravated his swollen left knee. Cowboy boot removed, he again dropped to his knees and joined a small group praying in tongues.

His rehabilitation program was at best unorthodox. Six days after the surgery, he rode his horse up a steep 700-foot hill and joined his friends, one of whom got stuck in a tangle of branches 10 feet up a tree. Without hesitation, Moraes wrapped his arms around the thick trunk, climbed up the tree, and freed his friend. Then he peered up at a cluster of branches, as if considering a higher climb.

"Justin McBride says to go a little higher," someone joked.

Down climbed Moraes.

Yet moments later, he and his friends were swinging on a vine. When they realized a tree impeded their swing path, Moraes brandished a small machete and whacked the offending arbor. *Tim-berrrr!* Down it came, but not before Moraes had swung on the vine and tried to dislodge the tree by crashing into it with his feet.

"How's the knee?" someone asked.

"Which one?" replied Moraes, grinning.

Leaving the junglelike brush unscathed, Moraes untied his horse and rode down the steep hill while declaring that only he could stop himself from capturing the PBR championship. Later in the week, driving a friend to the airport, the talk turned to bull riding.

He spoke about his loneliness on the PBR tour and his disappointment that riders like Justin McBride and Ross Coleman—both of whom had spent time with Moraes during a trip to Brazil—had never invited him for special trips to their own homes. During PBR events, McBride, Coleman, and the others were friendly with Moraes, but after the nightly competition, he often found himself alone—unless he was with fellow Brazilians or nonriders. Moraes's idea of socializing was to hang out in the hotel coffee shop, talking bull riding. McBride, Coleman, and many of the others usually headed for the bars.

Occasionally he joined the dozen or so devout Christian riders, including Mike Lee, at the weekly Bible studies. These riders were nondrinkers and nonsmokers who avoided the buckle bunnies and the PBR's after-event parties and seemed like the group to which Moraes would gravitate. Yet over time, Moraes grew isolated from them, too.

"I tell them they should pray more," said Moraes, who also urged the group to focus more on evangelization.

In some respects, Moraes's isolation mirrored the dynamics of bull riding. There were no teammates, no on-site coaches, no one to blame but oneself. Moraes understood this with only five regular-season events left until the PBR finals in Las Vegas.

"It's totally up to me," he said. "Nobody's as good as me right now. Nobody. That's a fact. That's why I can't afford to lose. If I lose, it means I failed."

Because of his powerful left arm, the one he used to grip the bull rope, and his strong legs, Moraes was known as a "power rider." He detested the label, because it suggested he relied more on brute force than balance. Perhaps to prove otherwise, Moraes walked across the top of the 6-foot-high panels of the back pen like a tightrope artist wearing cowboy boots and spurs.

Though they never joined Moraes on the panels, two other riders in the PBR showed exceptional balance and athleticism. They were the two riders Moraes considered his strongest competition—McBride and Lee.

"I love the way Justin rides," Moraes said, noting how McBride pinned his knees against the bull instead of clamping down with his full legs. "He neutralizes the bulls a lot. Has a lot of balance. Graceful rider. One of the best riders we have there now. If he wins, I'll be upset with myself. But I'll be very proud of him. He's going to represent (the PBR) very, very well.

"But not Mike Lee. Mike Lee cannot represent now. He's immature. He can't even talk. Rides well. But he does not know why he rides and how he rides. . . . He doesn't understand the fundamentals of riding. He just does it. That's pure ability. . . . I ride with my mind. He rides with his born ability."

The words came across harshly, considering that some riders saw Lee as a future superstar who might one day surpass Moraes.

"The next Adriano Moraes hasn't been born yet," Moraes said. "If he has been born, he's not riding. And if he's riding, he's not riding with us."

134

THIRTEEN

TUFF TIMES
FOR PBR

COLORADO SPRINGS, COLORADO
WEDNESDAY–FRIDAY, JULY 7–9, 2004

Back late from a business meeting, Randy Bernard strode
into his eighth-floor office, dumped his travel bag on the
ground, and settled into the leather chair behind his cher-
rywood desk. To his left was a spectacular view of Pikes
Peak. But he scarcely glanced at the snowcapped mountains.
With his tanned face, toothy smile, and full head of brown
hair, even at age 37 he looked as much a frat house president
as a chief executive officer, let alone the CEO of a company
with a budget of $35 million in 2004. He usually wore jeans
and cowboy boots but hardly cut the image of a stereotyp-
ical cowboy, with his PalmPilot, pocket-size digital camera,

and iPod. He could be as affable as a cruise ship director and as smooth as a marble countertop, but at the moment he seemed distracted as he flipped open his laptop computer while his executive assistant, Andee Lamoreaux, rattled off Bernard's phone messages. Bernard stared at his computer screen. Online, he clicked onto rodeo Web sites where he knew the message boards would be filled with chatter. He wanted to get the latest take on the news that a week earlier had rocked the PBR and sent his executive assistant scrambling.

IF ANYBODY COULD FIND BERNARD, it was Lamoreaux. She punched the numbers on her office phone.

"Hello?"

Got him.

Bernard, who was on business in London, answered his cell phone. Lamoreaux's urgent voice indicated there was no time for chitchat. Call Richard Perkins, she said, referring to the PBR's chief financial officer.

"Why? What's up?"

"We just got a letter—Tuff resigned."

Tuff resigned? It was enough to make a cowboy swallow his snuff.

"Oh, damn," Bernard said.

Less than 7 days into what was supposed to be a leisurely 6-week break between BFTS stops, Hedeman had terminated a contract that called for him to sign autographs at all of the tour's BFTS events and paid him more than $100,000 a year. His resignation letter, dated June 24 and sent by certified mail, contained a single sentence: "Gentlemen, I hereby tender my resignation as a member of the board of directors of the Professional Bull Riders, Inc., and as president of the Professional Bull Riders, Inc., to take effect immediately."

Bernard left three phone messages for Hedeman. None was returned.

Adding to the confusion, a British filmmaker working on a documentary about the PBR called Bernard to say that just days earlier, her crew had taped an interview with Hedeman during which he had said the PBR was "his life." Now he'd resigned? She didn't get it. Neither did Bernard.

All Bernard had to go on was an article in the *Empire-Tribune,* a newspaper in Stephenville, Texas. "The PBR is big business," Hedeman was quoted as saying. "I just have some fundamental differences about that. I will always choose what I think is best for the bull riders. Producing in a sport that is profitable is important and it's hard work. I enjoy doing that; but when it comes to what's good for business and what's good for the riders, I put the riders first every time. They are what the fans come to see."

The insinuation was clear: The riders had become a secondary concern to Bernard and the PBR's board of directors. But less than 24 hours after the article was published, Ron Pack, Hedeman's business partner and close friend, disavowed the quote that appeared in the Stephenville paper. Bernard wasn't convinced, and not long after his conversation with Pack, he got a call from a rodeo newspaper reporter who wanted to know what Bernard thought of Hedeman's resignation and the quote. The quote? Yes, the quote, replied the writer, reading to Bernard what the writer said Hedeman had sent him—the exact same quote that had run in the *Empire-Tribune.*

Bernard was upset but had no intention of canceling the meeting he'd arranged with Pack and Hedeman for July 12 at the Dallas/Fort Worth International Airport. There they would discuss Hedeman's future with the PBR. Bernard would bring Cody Lambert, the PBR's vice president and a grouchy but funny ex-rider who was as tough as Hedeman. He and Hedeman had once been friends. After all, they had grown up together, attended college together, and traveled together on the rodeo circuit. To this day, Lambert would say of Hedeman, "He's the best rider that ever got on a bull." But their friendship was over.

Before Bernard had taken over as the PBR's CEO in 1995, Pack said, Hedeman and Lambert had formed the political strength behind the tour. But as the years passed, they found themselves on opposite sides of issues, especially when, at Bernard's urging, the PBR began copromoting its own events. Hedeman was looking out for the original promoters and sponsors, Lambert was looking out for the PBR, and both contended they were looking out for the riders.

At the 1995 finals, only hours before Hedeman's infamous wreck with Bodacious, Lambert ripped off the arm of a chair and flung it across the room at Hedeman. It bounced off a metal locker. Just another PBR board meeting where the old friends turned nasty. "Tuff and Cody, without a doubt, run the board of directors," Pack said. "Two captains sailing a ship and a difference of opinions. Somebody's going to win and somebody's going to lose." Lambert had heard Pack's assertion before and vehemently denied it, saying neither he nor Hedeman had any more influence than the other board members.

Nonetheless, by 2004, it was clear Hedeman was headed for defeat.

As the word of Hedeman's resignation spread among the bull riding world, fans swamped the PBR's message board before Bernard ordered it shut down. "There was so much malicious gossip, and the PBR is not going to be a place to start false rumors," Bernard said. "We're not going to put the message board back up until fans understand that."

What Bernard had to understand was this: To many fans, Tuff Hedeman *was* the PBR.

IN 1992, AFTER THE JUSTIN BOOTS WORLD BULL RIDING Championship in Scottsdale, Arizona, Hedeman and about a dozen bull riders crammed into a motel room. It was the culmination of months of talks. Sam Applebaum, a California tax planner who'd befriended Hedeman and a handful of the other top bull riders, led the call to action: It was time to break away from the Professional Rodeo Cowboys Association (PRCA) and create their own bull riding tour.

A couple of years earlier, businessman Shaw Sullivan had done the same thing, creating a tour called Bull Riders Only (BRO). But Shaw wanted all the riders to sign contracts, essentially turning over control when it came to determining what sponsorship patches riders could wear, how the prize money would be distributed, and how the events would function.

Recalled Hedeman: "We basically said, 'Screw you.'" He and the other bull riders thought they, not the promoters, deserved control; and to make it happen, the riders in that motel room pitched in $1,000 apiece. The number of original investors eventually grew to 21, and the group set out to start its own bull riding tour.

With $21,000 in seed money and with Applebaum serving as president, the group founded the Professional Bull Riders. The riders knew little about business, but they knew enough to realize $21,000 wasn't going to get them far. So they hired a sports agency owned by David Falk, who then represented basketball star Michael Jordan, and paid him to find potential sponsors. Falk came back without a list; there were no takers.

Undaunted, Applebaum, Hedeman, and Lambert took things into their own hands. With the Gaylord family, owners of The Nashville Network (TNN), arranging the meeting, the three PBR executives went to the offices of Anheuser-Busch. It turned out the company wanted to break into the rodeo market, but the PRCA had an exclusive deal with Coors. Hedeman and Applebaum made their pitch and got what they wanted—a commitment from Bud Light. Then they got a deal with TNN to televise the PBR events, and the riders could hardly believe their good luck.

The inaugural season in 1994 included eight events and $660,000 in prize money. The tour culminated at the world finals, which offered a $275,000 purse. By 1995 the prize money had shot up to $1.2 million, but the PBR founders realized they had a problem: Sam Applebaum.

He was a smart and tough negotiator, but what he possessed in brainpower, he lacked in manners. Swaggering into corporate offices, he'd prop his cowboy boots on an executive's desk and squirt tobacco juice into the nearest waste can or office plant.

If the PBR hoped to make it into the American mainstream, the board decided, it needed a polished leader. Firing Applebaum in '95, the PBR board settled on an unlikely choice as the next CEO.

For starters, he was only 28 years old and had limited background in the rodeo business, much less corporate America. He'd grown up in San Ardo, California, a small town in the center of the state, where his family owned a 5,000-acre ranch and raised cattle and grew wheat, barley, and alfalfa. His name was Randy Bernard.

After getting married during his senior year of college, Bernard dropped out of Cal Poly State University in San Luis Obispo and took an internship with the Calgary Stampede, one of the world's best-known rodeos. That in turn led to a job at the California Mid-State Fair. While his marriage failed, Bernard's career took off. He earned a reputation as a can-do workaholic, helping book shows that included MC Hammer and George Strait concerts and bull riding events. At one of those bull riding events, he met two of rodeo's best-known cowboys—Lambert and Ty Murray, a seven-time world champion all-around cowboy who had established his Hall of Fame credentials competing on the PRCA circuit but also was a founding member of the PBR.

Hedeman, Lambert, and Murray. It was a powerful triumvirate; and when Murray and Lambert helped persuade Hedeman that Bernard was the right man for the job, the PBR hired him as its next CEO. His new title was more impressive than his new office, which Bernard later joked was little more than a broom closet, a card table for a desk, and a milk crate for a chair. In truth, it was a cramped space in downtown Colorado Springs donated by Douglas Quimby, a lawyer who worked part-time for the PBR. That's all they could come up with for an office, and it was unclear how they were going to come up with the money to pay for Bernard's starting salary of about $50,000 a year. When he took over, the PBR had $8,000 in the bank and $130,000 in bills.

Desperate to balance the books, Bernard focused on sponsorship and brought aboard Wrangler, Jack Daniel's, and the city of Las Vegas. He also dragged the tour out of the Old West and into the 20th century, replacing the rodeo-style show with high-tech pyrotechnics, lasers, fireworks, and rock music. The idea was to market bull riding as an extreme sport, with Bernard instructing the in-arena announcers to start shows with the following line: "This isn't a rodeo. This is the one and only PBR!"

Then, with urging from Hedeman, at the 1996 PBR finals, the tour put up $1 million in prize money, more than double the money the PRCA offered bull riders during its 10-day NFR championships. Also announcing plans for an 18-city, $2.2 million tour in 1997, the PBR reduced the PRCA to the minor leagues of bull riding.

When it came to ideas, Bernard begged, borrowed, and stole, studying the business model of the World Wrestling Federation under Vince McMahon and establishing ties with Brian France, chairman and CEO of NASCAR. And through Ken Hudgens of Clear Channel Entertainment, he formed a partnership with the company to help the PBR start promoting its own events. The tour was taking off—despite internal controversy.

In 2001, at Bernard's behest, the PBR bought back the TV rights it had sold in 1995 to Allen Reid, a TV producer who had put together the deal with TNN. The PBR had agreed to the 1995 sale before Bernard took over and at the time thought those rights were worth next to nothing. In fact, Hedeman, Lambert, and the rest of the founders could hardly believe their luck when Reid paid them $300,000 and guaranteed another $100,000 a year thereafter.

Six years later, Reid's investment looked awfully shrewd. When Bernard inquired about buying the rights back, Reid set a price: more than $6 million.

The board members were furious. They demanded Reid lower his price. He refused. Talks stalled.

Bernard and other board members worried that as time passed, the value of the PBR's TV rights—and Reid's asking price—would only increase. So despite concerns about the costs, they voted to buy.

To come up with the money, Bernard enlisted the help of Tom Teague, a multimillionaire from North Carolina who had made his fortune running a truck-leasing business. Teague, who'd met Bernard 7 years earlier and had expressed interest in the PBR, chipped in about $3 million in exchange for half ownership of the PBR's TV rights. A month later Teague joined the PBR board.

While Hedeman welcomed someone with the business savvy of

Teague onto the board, he and others outside the board grumbled about how much the PBR had paid Reid. In 2002, the PBR parted ways with TNN and negotiated a deal with the Outdoor Life Network. That wasn't the only change.

Donnie Gay, the eight-time world bull riding champion, had been the lead commentator of PBR broadcasts, taping a voice-over at an office in Nashville for the delayed telecasts. That wasn't going to cut it for Bernard, who wanted Gay and the rest of the three-person crew to do the telecasts live. But Gay turned down a raise of $1,000 an event, testing the PBR's resolve.

Bernard and the board fired the entire crew. Ignoring a hailstorm of angry e-mails from fans loyal to Gay, Bernard ushered in fresh faces meant to attract new and younger fans. The diehard fans bellyached, but not as loudly as some of the PBR's own employees did when the board, taking Bernard's advice, voted to pay $710,000 for a single 2-hour telecast on NBC. He argued it was more than worth it to put the tour on national TV and suspected that Hedeman was behind the ensuing resistance.

Objecting to the plan to pay for NBC airtime, five high-level employees walked into Bernard's office one day and threatened to quit unless Bernard did first. Bernard asked the men to remain in his office while he called Lambert and Murray and put them on speakerphone. Murray was the board member who had broken the board's deadlock vote that gave Bernard approval to buy back the PBR's TV rights. He was known to be a smart, blunt, take-no-bullshit cowboy.

"If I were you," he told Bernard loudly enough to be heard by the five employees, "I'd fire every one of them sons of bitches right now."

Bernard fired just one of the dissenters and moved forward. Though the PBR lost money on the first NBC broadcast, the tour negotiated better deals for future broadcasts with the hope that national exposure would attract more sponsors and fans. By 2003 the PBR had grown to 28 regular-season events plus the PBR world finals—which in 1999 moved from the MGM Grand Garden Arena to the larger Thomas & Mack Center to accommodate growing crowds—and had increased total prize money for the BFTS and minor-league events to more than $8 million.

Playing the dual role of corporate CEO and cowboy, Bernard kept a sport coat nearby and a cowboy hat on the back ledge of his Lincoln LS V8 sedan. But the cowboy decor is limited in his two-story house in Colorado Springs, with a barbecue on the wooden deck, dark fabrics on the living room furniture, a Buddha statue in front of the fireplace, and, stacked across a shelf near the kitchen, books that include *Patton on Leadership, The Millionaire Next Door, Business @ the Speed of Thought*, and *Sex, Lies and Headlocks*, the last being an unauthorized biography of Vince McMahon, who built a wrestling company into a billion-dollar juggernaut.

Keeping a round-the-clock work schedule, Bernard went weeks at a time without seeing his second wife, Cameo, a two-time Miss National Fitness Champion and a TV fitness spokesperson who lives in Southern California. He traveled more than 200 days a year, met with potential sponsors and investors, and paid attention to details, down to whether the arena suites needed vacuuming. Hanging prominently on a wall in Bernard's office was a charcoal print of Hedeman riding a bull, with the inscription, "To one of my best friends. Thanks for all your help. Best of luck." But the photo had been signed in 1995. The start of their rift had taken place at the 1996 PBR finals.

That week boxes of Cinch jeans arrived at the MGM Grand, then site of the PBR finals. It was like a shipment of Coca-Cola arriving at the offices of Pepsi. Cinch was a chief rival of Wrangler, one of the PBR's top sponsors. But Hedeman had an endorsement deal with Cinch jeans, and the boxes that arrived at the MGM Grand were addressed to him. When Bernard learned about the surprise delivery and that Hedeman intended to pass out the jeans to the PBR's riders, he confronted him in front of a few other people.

"What the hell do you think you're doing, Tuff? Wrangler is our sponsor, period. You don't do shit like that."

The public tongue-lashing enraged Hedeman.

"You and me are going outside," Hedeman said.

They exited through a nearby door.

He grabbed Bernard by the throat. "I ought to kick your ass."

Moments later Hedeman dropped his hands and walked away. Hedeman later claimed that his limo driver had inadvertently dropped three or four boxes of Cinch jeans at the arena and that somebody opened the boxes without asking his permission. He also said he had had no intention of passing out the jeans to fellow riders until he got back to the hotel. But his relationship with Bernard only worsened.

In 2002, with Bernard leading a meeting that included the riders and shareholders in Louisville, Kentucky, Hedeman had stood up, accused the board members of raking in most of the PBR's profits, and criticized Bernard and the board for voting against increasing prize money. Bernard explained that in the aftermath of the September 11 terrorist attacks and the economic downturn, he wanted to proceed cautiously. Board members chided Hedeman for his unexpected remarks, which led to a tense 6-hour meeting between Hedeman, Lambert, and Murray. After that meeting, Hedeman and Bernard coexisted without further controversy. But hope for permanent rapprochement ended in June 2004 after the PBR's stop in Nashville.

EVEN BEFORE BULLNANZA–NASHVILLE JUNE 12 AND 13, Hedeman had objected to Bernard's having dropped some original PBR sponsors who couldn't match the money offered by new sponsors. He also objected to Bernard's having cut ties with some promoters and having demanded others split the gate receipts with the PBR. The rift intensified when Bernard suggested the PBR should get 30 percent of the profits from the Tuff Hedeman Challenge instead of allowing Hedeman to keep 100 percent of the profits. The 70-30 split was the same deal the PBR had with the Ty Murray Invitational and the Bossier City event that Hedeman and Pack copromoted.

Ultimately, Bernard and the board backed away from demanding a split of the profits at Hedeman's signature event, but animosity festered.

When the rumors about Hedeman's badmouthing Bernard persisted, Lambert confronted Hedeman at a board meeting. "Do you think Randy should resign?" he asked.

"Yes."

But Hedeman found himself alone. All seven other board members, including Murray and Lambert, expressed support for Bernard. In private, Hedeman continued to gripe about Bernard's bottom-line-driven philosophy—a philosophy that in June 2004 ended the tour's relationship with one of its earliest partners, Gaylord Entertainment, producer of the Bullnanza bull riding events. Since Bullnanzas had become part of the PBR tour in '94, the event had assumed all the risk and reaped all of the profits. Under Bernard, that was about to change.

He presented a new deal: a 50-50 split.

A. G. Meyers, a friend of Hedeman's who had produced the four Bullnanzas in Nashville, Reno, Oklahoma City, and Guthrie, refused the deal, and that ended the PBR's 11-year relationship with Bullnanza and the Gaylord family.

A few days later, committed to producing the events in 2005 without the PBR, Meyers called the Oklahoma City arena to book his regular dates. No luck. Bernard, anticipating the PBR's split with Bullnanza, had booked the coveted dates months earlier.

Meyers retaliated by calling a handful of riders, including Justin McBride, trying to secure a commitment from them to ride in future Bullnanzas. PBR rules called for a 1-year suspension for any rider who missed a BFTS event without a medical excuse or permission from the PBR. But Meyers's politicking concerned Bernard enough that during the 2nd week of July, he was on the phone with McBride.

"He's badmouthing us pretty good, huh?" asked Bernard, smiling as he leaned back in his office chair. "That just pisses me off. Jesus Christ, all we're trying to do is make it the best deal for the PBR. We're kicking ass. I can promise you that."

While riders and fans continued to speculate about Hedeman's resignation, Bernard had turned his attention toward finding a replacement. Having lost one star, he and the PBR board grabbed at another—Murray, one of the PBR founders who had pushed for the hiring of Bernard. Since retiring, Murray had spent most of his time in semiseclusion in Stephenville, Texas, where he ran his 2,000-acre cattle and horse ranch, retired his parents, and built a boat and a guesthouse with his father. He enjoyed the spotlight about as much as he enjoyed a bull's horn in the ribs.

On the PBR's top circuit, any rider who skipped a postevent autograph session was fined $500. During his second-to-last season, Murray had blown off so many autograph sessions that his fines exceeded $10,000.

Bernard called Murray and, with help from Lambert, made his pitch. Then he scheduled a telephone conference with the voting board members, including Lambert; Cody Custer, a retired rider and the PBR's primary back judge; Aaron Semas, a retired rider and an original investor in the PBR; Teague, the multimillionaire from North Carolina; and active riders J. W. Hart and Michael Gaffney. The men needed less than 30 minutes to make Murray its unanimous selection as the PBR's next president. Then they called Murray.

"If you need me, I'll do it," he said.

The PBR immediately posted a story on its Web site heralding the appointment of Murray as the new president and another unanimous vote adding Adriano Moraes to the board. Hedeman's resignation was mentioned in the last sentence of the story. Yet the story failed to address concerns about replacing the fan-friendly Hedeman with someone like Murray.

But Bernard did his best, announcing that Murray had forfeited his six-figure salary and donated the money to top riders who signed autographs. Unlike Hedeman, however, Murray agreed to appear at no more than 12 events a year. On July 9, Bernard gathered his staff in a conference room, and they had to squeeze in. The two-person team when he took over in 1995 had mushroomed to an army of 47, none of whom had ever ridden a bull; they were hired to help run a business, not a rodeo. They were called in to hear Murray address them via speakerphone.

Before he called and began his remarks, someone must have told him about the staff's volleyball party scheduled for that night.

"You better buckle down," Murray said. "And if anybody drinks beer at the volleyball game, you're fired."

The staff cracked up, knowing if Murray had been at the party, he would've been pounding beers rather than the volleyball. Then he praised the PBR staff for all it had done and said he wanted the employees to know how much he appreciated them.

"I'm not just trying to blow smoke up your asses," he said.

"You ever going to leave the ranch?" piped up Sean Gleason, the PBR's chief operating officer.

"Not if I can help it," Murray shot back.

LESS THAN 2 WEEKS AFTER HEDEMAN STEPPED DOWN, Bernard gathered his senior staff members and called for a plan that showed how the PBR was going to increase its revenue in 4 years from $35 million to $100 million.

"I thought you said 5 years," Gleason said.

Bernard grinned. "Well, I'd like to do it in 4."

He asked each department head to look for ways to cut costs and increase revenue, and he wanted it on paper in 2 weeks. The PBR had 23 corporate sponsors, including the big three—Ford, Wrangler, and Bud Light—and a newcomer, in the US Army. But HealthSouth Corporation was trying to recover from a financial crisis after the government filed suit in 2003, accusing the company and its former CEO of massive accounting fraud. The company delayed payments and eventually pulled out altogether. Now some riders were carping about the reduced money on the Challenger Tour, which many of the top-45 riders depended on to make ends meet. And the prize money the PBR had advertised would be available during the 2004 season was on pace to fall about $800,000 short of the original projection of $9.5 million. As a result, Bernard wanted to come up with a presentation to convince the riders, the stockholders, and the board that the PBR would continue to grow with or without Hedeman.

Make no mistake; Bernard remained more than a little interested in what the industry and fans were saying about Hedeman's resignation. Sitting in his office chair, he turned to his laptop and clicked onto the rodeo sites, breaking into a grin as he pointed at his computer screen.

"Look at this."

It was a poll that got to the heart of the matter with one question: Will Tuff Hedeman's resignation hurt the PBR?

Of the 42 respondents, 34 had voted "No," 3 had voted "Yes," and 5 had voted "Wait and see." A half hour later, Bernard rechecked the poll. The results from a small sampling of fans were running about the same. But this time, Bernard moved his cursor in position to cast his own vote. He clicked on choice number three: "Wait and see."

FOURTEEN

THE BULL THAT
SAVED JOE BERGER

Camped out on a bar stool inside Lonesome Dove, where the patrons and bartenders were on a first-name basis, Joe Berger stirred the swizzle stick of his Black Velvet whiskey. He stared into his drink and contemplated the past 6 years of his life.

Ever since he'd suffered a massive heart attack in 1998, he'd carried a bottle of nitroglycerin in his pants pocket, kept another bottle on his nightstand, and kept a third bottle next to his easy chair. Sometimes it was hard to keep track of his bottles of medication. There were more than a dozen containing different-colored pills for different ailments, and Berger started each day by swallowing a handful. Sometimes the medication slowed his gait to a shuffle, slurred his speech, and left him looking every bit of 67 years old. Sometimes he didn't bother to take his medication and ate forbidden foods, such as ribs dripping with barbecue sauce.

While his health was failing, his marriage already had failed. He was months removed from a bitter divorce that had ended his 50-year marriage and strained relations with his five children.

Wearing blue jeans and a golf shirt that stretched over his ample gut, Berger, with his swept-back white hair and sad-eyed look, bore a resemblance to Rodney Dangerfield. Like Dangerfield, Berger had spent years looking for respect. Berger had finally gotten it—despite all of his tribulations along the way.

"I don't have a Learjet," he said, stirring the swizzle stick. "I don't have a ton of money. But I've got the buckle."

There it was around his waist, the gold championship buckle encrusted with diamonds, awarded to the owner of the PBR's Bull of the Year. Berger had won it for owning Little Yellow Jacket, the prized specimen at the Berger family's Rafter Arrow Ranch, in Mandan, North Dakota. He had a second Bull of the Year buckle, too, which he had given to his youngest son, Nevada, and now Berger was aiming for an unprecedented third buckle. Whether he'd win it depended on the fortunes of a crossbred bull that had survived a deadly blizzard, endured a grueling travel schedule, and produced semen that went for $500 a straw.

In April 2004, just as the PA announcer was introducing Little Yellow Jacket during the pre-event introductions at stop number 16 in Billings, Montana, the bull entered the arena and, as if on cue, reared up on his hind legs and shook his horns. Standing on the chutes, rider Ross Johnson elbowed one of Joe Berger's sons, Chad.

"Did you see that?" Johnson exclaimed. "He's human!"

Little Yellow Jacket weighed about as much as most NFL offensive lines—1,800 pounds, give or take a few helpings of alfalfa and oats. On all fours he stood 5 feet 3 inches tall, and when he bucked, his hind hooves stretched to almost the top of the 6-foot-tall chutes.

With brown eyes the size of half dollars, loose skin sagging beneath his chin, and a reddish brown coat, he blended into a pen of bulls. The key to picking him out of the crowd was the horns. The right one extended parallel to the ground and his left one curved down, as if it were borrowed from a ram. What separated him from his four-legged colleagues became clear when a rider climbed on his back and the chute gate swung open. Little Yellow Jacket unleashed a wicked combination of speed, power, and determination. As long as the rider was on his back, he never quit—like the man who had bred and raised him.

A cattle buyer by trade, Berger spent 20 years working for other people before buying his 2,000-acre ranch in Mandan, a town of about 17,000 that sits across the Missouri River from the state capital, Bismarck. It was the perfect place to raise cattle, but in 1976 Berger started breeding bulls full-time. It was risky business.

By the early '80s, the Bergers had fallen behind on loan payments and the bank threatened to foreclose on the family's ranch. The family avoided bankruptcy only after Joe's oldest son, Fred, helped take care of the bills and reorganized the debt. In a concession to his family and their strained finances, Joe loaded up 33 cows that he had wanted to use to breed to bulls and sent them to an auction to be sold by the pound and slaughtered. As the trailer pulled away, Joe wept.

The unpaid bills had piled up again by 1993, so Joe placed an ad in a rodeo publication, offering to sell his remaining cows for the modest price of $500 apiece. The sale would wipe out his bull-breeding program.

No one responded to the ad.

So Berger kept that herd, which included the mother of an unborn bull named Little Yellow Jacket. To pay the bills, Berger began taking his best bucking bulls to the Las Vegas sales held in conjunction with the NFR and PBR finals. Between 1995 and 1997, he sold Moody Blues, Locomotive Breath, and Skoal Yellow Jacket for a grand total of almost $40,000. Then came the agonizing twist.

With the bulls in the hands of other men, Berger watched Moody Blues, Locomotive Breath, and Skoal Yellow Jacket emerge as stars on the pro circuit. And after the bulls won their new owners thousands of dollars in bonuses, they resold the bulls for more than three times what they'd paid Berger.

After the 1998 PBR finals, where Moody Blues was voted Bull of the Year, Berger watched a TV interview with Terry Williams, who'd bought Moody Blues from Berger. The interviewer asked about the bull's impressive bucking.

"He's been that way ever since he was a calf," Williams said. As if Williams had raised him from birth!

Goddamn it, Joe thought to himself. *If I get another bull like that, I'm going to keep him.*

In the winter months of 1996 and 1997, deadly blizzards pounded North Dakota. Snow whipped across Mandan and sent the windchill factor plunging as low as 60 degrees below zero. Motorists stuck in snowdrifts froze to death. The cattle, unprotected from the elements, were at even greater risk. The Bergers lost more than half their herd.

One of the survivors was a brown-coated newborn bull. They named him Little Yellow Jacket, and Nevada grew particularly close to the bull. Once, on the Bergers' ranch, Little Yellow Jacket broke away from about a dozen bulls feeding inside a pen and sauntered toward an open gate. With a young ranch hand watching, Nevada barked, "Get back in here."

With his massive shoulders already out of the pen, Little Yellow Jacket turned around, dropped his head, and lumbered back to the feed bin. The ranch hand watched, mouth agape.

Two nights before the bull riding event in Bismarck, Joe Berger watched as Nevada affectionately rubbed Little Yellow Jacket's head, back, and rump, as if the bull were a pet beagle. But this was no lapdog. More than once, Little Yellow Jacket had charged at Joe Berger, forcing him to scramble over a fence or onto the bail feeder for safety.

"I wouldn't trust him," Joe told Nevada a little crossly.

Nevada shrugged. It was as if he and Little Yellow Jacket communicated through an unspoken language—the bull whisperer and the PBR champion.

Over the past decade, in part because of Joe's failing health, Nevada had taken over most of the duties of Berger Bucking Bulls. He branded them, fed them, weaned them, and, if they proved good enough to buck with the best, hauled them across the country to PBR events.

That weekend Joe Berger fussed when he learned Nevada had scheduled Little Yellow Jacket to buck on back-to-back nights. He fussed again when Nevada told him he was keeping Little Yellow Jacket and the other bulls not at the ranch but at the family's feed pen near downtown Mandan the night before the competition. Joe fussed a lot at his youngest son. But Nevada usually got his way. Without him, Little Yellow Jacket might have spent his best years grazing on the family ranch in anonymity. Of course, without the Bergers, Nevada might have spent his own life in anonymity—or worse.

STANDING ROCK RESERVATION. Nevada Berger no longer considered it home.

On a tour of the Sioux Indian reservation, he stopped at the new casino and pointed to it with pride. But when Nevada got back in his truck and continued the tour, the bleaker parts of the community came into full view. The boarded-up homes. The defunct steel plant. The stray dogs. An older man pedaled his bicycle through what looked like a ghost town.

Having seen enough, Nevada steered onto a two-lane highway and passed three teenagers hitchhiking in the middle of the road. "They'll do the same thing in the middle of the night," he said. "People get killed around here all the time, and they act like it's not a big deal."

He pushed on the gas pedal harder and drove away from the place where, 32 years ago, somewhere amid the dilapidated homes and run-down neighborhoods, Nevada had been born to Chuck Two Bears and Anna Martinez.

Darlene Berger first saw Nevada the day she drove to the reservation to buy some beaded jewelry. He was 3 months old, malnourished, and in the care of his destitute grandparents. They were hoping to find the boy a new home.

This boy has no chance, Darlene thought. Then the jewelry maker asked Darlene if she'd be willing to adopt the boy. The Bergers already had four children between the ages of 11 and 16, not to mention the pile of bills. But the next day, after talking it over with Joe, Darlene returned to Standing Rock Reservation and took the boy home. His grandparents had called him Arlen. But from that day forth, the boy was known as Nevada.

His new brothers and sisters adored him, in part because he rescued them from the regular drives around the ranch with their father. Joe Berger would take the kids for hours and often parked in one spot, gazing at his cattle as they grazed. Occasionally the bulls bellowed, and the unlucky Berger child groaned.

"When are we going in, Dad?"

Too young to know any better, Nevada happily joined Joe. When Joe baled hay or cleared the fields in his bulldozer, there was Nevada, sitting by his side. Darlene Berger and the children played only a peripheral role in the business.

At the age of 13, Nevada began riding bulls and in less than 2 years broke both of his arms—twice. He exhibited the good sense to give up riding but kept working with them. He was there when his father still was trying to figure out exactly what kind of bucker he had in Little Yellow Jacket. Surviving the blizzard proved he was sturdy, but the bull's first real test came at a small rodeo not far from Mandan. Little Yellow Jacket was 2½ years old.

He was barely out of the chute that day before he slam-dunked the rider, and the Bergers knew just as quick that Little Yellow Jacket had a chance to be among the country's elite bulls. Nevada, aware of the PBR, called Cody Lambert and left countless messages before Lambert finally called back. It was Lambert who determined which bulls got into the BFTS events, and in 1998 he agreed to let Nevada bring a small string of bulls that included Little Yellow Jacket to three events.

By 1999, Little Yellow Jacket was a rising star on the PBR tour.

Nevada worried about wearing out the young bull with all the travel, but not as much as he worried about squandering a chance to showcase Little Yellow Jacket. Week after week, he climbed behind the wheel of the family's 1993 Dodge truck, which had so many miles on it the odometer broke. "The King of the Road," Joe Berger called the bull, because from coast to coast, border to border, in and out of 45 states, Little Yellow Jacket bucked with consistency and ferocity rarely seen among young bulls. He threw off more than 85 percent of the riders before the 8-second buzzer, but he was the kind of bull almost every rider wanted to try, because those who held on for 8 seconds were virtually guaranteed scores of 90 points and up.

Deep-pocketed men began to drool. Tuff Hedeman offered $50,000 for the bull. Berger turned him down.

Terry Williams offered $65,000. Berger turned him down.

Then, relayed through Lambert, came an offer of $130,000, enough money for Berger to pay off the rest of his debt. Berger, who wanted a gold buckle, turned down the offer. The next morning, the phone rang. It was Fred, the son who'd saved his father from bankruptcy.

"Did you fall out of bed and hurt your head?" he asked.

"Why?"

"Someone offered you $130,000 and you didn't sell that goddamn bull? Are you crazy?"

Crazy? Maybe. But Berger had a feeling about this bull, which by the age of 5 had filled out to 1,600 pounds. In 2 years Little Yellow Jacket had gone from King of the Road to King of the PBR. At the 2001 PBR finals, he was named Bull of the Finals, finished runner-up to Dillinger in the rider vote for Bull of the Year, and earned $20,000 in bonuses. When Joe Berger accepted the gold buckle for Bull of the Finals at the PBR awards banquet, tears ran down his face.

The dividends kept coming. In 2002 Little Yellow Jacket won the vote for Bull of the Year in a landslide, making Joe Berger the first man to breed and raise a bull from birth that had gone on to be voted PBR Bull of the Year. As he knew all too well, the previous gold buckles had gone to wealthy men who bought promising young bulls from cash-strapped breeders like him. And suddenly yet another wealthy man sought out Berger.

Checkbook at the ready, Tom Teague, the North Carolina businessman who had helped the PBR buy back its TV rights, spent the next year pestering Berger about his interest in buying the bull. Berger kept resisting, to the point where Teague almost gave up.

Late at night at the 2003 finals, after a few drinks in the hospitality room, Berger approached Teague. "Tom, what will you give me today for a half interest in that bull?"

"Fifty thousand dollars."

Berger took a swig of his drink. "Sold," he said.

Teague, in turn, gave half of his share to Bernie Taupin. But in the world of bull riding, it was Little Yellow Jacket, not a famous songwriter, who remained the star. In 2003 he was voted Bull of the Year for the second straight season and joined Dillinger as the only bull to win the award twice. Soon he had his own line of merchandise—T-shirts, tank tops, sweatshirts, thermoses, Beanie bulls, art prints, greeting cards, key chains, ball caps, and visors—and a growing legion of fans.

The partnership with Teague allowed Berger to keep the bull at his farm in North Dakota and keep any gold buckles. Berger gave Nevada the gold buckle Little Yellow Jacket won as the 2003 Bull of the Year.

But Teague wanted a buckle of his own. So in Greensboro, North Carolina, at the PBR's fourth event of the 2004 season, he pulled aside Joe Berger and, looking to buy the Berger family's share of Little Yellow Jacket, made an offer he figured couldn't be refused. Name your price, he said.

But it wasn't so simple.

After the Bergers had divorced, Darlene got the house and a 50 percent interest in the bulls. She had the right to match any offer Joe got. Even if she couldn't match the offer, her share would keep Teague from taking full control of the bull—and she was adamant about keeping the bull for Nevada and the rest of the family. Tantalized by the thought of a six-figure check from Teague, Joe Berger mulled the offer. But with Darlene vowing to keep her share, he announced he was keeping the bull. The decision temporarily united the family during the July 16 and 17 Challenger Tour Event in Bismarck, with the PBR still in the middle of a 6-week break between BFTS events.

That weekend, an army of pickup trucks rattled across the Missouri River Bridge and into Bismarck to see Mandan's most famous resident in the flesh. Many of them had seen him only on TV.

On April 20, 2003, in Colorado Springs, NBC televised the Bud Light Million-Dollar Bounty, presented by Ford Trucks—a one-ride showdown between Chris Shivers and Little Yellow Jacket. Ride the bull for 8 seconds, and Shivers would win $1 million. Buck Shivers off before the buzzer, and Little Yellow Jacket would win his owners $50,000.

That weekend, Little Yellow Jacket roomed in a special tent with a pair of chandeliers at the upscale Broadmoor Hotel. He had round-the-clock security, and police escorted him to the arena.

The showdown had all the feel of a championship prizefight, with an official weigh-in behind the Broadmoor. Wearing his boots and oversize world championship buckle, Shivers tipped the scales at 146 pounds. Little Yellow Jacket almost crushed the scales despite weighing in at—for him—a relatively light 1,650 pounds.

The sellout crowd was rooting for Shivers, in part because they wanted to see the rider collect the oversize check for $1 million, which was already made out to Shivers and waiting in a nearby hall. Prior to the Million-Dollar Bounty, Little Yellow Jacket had been ridden just eight times in 54 attempts, and Shivers had failed in all four of his tries. In their last matchup, Little Yellow Jacket had dumped Shivers while spinning to the right. But it was foolish to predict what the bull would do.

With NBC's cameras rolling, the chute gate opened and Little Yellow Jacket spun to the left. He jolted Shivers forward and propelled the little cowboy into the air. When Shivers landed with a thud, the clock read 1.8 seconds—all the time the bull had needed to defeat Shivers. After scrambling to his feet and sprinting for the side fence, Shivers covered his face with his cowboy hat and wept. The residents of Mandan, North Dakota, watching on TV, cheered. Berger and Teague split the $50,000 bonus, and Berger's take from Little Yellow Jacket's earnings over the past 6 years climbed to over $275,000—more than enough to wipe out his debt.

The 1993 Dodge was long gone, replaced by new Ford F-350 trucks.

The rickety trailer used to haul Little Yellow Jacket was gone, too, replaced by a new model bearing the name of the Bergers' prize bull on the side.

In July 2004, Little Yellow Jacket came off the road to buck in front of his hometown fans at the fourth annual Challenger Tour event, a two-night PBR minor-league stop in the Bismarck Civic Center. Each night crowds of more than 8,000 cheered loud for the 45 riders and even louder for their favorite bull.

On night one, Little Yellow Jacket squared off against Cory Turnbow, a 38-year-old rider with Elvis sideburns who ran his own sewage treatment plant in Cleburne, Texas. Turnbow had driven 18 hours to get to the PBR Bull Riding Challenge at the Bismarck Civic Center, and in the first round he broke his bull rope in the chutes. Taking advice from Hedeman and Lambert, he tied the rope in a square knot, rode his first-round bull, and scored an 85, good enough to make the first-night championship round. His reward: a matchup with the PBR's two-time Bull of the Year.

With his broken rope, Turnbow boarded Little Yellow Jacket and tried to maneuver him off the back of the chute. The bull never bucked or thrashed in the chute before the gate opened, but he did lean, making it hard for a rider to slide down one of his boots. Surrendering to the bull's strength, Turnbow called for the gate. Little Yellow Jacket turned back to the left, shook Turnbow's feet from his sides, and hurled him headfirst into a metal post. Blood poured down the rider's face.

After the medical team helped Turnbow out of the arena, Joe Berger lifted his white cowboy hat, acknowledging the crowd's cheers.

On night two, Rogerio Ferreira, the long-legged Brazilian, advanced to the championship round and found himself matched up with Little Yellow Jacket. This was Ferreira's fourth full season on the PBR and his first shot at riding Little Yellow Jacket. He was so excited he could barely wait. When the gate opened, Little Yellow Jacket took one jump, hop-skipped to the left, and slammed Ferreira to the ground. The Brazilian left the arena with his head bowed, and again Berger lifted his cowboy hat to acknowledge the crowd's cheers.

North Dakota's favorite bull was at his best, but the 2-day event was compelling for other reasons, too. Only a week after resigning as president of the PBR, Hedeman made his first public appearance, hired by the Bergers to help promote the event. "So I hear you quit on me," Bobby "Jinx" Clower, a member of the PBR's traveling crew, said by way of greeting Hedeman.

"I guess so," Hedeman said.

Normally surrounded by fans, Hedeman at first kept his distance while nursing a Bud Light at the Lonesome Dove bar. He talked quietly with a few friends. To others he offered cryptic answers as to why he'd resigned.

"I'm a cowboy," he said. "I'm looking out for the best interests of the cowboy. I'm no politician. Some people on the board think things are better off without me. We'll see."

Watching from afar were Bill and Peggy Duvall, the die-hard fans with the matching PBR jackets who already had attended 13 of the 23 BFTS events during the 2004 season. They'd come to Mandan to see the home of Little Yellow Jacket, but they looked just as pleased to see Hedeman and enjoyed the gossip stemming from his presence. Later, Hedeman joined the crowd and regained his form, drinking beer until the wee hours of the morning and getting up by 5:45, in time to fulfill his promotional obligation of TV and radio interviews.

The lineup of riders on night one included James White, the star-crossed rookie returning to action just 2 weeks after a bull had flipped him three times, chipped his front tooth, and split his lip. He arrived looking uncharacteristically dull eyed and distracted.

Five weeks after his BFTS debut in Anaheim, he was one of three riders who had landed an endorsement deal with the US Army. But soon after, White broke his hand, which kept him out for 3 weeks. Then came tragedy.

On May 24, a drunk driver swerved across a highway and collided with the car White's mother was driving. She was killed instantly, while the two other passengers in her car survived. White had lost not only his mother but also his biggest supporter. Since then, he'd fallen out of the top 45 and needed to win on the minor-league circuit to get back on the BFTS. But in the first round at Bismarck, White got bucked off again. He packed up his equipment bag and headed for the next minor-league stop.

Later that night, in the hallway, someone asked a passing rider, "How's the leg?"

"We'll know when I get on."

The rider was Jody Newberry, who'd been out 11 weeks after having knee surgery to repair torn ligaments. His June 5 wedding and honeymoon in Hawaii kept him preoccupied only so long. In seventh place in the BFTS standings and with an outside shot at a $1 million bonus, Newberry was itching to get back. "I hope I haven't forgotten how to ride," he said before getting aboard Huskers Red against the advice of his doctors, who told him he needed to rest his knee for several more weeks. By riding, he risked another trip to the operating room. But risking more surgery struck Newberry's family members as typical Jody.

As a 6-year-old, after watching a movie called *Rad*—which featured teenagers on motocross bicycles doing tricks such as backflips off of ramps—Newberry found two cinderblocks and a wooden board and assembled his own ramp. Helmetless, he pedaled furiously down the driveway, up the ramp, pulled back on the handlebars, flipped in the air and . . . landed square on his back.

Holding her breath, Jody's mother, June, watched the fiasco through her bedroom window. Relieved to see her son standing up and dusting himself off, June shouted, "Jody, you can't do these things just because they did it in the movie. You don't have the right ramp. And they practiced."

Ignoring the lecture, Jody pounded one fist into the palm of his hand.

"I know where I went wrong," he muttered, then told his brother to get another cinderblock. They readjusted the ramp, making it even steeper.

June ran outside. Too late.

Back down the driveway he sped. Up and off the ramp he flew, sailing into the air as he pulled back on the handlebars and . . . landed on his head. When his mother emerged from the house, Jody, elbows bleeding, was lining up for a third attempt. His mother ordered him to stop. But she knew it was only temporary. He tried and tried and tried again and eventually executed a backflip. He failed to land on his bicycle, however, and finally came inside skinned up from head to toe. Of course, this was the same kid who would run into a wall, fall, rub his head, grin, and take off running again.

Another time, when the husband of Jody's older sister regaled the twin brothers with how his cousins used to ride their bikes off the barn roof, there went Jody, tying his bike to a rope and . . . his mother emerged from the house just in time to see Jody and his bike on top of the barn roof.

Ten feet above the ground.

"Jody, what do you think you're doing?" she shouted.

"Gonna ride my bike off the roof," he answered.

"Get down here!"

Grudgingly, bike in hand, Newberry rappelled down the side of the barn. What the brother-in-law had neglected to mention was that the barn was built against a hill.

So, almost two decades later and now inside the Bismarck Civic Center, here was Newberry climbing onto Huskers Red instead of his motocross bike.

Two jumps and a turn to the left by the bull, and off Newberry fell. But he walked out of the arena smiling. His surgically repaired knee felt fine. He felt ready for the rest of the season.

Then there was Eathan Graves, the pint-size rider who'd outridden McBride and three other regular riders on the BFTS at the Humps N' Horns event in Thibodaux. Still carrying the fake $1 million bill, he would have settled for a lot less than that in recent weeks. In nine events since Thibodaux, Graves had failed to win any money. He also left Bismarck without any money after getting bucked off Western Wishes. But he did leave with some consolation after Hedeman walked by and said, "Man, you really did a good job. He bucked you off like he bucks off some of the best."

Adriano Moraes competed, and so did several other regular riders on the BFTS. But the biggest draw that weekend was Little Yellow Jacket. It was the sole reason Michael Axt drove with his wife and their three children 65 miles from their home in McClusky, North Dakota. Axt said they wanted to watch "the greatest athlete in the state of North Dakota."

Of course, he meant Little Yellow Jacket.

And before night two, Axt was among the fans swarming Darlene Berger's merchandise stand. He inspected one of the ball caps and announced, "This is going to be obsolete next year."

A woman helping with the sales looked startled. "Why's that?" she asked.

Axt pointed to the side of the cap and the embroidery that read *Two-Time PBR Bull of the Year*. "Because he'll be a three-time champion."

That remained to be seen. Little Yellow Jacket had effortlessly bucked off both of his riders at that weekend's event. But Pandora's Box had been spectacular, bucking off his two riders—including veteran J. W. Hart—with dynamic force. On Little Yellow Jacket's home turf, it was Pandora's Box who earned Bull of the Event honors.

As the fans filed out of the Civic Center, Winston Loe, an oil-field consultant from Texas who had bought Pandora's Box in 2001 for $13,000, accepted the buckle awarded to the owner of the Bull of the Event. But Loe wanted more. He wanted the gold championship buckle won by the man who owned the Bull of the Year. So far, Pandora's Box had gone unridden in 13 attempts on the BFTS. Little Yellow Jacket had been ridden once in 13 attempts, by former world champ Michael Gaffney.

Saturday night in Bismarck, Joe and Nevada Berger were among the first to congratulate Loe, a husky man whose beard concealed his double chin and whose stoic nature concealed any excitement. He allowed a smile only after the Bergers had moved out of sight.

"Everybody's pretty high on him," Loe said, looking at Pandora's Box. "But again, you've got the Little Yellow Jacket problem. You've got to knock the champion out. In my opinion, that hasn't happened yet."

But with five BFTS events left before the finals, there was plenty of time for a knockout punch.

CONCESSIONS

Cowboy Hall of Fame hot dog (with part of the proceeds going to the Cowboy Hall of Fame, under construction)	$3.65
Taco-in-a-bag (think taco without the shell)	$3.25
Flying-style pizza burger (a hamburger patty with pizza sauce and mozzarella cheese)	$4

"Other than that," concessions manager Darryl Dolan said, "we don't really have anything that's peculiar." Well, nothing as peculiar as deep-fried Twinkies.

FIFTEEN

RUMBLINGS FROM
THE RIDERS

Oklahoma City, Oklahoma
Friday & Saturday, August 6 & 7, 2004

Boycott.

The ugly word spread through the halls at the Westin Hotel where the PBR riders were staying the weekend of Bullnanza–Oklahoma City. As the war between Tuff Hedeman and the PBR board looked ready to erupt, some riders discussed whether a boycott of a BFTS event, maybe even the finals, would amount to treason or liberation.

During the 6-week break since Bullnanza–Nashville, the last BFTS event, Hedeman's resignation had dominated talk in the world of bull riding. A quote that appeared in two newspapers suggested Hedeman had quit at least in part because he thought the PBR board was taking the riders for granted, and some of the riders were looking for a leader to press the board on their behalf.

They wanted more insurance coverage. They wanted a say in what bulls were picked for events. They wanted to get rid of a rule that subjected riders to a 1-year suspension if they missed a BFTS event without a medical reason or permission from the PBR. It appeared the riders would have a chance to discuss all of that and organize themselves when Hedeman scheduled a riders-only meeting for the day after Bullnanza–Oklahoma City ended. It was no secret.

Randy Bernard and the board members had caught wind of the meeting and, like many of the riders, wondered why exactly Hedeman had called it. To simply explain why he'd resigned as president of the PBR but stayed on board as a commentator on the OLN telecasts? To announce he was starting his own bull riding tour and attempt to persuade the riders to defect from the PBR? To try to organize the riders into a union and make demands of the PBR board? And if the PBR refused to make any concessions, would Hedeman call for a boycott of a BFTS event or even the finals as some riders had heard he was contemplating?

Pressing Hedeman for details proved as futile as asking him to trade in his Cinch jeans for Wranglers. J. W. Hart, Michael Gaffney, and Adriano Moraes, active riders who also were members of the PBR board, planned to attend Hedeman's meeting and report back to Bernard and the rest of the board members. But there were still 2 days of bull riding ahead and an event that kicked off the homestretch of the 2004 season. Only five regular-season events remained until the finals, with Moraes, Justin McBride, and Mike Lee running 1-2-3 in the overall standings and still the top contenders. But a familiar face and a long-shot contender showed up on the scene that weekend.

Equipment bag slung over his shoulder, the short but muscled rider strode into the locker room and into the path of B. J. Kramps. "Hey, pip-squeak," Kramps said.

It was the PBR's most popular pip-squeak, and the reigning champion. Chris Shivers was back. But it was too early to determine which

Shivers—the determined champ from 2003 or the distracted defending champ from 2004. After breaking his right shoulder blade February 6 in Tampa, then having surgery not only on the shoulder but also for a nagging hip injury, he'd been recuperating at his ranch in Jonesville and missed 15 BFTS events. He arrived in Oklahoma City with his wife, Kylie, and their 18-month-old son, Brand. But they parted ways after getting to the Ford Center, knowing Shivers would be in demand.

First came the well-wishers, then came the TV folks, and off he went for a pre-event interview with OLN's Leah Garcia. He waited under the hot klieg lights. Garcia welcomed him back and asked about his plans.

"The goal is always to win the world championship," he said. Off camera, he added, "I didn't show up to half-ass it and not win."

With the new scoring system at the finals, Shivers had an outside chance at catching Moraes. But first he needed to qualify for the finals. He stood in 55th place in the qualifier standings with $13,286.40 and, riding with an injury exemption, found himself almost $5,000 behind Jason Bennett and the 45th and last spot for the finals, for which he'd qualified for 7 straight years. "I'll be back," Shivers promised.

But to catch Moraes, Shivers needed to rack up points in a hurry. He trailed by more than 7,000 points. Yet he looked unconcerned and care-free. Outside their locker room, he and Mike White, Shivers's best friend on tour, traded barbs and took turns roping each other as if they were calves. During introductions, White felt the back of his chaps pull tight with each step he took across an elevated ramp. When the arena lights came on, he realized somebody had knotted the fringe on the back of his chaps.

Shivers flashed a shit-eating grin.

White's look said it all: Damn you, Shivers.

Later, grabbing an electric prod used in emergency cases to move recalcitrant bulls in the back pens, Shivers jolted White on the ass. White shrieked, but he resisted retaliating. He looked happy to see that Shivers was enjoying himself, unlike the vibe he had gotten from his buddy earlier in the season. It wouldn't take long to see what effect the mood might have on his riding.

On the second ride of the night, Shivers settled on top of Gator, unridden in nine outs. The bull lunged out of the chute and took a series of long, powerful jumps. Shivers found his rhythm and effortlessly moved with the bull. No flashy spurring. No crowd-pleasing arm whip. Just a solid, mistake-free ride to the 8-second buzzer.

Lazily, almost contemptuously, he tossed his cowboy hat toward Gator as if to say, "That's all you got, big bull?"

In came the judges' scores—87 points—and up went the cheers.

Though fans were eager to see Shivers, the riders were waiting almost as eagerly to see somebody else—Jared Farley. In the 6 weeks between Bullnanza–Nashville and Bullnanza–Oklahoma City, Farley had dominated the PBR's minor-league circuit, winning three of his last five events and prompting a resounding question: "Who the heck is this guy?"

He was an 18-year-old Aussie and, like NFL quarterbacks Peyton and Eli Manning, had all the requisite genes to be a champion. His father, Paul, had won six Australian national championships and ridden in the Calgary Stampede. But Paul Farley lacked the crowning jewel, a US championship. In fact, Paul Farley never even competed on US soil—the primary place his son intended to compete.

In a 3-week span, he'd won $35,000, and the total moved him into the top 45 and secured him a spot on the BFTS circuit for the rest of the season. But until Bullnanza–Oklahoma City, Farley had yet to ride in a BFTS event.

During the first round, when Farley slid onto Camo in the chute, the bull squirmed and wriggled and bucked. He refused to cooperate, and Farley finally hopped out of the chute.

A couple of riders watching chuckled. "I guess he don't want to be next," one of them said, referring to the bull.

But now Farley was limping as he waited for a reride bull. Twenty minutes later he hopped aboard Armadillo Willie, the gate opened, and the two soared into the arena. The unshakable Farley would not budge, making the 8-second buzzer for a score of 84 points. One bull and it was clear: The Aussie rookie was for real. So, too, it appeared, was the army of Brazilians.

There they were, now six strong, yakking away in Portuguese. The group included Adriano Moraes and his two younger brothers, Allan and Andre, who were making history as the first three brothers to qualify for a BFTS event. They also became the first three brothers to get bucked off in the first round. Adriano Moraes was furious.

Aboard Bomber, Adriano Moraes looked on his way to a 90-point ride before the bull's last-second belly roll dumped him off the side and onto the dirt. His air of invincibility was gone, and so was that easygoing smile. Later, passing Justin McBride on the chutes, Moraes grumbled about how easy a ride Bomber should have been.

"The easiest bull here," Moraes said.

"Yeah, sure looked like it to me," said McBride, rolling his eyes and shaking his head as the Brazilian walked away; then he added, "Goofy bastard."

Adam Carrillo won the round with an 89-point ride, and McBride trailed by only a half point. But during the postevent autograph session, one never would have known it.

"Ay-dree-ah-noooo! Ay-dree-ah-nooo!"

"What?" he barked in jest, signing autographs and chatting up fans.

"I'm coming to Vegas," one told him.

"Coo-ooo-oool. Hopefully I'll be riding better than I was tonight."

Shivers was signing autographs only a few feet behind Moraes.

"Chris, are you healthy again?" a fan asked.

Overhearing the question, Moraes answered before Shivers had a chance.

"I think so," Moraes said with a wink, and Shivers smiled.

Without so much as a trace of a smile, Mike Lee returned to the arena. His wife, Jamie, making a rare appearance at a BFTS event, stood next to Pastor Todd Pierce and watched her husband with a look of concern as he joined the autograph session. "He needs to be around people," she said.

But Lee, who'd gotten bucked off Paleface that night, engaged in no banter with the fans or other riders as he dutifully signed autographs. He served as the ultimate contrast to Moraes, who was lifting children over the arena railing and posing with them as their camera-toting parents snapped pictures.

"Think about that million-dollar smile," someone shouted at Moraes.

"I just want to ride all my bulls," he said.

Since the stop in Albuquerque, New Mexico, he'd ridden only six of his past 16 bulls, a stretch that included four straight buck-offs. Despite his lead in the standings, Moraes knew he needed to find his old groove to keep challengers from overtaking him. That is, unless some of the challengers boycotted the finals.

SATURDAY MORNING IN THE HOTEL RESTAURANT, Pastor Todd Pierce picked over his grits and paged through his Bible. He was worried about the feud between Hedeman and the PBR board and likened the situation to a bitter divorce where the parents waged their battle through their children.

"You've got to decide who's really got the riders' best interest at heart," said Pierce, who like many of the riders found himself torn.

Yet Pierce feared that the riders-only meeting Hedeman had called for Sunday might split the riders. So later that morning, during his sermon at the Cowboy Church service, Pierce urged the riders to watch out for Satan, suggesting that the angel of darkness was hiding behind the brewing controversy.

To other people, Satan was the rodeo's first full-fledged agent—Mark Nestlen, the paunchy man with the wire-rimmed glasses who walked into the hotel lounge at 1:30 that afternoon. Nestlen, according to PBR insiders, settled disputes with legal threats and litigation, whereas some cowboys settled disputes with their fists.

Curt Lyons, a lanky 32-year-old rider from Oklahoma, was still bitter about a deal gone bad when he spotted Nestlen in 2000 during a PBR autograph session in Laughlin, Nevada. When the session ended, Lyons recalled, he walked up to Nestlen and with one punch decked him.

But most of the time, Nestlen was able to roll with the punches. He knew the rider contracts he signed better than the riders did, and he knew PBR rules on sponsorship and rider endorsements better than the

PBR officials did—and he never hesitated to take action any time he felt his clients had been cheated out of money.

Every time Clint Branger heard the latest dustup involving Nestlen, Branger cursed himself. He felt partly responsible. In 1997, the two met on a connecting plane in Charlotte, North Carolina, with Branger explaining he was a professional bull rider and Nestlen explaining he'd spent the past 13 years working as a lobbyist for the agriculture industry. The two got to talking about how the cowboys needed help managing their sponsorships and endorsements. Nestlen expressed an interest in the matter and said he was ready to leave Washington, DC.

"Next thing I know," Branger said, "he's calling up and wanting me to sign on with him." Branger did.

Until then only stars like Tuff Hedeman and Ty Murray commanded significant endorsement deals. But that was about to change. Later that year Nestlen quit his lobbyist job, moved to Oklahoma, and, with help from his new wife, started a firm called Cowboy Sports Agents.

At the 2000 finals, Branger's endorsement deal with DeWALT Power Tools had expired. He was set to be inducted into the PBR's Ring of Honor that weekend, and a friend of his with DeWALT asked if Branger would mind riding in a DeWALT truck as part of a promotional deal. No problem, said Branger, though he mentioned that Nestlen wouldn't like the idea.

Branger was right. "He was madder than hell," Branger recalled. "You could see like the blood vessels bursting through his eyes. He was almost threatening to sue."

The two men parted ways and never spoke again. But by that time, Branger's defection was no big deal for Nestlen, who had a foothold in the world of bull riding. His star client was Shivers; and with Nestlen's help, the young rider landed a six-figure deal when he became the exclusive endorsee of the Ford Motor Company. For his 28 clients, Nestlen said, he had brought $1.2 million in endorsement deals, with Cowboy Sports Agents getting a 15 percent commission.

By the 2004 season, the company's stable of clients featured 18 bull riders, including Owen Washburn, the 1996 PBR champion; Luke Snyder, the 2001 PBR Rookie of the Year; Mike White, the 1999 PRCA champion; and Greg Potter, a standout rider from Australia. The riders Nestlen helped make money tolerated his behavior, but many PBR officials loathed him. With disregard for the tour's primary sponsors, such as Wrangler and Jack Daniel's, Nestlen cut deals for his clients with Wrangler rival Cinch jeans and Jack Daniel's rival Jim Beam. Of course, that didn't keep him from cutting deals with Wrangler and Jack Daniel's—for the right money.

By the middle of 2004, every rider who started the season in the top 10 had at least one sponsor, and more than half of the riders who started the season ranked between 11th and 55th had sponsors. The increasing corporate interest in sponsoring riders stemmed in part from the eight BFTS events to be televised on NBC. With the exposure making them valuable billboards, the riders plastered stickers on their protective vests like NASCAR drivers plastered stickers on their cars.

Encouraged by Nestlen's success and, in some cases, prodded by PBR officials hoping to limit Nestlen's influence, others joined the agent game. But no one operated with as much power or instilled as much fear.

"Piece of shit" is how Hedeman referred to Nestlen. Adriano Moraes chose more polite words to express the same sentiment, but later that year he enlisted Nestlen's help when his deal with Resistol was set to expire. Moraes knew no one worked harder for clients than Nestlen. And there he was Saturday afternoon in Oklahoma City, meeting with Joe Loverro, producer of the Outdoor Life Network's PBR telecasts. It was Nestlen in prime form.

Arriving with a representative from Theragenics Corporation, Nestlen told Loverro that Washburn was serving as a spokesman for the Atlanta-based company, which sells implantable radiation devices. A can't-miss story for OLN, Nestlen assured him, but Loverro had some questions.

Did Washburn have cancer and use the devices? No.

Did anybody close to him need the radiation devices or use them? No.

Loverro didn't see the point of the story, but Nestlen continued to push. Wearing down, Loverro said he might be able to squeeze something in during the finals telecasts. No surprise there. More often than not, Nestlen got what he wanted.

Loverro looked drained. Earlier that morning, he'd huddled with Bernard and Lambert in the presidential suite of the Renaissance Hotel, across the street from the Westin. The talk centered on Hedeman and his future role with the PBR and OLN. Bernard and Lambert wanted Hedeman off the broadcast team. For one, they hated that Hedeman was still making money off the PBR while privately attacking Bernard and the board. They also feared Hedeman might air his beefs during a broadcast. But Loverro worried about something else.

Pulling Hedeman from the broadcasts without explanation in mid-season, Loverro said, could cause a backlash from TV viewers. The three men met for 3 hours and arrived at no decision except to hold off until they got details from Hedeman's riders-only meeting Sunday.

That night, inside the Ford Center, Moraes was trying to redeem himself. All season, when making it to the 8-second buzzer or getting bucked off, he'd acted as cool as a running back crossing the goal line for a touchdown. But in the second round, when Moraes rode King's Court, he pounded his chest with both fists, releasing 6 weeks' worth of frustration.

The 88.5-point ride earned him a spot in the championship round on Smokeless Wardance. During that ride, Moraes stayed in the middle of the bull and leaned forward, trying to neutralize Smokeless Wardance's power. He strained with his powerful left forearm, and his thick legs gave way. The bull jerked forward. Momentum pulled Moraes. There was no holding on.

Moraes slammed face-first into Smokeless Wardance's right horn, and the ride ended with Moraes tossed to the ground before the 8-second buzzer. He looked dazed as he headed for the sports medicine room.

X-rays showed that the force of the blow had cracked his eye socket and fractured his upper jaw. Pressing an ice bag against the left side of his face, Adriano Moraes emitted garbled words between his bloody lips. As Moraes eased himself off the examination table and got dressed, Tandy Freeman called a specialist to schedule surgery. For the second straight BFTS event, Moraes would leave needing surgery—first for his knee and now for his face.

Five concerned Brazilians stood huddled outside the sports medicine room when Moraes emerged. He muttered a few words in Portuguese and walked past. Alone, he headed toward the arena exit and every few steps spit blood on the concrete floor.

Mike Mathis, an in-arena announcer, stopped Moraes in the corridor.

"Are you okay?"

"I'm fine," Moraes said. "Hey, who won?"

"Brendon Clark."

"Really? Cool."

Two steps later, the co-owner of Smokeless Wardance wrapped his arm around Moraes's shoulder. "I'm sorry," he said.

Moraes shook his head, indicating there was no need for an apology. "That is a good bull. I'll be fine."

Off he went, out a back door and up a ramp that led to a parking lot. A young member of the PBR crew caught up to Moraes and stared at the rider's puffy red face.

"Champ," the kid said, "you look like Rocky Balboa."

Yet once again, Moraes's top challengers failed to land anything resembling a knockout punch. After opening the competition with an 88.5-point ride, McBride fell off his last two bulls. Lee got bucked off both of his bulls and failed to make the championship round. And after Shivers's 87-point ride in the first round, he fell off his last two bulls. Though Farley rode two bulls and served notice that he was more than a minor leaguer, the $1 million bonus was out of reach for him and most of the other riders. But that didn't stop several of the cowboys from partying later that night.

With music throbbing in Club Rodeo, the PBR crew gathered on the second floor. In walked Bernard. He wasn't there to drink but rather to gauge the mood of the riders less than 10 hours before Hedeman's meeting.

At 9:45 Sunday morning, the cars began pulling into the parking lot at Chelino's Mexican Restaurant. By 10:30, more than 40 riders had gathered in a second-floor room. Instead of a buffet, the breakfast fare was an open bar. Ross Coleman sipped a margarita as the meeting came to order.

Hedeman sat behind a table in front of the room. Sitting alongside him were Ron Pack, Hedeman's close friend and business advisor; Tommy Joe Lucia, the PBR's outgoing production officer; and Terry Williams, a stock contractor and friend of Hedeman's who had started his own tour, Championship Bull Riding (CBR). The men passed out a six-page overview of their goal on letterhead with a logo for the "Bull Riders Alliance."

Hedeman spoke for less than 10 minutes before turning things over to Pack and Lucia. One of the riders interjected, saying he didn't think the PBR had the riders' best interest at heart. Gaffney, one of the three active riders and PBR board members, spoke out.

"I beg to differ."

"How are you trying to make things better?" Hedeman demanded.

"Why are you insinuating we're not doing anything for the riders?" Gaffney asked.

"Give me some examples of what you're doing."

Gaffney glared. Hedeman glared back. Lucia interrupted the showdown.

"The purpose of this meeting is not to get into personal deals," he said. "It's to find out how to help the bull riders."

Among the list of things they wanted for the riders, Pack and Lucia said, was better insurance coverage, more say in picking bulls, a retirement fund, and to get rid of the competition clause that subjected riders to a 1-year suspension if they missed a BFTS event without a medical excuse or PBR permission. They talked about taking these demands to the PBR with the following ammunition: Give us what we want or we're not going to ride.

"Basically, what you're telling us is if we join this, we're going to have to boycott," rider Lee Akin said. "In my opinion, the PBR will call our bluff."

"Unfortunately," Lucia said, "that sounds like something that could happen. Hopefully it won't."

Akin wanted to make sure he understood. "Once we take this stand and join the alliance, if the PBR doesn't agree to go by our regulations, we are not to go (to the next event)?"

"Yes," Lucia responded. "That means we'd have to boycott."

More than 25 riders signed a sheet expressing interest in the Bull Riders Alliance, and they agreed to meet again in Reno. McBride was among those voicing strong support for Hedeman. But Akin and B. J. Kramps were among the riders who left the meeting thinking it had raised more questions than it had provided answers.

The next day, the board of directors held a teleconference and discussed Hedeman's meeting and the actions of Pack, Williams, and Lucia. "Traitors," Bernard branded them. Yet the board members knew they had to address the riders' concerns or risk a boycott. So they agreed to create a rider advisory committee to help pick the bulls and discussed contributing more money toward rider insurance coverage. In short, they planned to do everything in their power to head off a mutiny and undercut Hedeman's Bull Riders Alliance.

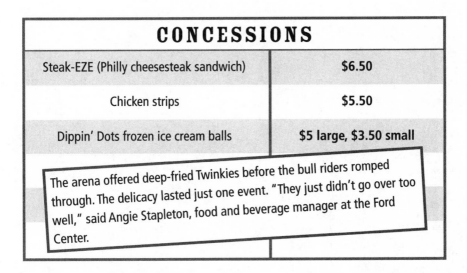

CONCESSIONS

Steak-EZE (Philly cheesesteak sandwich)	**$6.50**
Chicken strips	**$5.50**
Dippin' Dots frozen ice cream balls	**$5 large, $3.50 small**

The arena offered deep-fried Twinkies before the bull riders romped through. The delicacy lasted just one event. "They just didn't go over too well," said Angie Stapleton, food and beverage manager at the Ford Center.

STANDINGS

1	Adriano Moraes	8,117 points	6	Mike White	4,541.5 points
2	Justin McBride	6,547.5 points	7	Mike Collins	4,370 points
3	Mike Lee	6,205.5 points	8	Jody Newberry	4,355 points
4	Ross Coleman	4,746 points	9	Greg Potter	3,937.5 points
5	Brendon Clark	4,681 points	10	Owen Washburn	3,690 points

SIXTEEN

CONTENDERS & PRETENDERS

They gathered in a conference room at the headquarters hotel for another riders-only meeting. But this time there was no open bar and no sign of Tuff Hedeman and the other men behind the proposed Bull Riders Alliance.

Called by Bernard and the PBR board, the meeting was set up to end any chance of a rider boycott. A PowerPoint presentation included reams of information, much of it countering Hedeman's claims that the board was looking out for itself, not the riders. One slide showed that since its inception, the PBR had paid out $37 million to the riders and only $1.2 million to its shareholders. Then Bernard told the riders the floor was open and encouraged them to air their concerns and grievances. At one point, Mike Lee stood up and said he felt like the PBR executives were acting like "big dogs" and treating the riders like "little dogs"; then he sat back down. Looking irritated by the comment, Moraes stood up and defended the board while jabbing a finger into the air. Lee came back out of his seat. "Don't point your finger at me," he told Moraes.

As Lee inched closer to Moraes in the standings and as the finals approached, the relationship between the two looked strained. In recent weeks, Lee had stopped attending the weekly prayer sessions at Moraes's house. They suddenly looked more like rivals than friends. But the tense moment diffused, and the meeting came to a civil end, with Bernard and the PBR board feeling encouraged. They promised to pay more attention to the riders' concerns and encouraged them to pick four representatives who would be responsible for meeting regularly with the board to express those wants and needs. The riders agreed, selecting as their representatives Bart Jackson, B. J. Kramps, Cody Whitney, and Cody Hart.

When the riders filed out of the room, the Bull Riders Alliance looked to be on life support. Issues like insurance coverage and prize money remained unresolved, but most of the riders seemed ready to turn their attention back to bull riding and the beginning of that weekend's Bullnanza–Reno event.

Later that day, Justin McBride was in the locker room at the Lawlor Events Center and pulling on his riding boots when Jay Daugherty approached. Daugherty, who tracked the pre-event bull draws and postevent results from PBR's headquarters in Colorado Springs, was making a rare appearance on the road and catching up with the riders.

"Still hooked with Michelle?" he asked.

"No," McBride said flatly, staring at his cowboy boots.

Daugherty broke an awkward silence. "Back on the prowl?"

McBride lifted his head and flashed a grin, then half-shouted, "Yeah."

When Daugherty walked away, McBride gritted his teeth as he pulled one boot over a sore ankle. "Never let them see you sweat," he said.

He sure as hell wasn't about to let anybody see him suffer over a breakup. Definitely not in the locker room at Lawlor Events Center, where, after a 5-week interlude since the last BFTS event, riders were preparing for the 24th stop of the season.

Time was running out on those hoping to catch Moraes. In just 6 weeks, the PBR and the top 45 riders would converge on Las Vegas for the finals. But the news about McBride's romantic life provided a little conversational diversion.

There was no mention of McBride's and Michelle Beadle's breakup in *People* magazine, but on the PBR tour it was headline news. Beadle, an effervescent and quick-witted blonde, and McBride had met in 2002, when she did a stint as a commentator for the PBR telecasts. They'd been dating ever since. McBride had even given Beadle a promise ring. Semiengaged is what McBride said it meant.

The relationship was serious enough for Beadle to have left her apartment in New York and moved in with McBride in Elk City, where he was building a two-story stone house on 400 acres of property. The two had talked about making that house their permanent home, and McBride had even talked about the town near Elk City where he wanted to hold the wedding. But Beadle, 29 years old, wasn't sure she was ready to give up her career in television to settle down and start a family.

In July, about 2 weeks before McBride's 25th birthday, College Sports TV, a new cable network, called Beadle and offered her a job hosting a regular hour-long show. She accepted even though she knew McBride would never move to New York City.

The first weekend of August, the weekend of McBride's 25th birthday, Beadle packed her belongings and brought two suitcases to the Bullnanza–Oklahoma City. She was leaving for New York on August 7, the day of McBride's birthday. He was angry but made no plea for her to stay—and he had no interest in continuing the relationship long-distance.

The split came as no surprise to Rich Blyn, one of the PBR's athletic trainers.

"You ever hear of the expression 'She's a little bit country and he's a little bit rock 'n' roll'?" Blyn asked. "Well, he's a lot country."

Only 5 weeks after the split, McBride was in Reno and waiting on the arrival of Jill Ericksen, a former schoolmate of his in Mullen, Nebraska. She was living in Austin, Texas, and working as a graphic designer, and she and McBride had started talking more frequently. The weekend of Bullnanza–Reno, McBride paid for Ericksen to fly in and stay with him. It looked as if he'd already put the breakup with Beadle behind him; but Leah Garcia, one of the commentators for OLN, was among those who suspected he was still hurting. She and others also speculated about how the breakup might affect his riding, while others wondered if the broken cheekbone and eye socket Moraes had suffered 5 weeks earlier might affect *his* riding.

About an hour before introductions, Moraes was posing for photos to be used on a promotional poster for the finals. He positioned himself in front of the camera so as to hide the red, swollen area on his face—the lingering signs of the broken left cheekbone and eye socket he'd suffered 5 weeks ago. But that wasn't his only concern.

Moraes grabbed the loose skin under his chin. "I hate it," he said. "I'm going to do liposuction on that."

Mark Scott, the photographer, smirked. "I forgot you're not young," he said. At 34, Moraes was among the oldest riders on tour. But he still felt confident about his chances of winning the 2004 championship, despite his latest injury.

Outside the sports medicine room, rider Rob Bell entered the foyer with his right hand between his legs. "You ever get poison ivy on your nuts?" he asked the three riders relaxing in chairs. "Keeps you scratching."

Bell said he'd been clearing brush at his house when he got poison ivy on his stomach, legs, and crotch. Not much Tandy Freeman could do for him other than offer some cream. Then Moraes arrived.

"Where's your helmet?" Freeman asked.

"Who, me?" Moraes replied with a thin smile.

"Yeah, you."

"What for?"

"Your head, I think."

"If I wear a helmet," Moraes said, "Justin and the boys won't talk to me anymore."

He was only half-joking. They'd still talk to him, but helmets were decidedly uncool in the view of McBride and most of the other riders. Moraes continued to rationalize his decision not to wear a helmet.

"It took 20 years to break," Moraes reasoned about his cheekbone injury. "You think it's going to break again? It's going to take another 20 years."

Then Moraes claimed he was worried a helmet would impede his vision, prompting Freeman to roll his eyes. What everybody could see—with or without a helmet—Moraes was closing in on an unprecedented third PBR championship.

During the introductions that first night, the PBR executives watched through clenched teeth. Because it was a Bullnanza event, the PBR had only partial control of the opening and no way to stop the ending. Last man out and under the spotlight: Tuff Hedeman.

The crowd cheered long and loud. But instead of taking his usual spot behind the chutes and putting on his TV headset, Hedeman stayed in the arena and helped work the chutes. It wasn't by choice.

With Hedeman falling out of favor with the PBR, he and OLN had parted ways. Since his riders-only meeting in Oklahoma City, he'd made no effort to mend fences. In fact, on the second weekend of August, at a Challenger Tour event in Weatherford, Texas, Hedeman had convened yet another riders-only meeting and continued to urge them to pursue the Bull Riders Alliance. Bernard and the board were tired of the distraction and thought removing Hedeman from the broadcast crew would help refocus attention on the race for $1 million.

On the first night of competition, Lee rode Grumpy for 86.5 points, McBride rode Artemus for 85.5 points, and Moraes rode Sheep Dip for 84 points, with all three riders looking in prime form. But it was a rookie, Zack Brown, who took the first-round lead, with a 90-point ride on Desert Storm.

The next day, Hedeman huddled with a handful of riders, including McBride. He wasn't ready to give up on the Bull Riders Alliance or the idea of serving as the riders' representative in negotiations with the PBR. But the bulk of riders looked headed in another direction. Before the second round, about 25 riders gathered for a meeting in the locker room at the Lawlor Events Center and sounded comfortable with their four new representatives—Jackson, Kramps, Whitney, and Hart—addressing their concerns with the board. But McBride and Shivers were conspicuously absent, along with about a dozen other riders who had skipped the meeting. But all 45 were on hand when the second round of Bullnanza–Reno began.

Riding Grumpy to the 8-second buzzer, McBride hit the dirt, and the bull's back hooves came down hard. The quick-spinning McBride avoided getting stomped by just inches.

Exiting the arena, he was far more excited about the close call than his score of 82.5 points.

"I'm glad you rolled over when you did," Freeman said.

"Me, too," said McBride, breathing hard. "That's why it's an exciting sport, Doc."

Jody Newberry was less fortunate. Thrown off the right side of Kryptonite less than 3 seconds to the buzzer, he found himself facedown in the dirt when the bull stomped on the middle of Newberry's back.

After a visit to the sports medicine room, he came out with his right arm wrapped. "You okay?" Ross Coleman asked.

"I got a broken rib, but I feel like I got a broken arm," Newberry said. "I hurt bad."

Then, after a brief pause, Newberry asked, "You got any snuff?" Ah, Copenhagen, one of the riders' favorite antidotes for pain. But Chris Shivers looked like he needed a pep talk more than a chew.

He sat alone, head bowed. After getting bucked off by Lying Eyes in the first round, Shivers, having fallen to 62nd in the rankings, had needed a qualified ride when he'd boarded Foul Play. Three bucks to the left, Shivers appeared in control. But the bull reversed direction and shot Shivers off his left side before the buzzer sounded.

Shivers pounded his right fist into his left hand. Though he tipped his hat to acknowledge the crowd as he left the arena, he found a quiet place to ponder his situation: With four regular-season events left, he was in serious danger of missing the finals for the first time in 8 years.

While Shivers had failed to qualify for the championship round, all the riders in position to unseat him as champion had made it. In that final round, riding Stretcher, McBride had held on when the bull staggered before slipping off the left side. The bull nailed McBride on the back pockets of his Wranglers before McBride could scramble to safety. Then he checked the clock: 7.4 seconds. Damn.

Moraes, riding Sheep Dip, had fought to hang on until the buzzer as his bull rope slipped out of his left hand. He hit the dirt and checked the clock: 7.9 seconds. Double damn.

The two riders crossed paths behind the chutes. "You suck, as I did," Moraes said.

McBride winced. "Took me a shot in the shorts. My ass hurts."

Two riders left. First up, Zack Brown, the surfer-turned-bull-rider and a rookie from California. He looked like a seasoned veteran atop Red Alert, staying in rhythm with the massive bull until the 8-second buzzer. The 89-point ride catapulted him into the lead. But there was still one man left—Mike Lee, with yet another chance to win his first event of the season.

In the chutes, Lee slapped Spinner Bait, who was leaning against the back of the chute. Lee finally squeezed his cowboy boot down the backside and called for the gate.

Spinner Bait made two huge leaps to the right, lifting Lee off the bull's back. Gravity brought Lee back down, and he settled back into the pocket. The bull turned left with another series of bucks, none of which could unseat Lee.

"Mike Lee makes the whistle," shouted OLN commentator Brett Haber. "Will it be enough?"

Lee performed his signature pirouette with extra spunk before dropping onto his right knee in prayer. Then came the score: 88 points—a half point shy of tying Brown, relegating Lee to his fourth second-place finish of the year. Though Lee remained a paragon of consistency, some wondered how he could win the finals if he couldn't even win one regular-season event.

CONCESSIONS

Personal pan pizza	$4.75
Beer bratwurst	$4.50
Jumbo hot dog	$3

No deep-fried Twinkies? "No, not us," said Annie Monticelli, operations manager for concessions at the Lawlor Events Center. "We're pretty straightforward."

STANDINGS

1	Adriano Moraes	8,314 points	6	Ross Coleman	4,746 points
2	Mike Lee	6,936 points	7	Greg Potter	4,551 points
3	Justin McBride	6,830.5 points	8	Mike Collins	4,520.5 points
4	Mike White	5,226 points	9	Jody Newberry	4,436 points
5	Brendon Clark	4,758.5 points	10	Rob Bell	4,193 points

SEVENTEEN
THE GRAND RAPIDS JINX

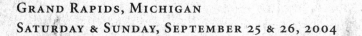

GRAND RAPIDS, MICHIGAN
SATURDAY & SUNDAY, SEPTEMBER 25 & 26, 2004

Justin McBride pushed open the door and strode into the room filled with camera equipment. A film crew was waiting. They were making a video tribute to the American soldier that would air during the PBR finals, and McBride was honored to participate. Three of his former high school classmates were fighting in Iraq, and at times he spoke eloquently about the sacrifice they were making on behalf of America.

The producer, who had filmed a few other videos for the PBR, reintroduced himself to McBride. They hadn't seen each other in 2 years.

"You're having a hell of a year," the producer gushed.

"Okay, I guess."

"You're right there," the producer said, referring to the standings. "Where do you want to be?"

It was a silly question. Everyone knew exactly where McBride wanted to be—atop the overall standings and on the way to his first PBR championship. Instead he was in third place, trailing Adriano Moraes and Mike Lee, and in a building that dredged up painful memories. A year earlier, he'd arrived at Van Andel Arena in Grand Rapids having just overtaken Chris Shivers for the lead in the overall standings. But that weekend, McBride got stomped by a bull and suffered a punctured lung and a broken rib—injuries that essentially cleared the way for Shivers and relegated McBride to 2003 reserve champion.

"Nobody remembers who won second," McBride grumbled.

Yet inside that room in Van Andel Arena, before the first round of the Grand Rapids Invitational—the 26th BFTS event of the 27-stop regular season—he refused to let any of that spoil his mood as the taping was set to begin. "Hey, can I swear when I do this?" McBride joked.

The producer handed McBride a script, part of a patriotic poem he was to read. "That's good," he said, "rather than letting my dumb ass try to figure out what to say."

It looked and sounded like the same old McBride—cocksure, profane, loose, the consummate cutup. But privately he lamented the failed rides from earlier that year that had him sitting third in the standings, rather than first.

Referring to some of those rides, Justin McKee, the color commentator for OLN, called McBride one of the PBR's "best 7-second riders." It wasn't meant to be a compliment.

The last-second buck-offs were the most frustrating—not only for McBride but also for his supporters, like Tuff Hedeman. From the first time Hedeman had seen McBride on a bull, he'd loved the way the kid rode. So Hedeman pushed him, sometimes chewing out McBride when he felt the young rider could have performed better. McBride would turn quiet and angry. And Hedeman would just keep chewing.

"You can take it or just quit," McBride recalled Hedeman once railing after McBride had fallen off a rideable bull. "I'm telling you because you got the potential to do it. So go and do it."

In recent years, as the finals approached and the gold buckle hung in the balance, McBride found himself tightening up—"riding not to lose it instead of riding to win it," he said. At the start of 2004, he vowed it would be different. But for all of McBride's aggressiveness, the avoidable miscues and lapses continued. Like the one at the February 7 Atlanta Classic, where, in the championship round, McBride got bucked off Slim's Ghost, a bull he could've ridden blindfolded. And the Colorado Springs Invitational in April, when he got bucked off twice less than a second from the buzzer. And at Bullnanza–Reno earlier in the month, when in the championship round McBride loosened up on a bull named Stretcher and fell off a half second before the buzzer.

Untimely buck-offs didn't keep McBride from being considered one of the PBR's best riders, but they did keep him from gaining ground on Moraes. In Kansas City, when Moraes got bucked off one of his two bulls, McBride went 0 for 2. When Moraes failed to ride a bull in Nashville, so did McBride. But after reviewing his regrettable moments from that season, McBride made a prediction about the finals: "I'm going to leave Las Vegas with a pocketful of cash and all the girls."

The crowd inside Van Andel Arena on hand for the first round of the Grand Rapids Invitational could have used some of McBride's vigor. The tour had circled back to the Midwest for the first time since its March stop in Indianapolis; and even with many of the spectators wearing cowboy hats and flannel shirts, it felt like Valium Night—free sedatives for the first 10,000 fans. Finally, McBride and Scar Face helped bring the crowd to life.

With McBride aboard the bull, Scar Face lunged out of the chutes, spun left, and then threw it into reverse, bucking backward for two jumps. Yes, backward.

With the grace of Fred Astaire in his prime, McBride moved with the bull and stayed in rhythm with Scar Face all the way to the buzzer. The 88.5-point ride held up as the round's best, qualifying McBride for the Mossy Oak Shootout and a chance to ride Lefty for $5,000 on the last ride of the night.

"Git 'er done, Justin," a fan screamed out as McBride boarded Lefty. "Git 'er done."

McBride stretched out his legs and lowered himself onto the bull that he'd failed to ride in two attempts, failures that made him only more determined to stay on the bull for 8 seconds. The chute gate opened, and out burst Lefty. Two jumps straight ahead, and then the bull turned hard to the left. McBride turned, too, quick enough to make the corner, and the bull kept spinning. Three seconds from the buzzer, the bull rope began slipping out of McBride's riding hand, and the centrifugal force of the bull's spinning shot McBride off the bull's back.

As McBride hit the ground, Lefty's right hind hoof smashed down on McBride's right leg. McBride speed-crawled away from the bucking bull, popped to his feet, and hobbled to the corner of the arena.

He pounded his fist on the metal chute, then limped through the exit gate. And that was as far as he would make it alone. Two athletic trainers carried him to the sports medicine room and set him down on an examination table.

"Smashed the fuck out of my spur," McBride said, squeezing his eyes shut.

Tandy Freeman took McBride's right leg into his hand. "Can you feel your toes?"

"I can't feel them real good."

Freeman lowered his voice as if prepared to tell a patient he had a malignant tumor. "Broke both bones," he said.

"What?" McBride screamed. "I don't got but one leg bone."

Freeman didn't need to see the x-rays to know what had happened. The force of the bull's hind leg had broken McBride's ankle, a fracture of the tibia and fibula that would require surgery and at least 3 weeks of rehabilitation before McBride could even consider riding again. For the second straight year and the third time of his career, McBride had been in contention for the title, only to suffer a late-season injury.

Watching his right leg swell up, McBride let out a primal scream and looked on the verge of tears.

"I'm everybody's favorite loser," he wailed.

"Only thing is, this year they made it where you got a chance," Freeman said, referring to the new point system for the finals. "You still got a chance."

McBride looked up at Freeman.

"Thanks, Doc."

Adriano Moraes entered the sports medicine room and looked like somebody had just shot his favorite dog. He hugged McBride and whispered into his ear, and McBride hugged Moraes around the neck.

"See you, Champ," Moraes said. "I'll be praying for you."

Few appreciated McBride's determination as much as Moraes did. But the person who understood that determination best was John Howell.

Howell and McBride were best friends growing up in Mullen, Nebraska, and the two small-town boys had oversize dreams. McBride wanted to win the world bull riding championship, and Howell wanted to win a Super Bowl ring. Together they hunted for white-tailed deer and coyote, fished for catfish and bass, canoed down the Red River, rode horses and four-wheelers, and talked incessantly about their goals.

While McBride earned a scholarship to the University of Nevada at Las Vegas, Howell turned down scholarship offers from several small schools. He thought he was good enough to play Division I football, and McBride encouraged him to take his chances. So as an undersize free safety, Howell did just that and walked on at Colorado State.

By Howell's senior year in 2001, the same year McBride was in contention for the PBR championship before breaking his riding hand, Howell had emerged as one of Colorado State's best players and was picked in the fourth round of the NFL draft by the Tampa Bay Buccaneers.

Then came January 26, 2003.

That day, the Buccaneers beat the Oakland Raiders for their first Super Bowl victory. Confetti was falling, a Jon Bon Jovi song was blaring, and Howell, then a 3rd-year defensive back and special teams stalwart for Tampa Bay, was on a raised platform and celebrating with his teammates when he saw McBride.

McBride, who'd watched the game from the stands, had gotten down on the field. Howell stepped off the platform and greeted his friend. The two embraced.

"Man, I'm so proud of you," McBride said.

Howell fought back tears. "Now it's your turn," he said.

Ever since then, Howell had noticed something about his best friend: McBride no longer was hungry for the championship—he was starving for it. The bull rider, starving for a championship, refused to pull out of the 2003 finals just because he'd broken a rib and punctured his lung less than a month before the event. So that same bull rider, still starving for a championship, sure as hell wasn't going to let a little broken ankle stop him.

Back in the sports medicine room in Grand Rapids, McBride glared at that right ankle. His entire leg had begun to quiver.

"Quit shaking, you scrawny leg," he yelled. "This is going to mess up my hunting again, too. I ain't going to be able to climb a tree with this."

Laughter shot across the room. Setting down a pouch of pain pills and a can of beer, McBride tried out a pair of crutches. "I hate these damn things," he said.

"Throw 'em down."

It was Hedeman, who'd entered the room to check on one of his favorite riders. McBride smiled at the icon who'd cussed him out more than a few times but now was there to comfort him. After all, this was Hedeman's kind of cowboy, cursing at misfortune, cracking up those around him, and showing the dexterity to exit the arena on crutches while carrying a beer.

The next night, Ross Coleman, McBride's best friend on tour, won the event for his first victory in 2 years. It was almost as if Coleman had ridden to protect McBride's spot in the standings. In fact, with Moraes and Lee each riding only one of two bulls, McBride actually gained ground in the standings on the strength of his 88.5-point ride on Scar Face.

Inside the sports medicine room, with McBride sitting on an examination table a few feet away, Freeman told an OLN reporter that McBride would need surgery but "he'll probably ride in the finals."

"Probably, his ass!" McBride snarled.

Broken ankle or not, he was going to the finals. And McBride was going with one plan: to win the prized gold buckle that he knew belonged on his belt.

CONCESSIONS

Chili cheese fries	$5
Boneless barbecued chicken strips	$5.25
Chicken Caesar wrap	$6
Jalapeño-and-cheese-stuffed pretzel	$3.50

Deep-fried Twinkies? Close, but no cigar. "They have them at the ballpark down the road," Mike Wojcaikowski, concessions manager at Van Andel Arena, said, referring to the minor-league baseball stadium. "But we've never got into that."

STANDINGS

1	Adriano Moraes	8,869.5 points	6	Brendon Clark	5,433.5 points
2	Justin McBride	7,222.5 points	7	Greg Potter	5,057.5 points
3	Mike Lee	7,152.5 points	8	Jody Newberry	4,900.5 points
4	Mike White	5,775.5 points	9	Mike Collins	4,520.5 points
5	Ross Coleman	5,533 points	10	Rob Bell	4,328.5 points

EIGHTEEN
SETTING THE STAGE

Huddled near the bathroom in the locker room, the three Brazilian riders laughed when they heard someone in the stalls erupting like Mount Saint Helens. Moments later, Mike Lee pushed open the stall door and strode up to the Brazilians.

"Were you laughing at me?" he asked.

Paulo Crimber and Guilherme Marchi stood next to Andre Moraes, younger brother of Adriano, who laughed again. WHAP!

Lee slapped Moraes across the face. WHAP!

Before Moraes could cover up, Lee slapped him again.

Moraes picked up a metal chair. He moved toward Lee. Then he put down the chair—too soon.

Lee wrapped his arms around Moraes. Picked him up,

carried him into the bathroom, and began shoving him against a stall door.

"Stop!" Moraes shouted.

Lee lowered him to the ground, and Moraes walked back into the locker room and sat in a chair. Lee came up from behind and hugged Moraes.

"I love you," Lee said. "I love you."

Love you? The Brazilians rolled their eyes, thinking what many people thought about Lee—that he was nuts. News of the incident angered Adriano Moraes, but he let Andre fend for himself.

It wasn't the first fight between riders. In 2003 at a bar in Raleigh, North Carolina, Chris Shivers decked Gilbert Carrillo and, with three punches to the face, did about $10,000 worth of dental damage. And at the Colorado Springs Invitational in April, at another after-event party, Gary Richard flattened Cory Rasch. But this outburst before the Columbus Invitational, the PBR's regular-season finale, was about more than tempers flaring. It was about a pattern of strange behavior that defined Lee and one reason that, despite all of his talent, some doubted he was ready to win the championship.

Thoughts of sin, lust, and guilt swirled in his head; and Lee found himself as confused as ever. During the introductions before the Columbus Invitational, Lee later recalled, he tuned out the explosions, the pyrotechnics, the crowd's cheers, and appealed to God.

Why are you sending me in this direction? Lee silently asked. *Why are you subjecting me to so much confusion? What's the point of all this?*

He wanted answers. He said he finally got them.

God, according to Lee, sent him a message: Lee had drifted too far from Jesus, become too concerned with his own success, and neglected the deeper truth that he was riding not for himself but for God and Jesus Christ.

During first-round action, Lee got bucked off Camo and accepted the fall as God's will and later that night joined 11 others in a hotel conference room for Bible study. At one point, the 12 men clasped hands and Pastor Todd Pierce led them in prayer. When Pierce finished, it was a chance for the others to speak their minds.

"Thank you, Lord, for making my heart free again," Lee said, "for making me realize the struggles aren't pointless."

But Lee's renewed inner peace had gone unnoticed by the fans inside Nationwide Arena, because most people were focused on Adriano Moraes, Justin McBride, and Mike White. Small even by bull rider standards, White stood 5 feet 6 inches tall and weighed 145 pounds. He had light brown hair and a smile bright enough to serve as a pitchman for Crest. With his cobalt blue eyes and angelic face, he looked almost fragile. But they didn't call him "Mighty Mike" for nothing.

Recently White had looked mightier than ever. He'd ridden all three bulls at the PBR's 24th stop, Bullnanza–Reno, where he'd finished third. The next week he'd covered all three bulls at the Laughlin Invitational in Laughlin, Nevada, and finished fourth. Though he fell off both of his bulls the following week in Grand Rapids, he still looked impressive— particularly on a wild ride atop Slider, who had been ridden only twice in 25 attempts. White made the buzzer, but back judge Cody Custer ruled White had touched the bull with his free hand, disqualifying the score. The ruling infuriated White, and Cody Lambert later acknowledged the ruling was an error. Though he left Grand Rapids without a point, White arrived in Columbus with unmistakable confidence. A few hours before the competition started, White happened upon Justin McKee, OLN's color commentator.

"Hey, I've got news for you," White said. "I'm going to go into the short round winning it."

For Joe Namath and Muhammad Ali, predictions were one thing. But for bull riders, they were taboo. Some riders believed predictions invited trouble, while others considered it bad form to disregard the role an 1,800-pound bull would play in determining the outcome. But White possessed the balance of a gymnast, the reflexes of a bantamweight boxer, and surprising power—a combination that enabled him to ride the sport's rankest bulls. And he was riding as well as he had since 1999, when at age 23 he had won the PRCA world bull riding championship and was the PBR's Rookie of the Year.

He was a rising star, yet never rose as fast or as far as most people expected. Mighty as he was, White's body kept breaking down.

A broken neck. A blown-out knee. A broken kneecap. The injuries had kept him on the sidelines for months at a time between 2000 and 2001. Additionally, some thought White spent too much time complaining when he drew a bad bull and fussing over how much media coverage he got. The best riders stayed above it all, and the PBR's brass wondered if White had what it took to be the best.

Finally in good health in 2002, he won two events that season and finished 10th overall, followed by four more victories in 2003 and a fourth-place finish. By the 2004 regular-season finale in Columbus, he looked primed for a strong run at the championship. Others simply wanted to get to the finals.

The most prominent rider on the bubble was Chris Shivers, the reigning world champion. He'd missed 16 of the past 26 regular-season events with injuries, putting himself in jeopardy of missing his first finals. At 57th in the qualifier standings, Shivers needed to win at least $6,000 over 2 days to catapult into the top 45. If he didn't, he would become only the second reigning world champion to fail to qualify for finals.

Three days before the Columbus Invitational, agent Mark Nestlen approached OLN producer Joe Loverro about using his star client as a commentator during the finals. Shivers's sponsors wouldn't be happy unless their highly paid cowboy was getting airtime—preferably while riding bulls, but at a minimum while appearing on TV as a commentator.

"What, you don't think he's going to qualify?" Loverro asked.

"I'm just doing my job and looking at all the options," Nestlen said.

But Shivers had no intention of doing TV commentary in Vegas. He planned to be riding in the finals. Stretching, fidgeting, pacing, he waited behind the chutes for his first-round ride Saturday night with two TV cameras inches from his face. Thinking it was finally time, Shivers approached the chute.

"Four and a half minutes," a PBR official yelled.

Commercial break. Damn. Shivers resumed his stretching, fidgeting, and pacing before the time finally came. He settled on top of Woodstock and tightened his grip on the bull rope.

"Go have fun, little fella," Custer told Shivers.

The gate swung open and the fun began. Within seconds, Shivers looked done, tipping right and starting to slip off the bull. The seconds felt like minutes as Shivers tried to hold on for the 8-second buzzer. His riding arm strained. His face muscles strained. He refused to let go of the rope.

Inches from the dirt, with the rope still in hand, Shivers held on until the 8-second buzzer. The crowd roared as he scrambled to his feet and shot his fists into the air. Then came the official score: 87.5 points.

The crowd cheered again. The reigning champ's chances of making the finals were still alive.

Ednei Caminhas won the round with an 89.5-point ride on Indian Outlaw. But White had no intention of backing off his prediction after scoring 89 points on Kryptonite.

The next night, despite the intensifying race for the world championship, the TV cameras again trained themselves on Shivers. His 87.5 ride the night before was impressive, but advancing to the championship round was his only chance of earning enough money to qualify for the finals.

Matched up against Complete Control, who was making his BFTS debut, Shivers climbed aboard the bull, settled in, and prepared to nod.

"Have fun!" White shouted.

The gate swung open, and out they went. But it was the bull, not Shivers, who looked like the seasoned pro. The reigning champ hit the dirt well before the 8-second mark, and one could feel the fans' energy deflate. Shivers tipped his cap to the crowd and briskly exited the arena. The TV cameras tried to follow him, but he walked beyond their reach and into a tunnel, where he found a quiet corner. He leaned against a concrete wall, buried his face in his cowboy hat, and let the tears fall.

Five minutes passed.

Tears finally dried, Shivers dragged his bull rope back up the tunnel, down the hall, and into the locker room, where he passed seven men. None of them said a word.

Ten minutes later, Shivers returned to the arena in time to pull White's rope and help his buddy prepare for his second-round ride. White lowered himself on Easy Money, an aptly named bull. He rode it for 87 points and, with that, made good on his prediction that he'd be leading the event going into the championship round. White sprinted to the sideboards and bumped fists with Nestlen.

Soon Nestlen had surprising news for Shivers: He still had a shot to get into the championship round. Shivers's first-round score of 87.5 left him tied with four other riders for the final spot of the 15-rider championship round. Scores from the back judge, Cody Custer, would break the tie. It took Nestlen 5 minutes to find the results—not the results for which he was hoping. Shivers's score was the lowest of all four riders, meaning he'd failed to make the championship round and failed to qualify for the finals.

Tears dried, Shivers did a TV interview and said he, not the judges, was the only one to blame. Even though he was out of contention, Shivers had a rooting interest. He headed back to the chutes and helped White prepare for what promised to be the best showdown of the round. He'd drawn High Tide, a bull unridden in 123 attempts. But man versus bull was just one of the battles playing out.

Little Yellow Jacket and Pandora's Box were dueling for Bull of the Year honors; and after the Columbus Invitational, the riders would cast their votes. The night before, Joe Berger, owner of Little Yellow Jacket, and Winston Loe, owner of Pandora's Box, sat side by side, drinking beer as if immune to any tension over whose bull would win the $20,000 bonus for Bull of the Year. But the next night, when Little Yellow Jacket and Pandora's Box were loaded into the chutes for the championship round, Berger and Loe watched from separate vantage points.

With Brendon Clark on his back, Little Yellow Jacket bucked off Clark with authority, the kind riders had come to expect from the two-time defending champion. Pandora's Box bucked off Mike Lee, but without the awesome power he'd shown all year while often overshadowing his chief rival. Little Yellow Jacket or Pandora's Box? Now it would be up to the riders.

But there was another bull waiting in the chutes. An unrideable bull, some thought. High Tide.

When nine of the first 10 riders of the championship round were bucked off, it looked as if White might win even if he fell off High Tide. But Ross Johnson rode Huskers Red for 85.5 points and moved into first place. The only way White could win was to become the first man to stay on High Tide for 8 seconds.

He climbed into the chutes and onto the bull's back. While the bull calmly waited, White wrapped the bull rope around his right hand as OLN's cameras moved in for a close-up.

"In one word, unrideable," said Brett Haber, OLN's lead commentator.

White pushed down on the back of his black cowboy hat and secured his position in the center of High Tide's back.

He can do whatever he wants, but he ain't going to throw me, White told himself.

Then he nodded to the gateman. The chute gate swung open, and out leapt the bull, taking three powerful jumps forward before turning back to the right.

With High Tide's speed and power building, the bull spun hard. White stayed centered as if glued to the bull's back. But as the clock neared 8 seconds, the bull turned back to the left, jerking White out of position.

I'm not turning loose, White told himself. *I'm going to ride this sucker.*

White squeezed tight to his bull rope as he tipped off the right side of the bull.

At last, the buzzer sounded.

Mike White had ridden the unrideable High Tide!

Even Johnson, bumped into second place and denied what would have been his first BFTS victory after White's ride, broke into a smile and applauded. After dismounting, White sailed his cowboy hat into the air, and seconds later another cowboy hat flew into the ring. The second hat belonged to Shivers; if he couldn't win the $1 million, by God, there was no one else he'd rather win it than White. Then came the score: 92 points, certifying the ride as one of the year's best.

Watching from his home in Elk City, Justin McBride was resting his broken right ankle and monitoring the race. Adriano Moraes rode two bulls but got bucked off in the championship round. Lee scored 89 points for his second-round ride on Gator but fell off Pandora's Box in the championship and finished tied for eighth. With his third victory of the season, White earned $36,667 and put Moraes on notice: Mighty Mike was in the hunt for the championship.

As White posed for pictures and signed autographs, other riders hustled into the hallway, where a PBR official was posting a sheet of the updated rankings determining which 45 riders had qualified for the finals.

Paul Gavin, the first rookie to break onto the tour in 2004, squinted through his left eye, the lid swollen and stitched from his ride and wreck earlier that night. He scanned at the posted standings but couldn't find his name.

J. W. Hart found it for him. Paul Gavin. Number 45.

"That means you're going to Las Vegas," Hart said, and Gavin grinned.

Riders clustered around the standings for the ultimate good-news-and-bad-news moment.

In: **Adam Carrillo,** who'd spent 11 years on tour almost conjoined with his twin brother, Gilbert.

Out: **Gilbert Carrillo,** who'd still go to Vegas as the first alternate.

In: **J. W. Hart,** the "Iron Man."

Out: **Troy Dunn,** who this year wouldn't be swooping in for the money and jetting back to Australia with bagfuls of it.

In: **B. J. Kramps,** the wiseacre from Canada who was rescued by Pastor Todd Pierce during his hangup in Anaheim.

In: **Zack Brown,** the surfer-turned-bull-rider and rookie from California.

In: **Jared Farley,** the rookie from Australia.

Out: **Gary Richard,** the rider nicknamed "Grandpa" who had turned 42 and failed in his quest to reach the finals one last time.

In: **Cory Rasch,** the Jack Daniel's pitchman who was overly dedicated to the company's product.

Out: **Evan Rasch,** Cory's younger brother.

In: **Lee Akin,** still trying to make heads or tails out of his bull riding luck after winning an event and then missing 4 months with a hip injury.

Out: **James White**, the rookie whose bittersweet year included an impressive debut at the Anaheim Open, landing an endorsement deal with the US Army, a broken hand that sidelined him for several weeks, and the death of his mother.

In: **Ross Johnson**, who survived the most frightening moment of the season during his wreck at the "Fort Worth Massacre."

Out: **Eathan Graves**, the waiflike 18-year-old from California who made a splash at a Humps N' Horns event in Thibodaux, Louisiana, but didn't even come close to qualifying for a single BFTS event, much less the finals.

In: **Jody Newberry**, who rushed back from his knee surgery, remained in the top 10, and dispelled the notion of a sophomore jinx.

Out: **Jim Sharp**, a two-time PRCA world champion bull rider who, at age 38, came back from an injury with two-thirds of the season over and failed to win enough money.

In: **Luke Snyder**, who despite his declining success still managed to qualify for his fourth straight finals.

In: **Owen Washburn**, who midway through the season started living up to his nickname of Captain Consistency.

Out: **Cody Hart**, the rider trampled by Jerome Davis's bull in Greensboro and beset by injuries that included a broken arm.

In: **Corey Navarre**, who broke through in Bossier City for his first victory in almost 3 years.

Out: **Cory Turnbow**, who tried to ride Little Yellow Jacket with a broken bull rope at a Challenger Tour event in Bismarck and ended up with a bloody gash on his forehead.

In: **Rob Bell**, who needed his chin stitched after becoming Little Yellow Jacket's first victim of the year.

Out: **Spud Whitman**, another one of Little Yellow Jacket's early-season victims.

In: **Brent Vincent**, who in Greensboro came within $\frac{2}{10}$ second of capturing his first BFTS victory.

Out: **Craig Sasse**, yet another victim of Little Yellow Jacket.

In: **Reuben Geleynse**, whose choirboy demeanor set up the ultimate yin-yang photo op when he tied McBride for the victory in Greensboro.

Out: **Tater Porter**, the 9-year veteran and former PBR standout whose inspired comeback ended short of his returning to the finals.

In: **Cory Melton**, the King of Buckle Bunnies.

Out: **Bart Jackson**, who dominated Drifter in Jacksonville on the first ride of the season but got cut from the BFTS late in the season.

In: **Ross Coleman**, who in 2004 abdicated his throne as King of Buckle Bunnies to Melton.

Out: **Kendall Galmiche**, who turned down a college baseball scholarship from Mississippi State to pursue bull riding and, while riding in front of mentor Donnie Gay in Thibodaux, broke his leg.

In: **Cody Whitney**, who, when once propositioned by a buckle bunny, replied by telling the woman she should call Whitney's wife to see if it'd be okay.

Out: **Jacob "Spook" Wiggins**, whose knack for storytelling was no help in trying to make the fairy-tale leap to the BFTS.

In: **Allan Moraes**, the youngest of the Moraes brothers.

Out: **Andre Moraes**, the second youngest of the Moraes brothers.

In: **Guilherme Marchi**, a member of the PBR's Brazilian army.

Out: **Robby Shriver**, the relentlessly upbeat rider from Georgia who, despite the power of positive thinking, failed to qualify for the BFTS.

In: **Paulo Crimber**, whose dance moves after a successful ride showed he might have a post-bull-riding career on *Soul Train*.

In: **Brendon Clark**, Troy Dunn's understudy who broke through for his first BFTS victory in Oklahoma City.

And yet more in: **Ednei Caminhas**, who'd sparked the controversy over sharp spurs; **Dave Samsel**, one of the American riders using a Brazilian rope; **Tony Mendes**, the bespectacled kid from Utah; **Brian Herman**, who broke through for a victory in Albuquerque while almost breaking open his head; **Michael Gaffney**, who in Nampa matched the PBR's highest score ever with a 96.5-point ride on Little Yellow Jacket.

As White exited the arena, clutching his oversize winner's check, Cody Custer walked past and pointed at Mighty Mike.

"Way to set the stage, dude," Custer said.

In two weeks, the PBR would descend on Las Vegas.

CONCESSIONS

Sliced prime rib sandwich	$13
Half-pound hot dog	$5.75
Half-pound cheeseburger	$6.25

The only things deep-fried are the special Buffalo wings ladled in secret hot sauce. Tried deep-fried Snickers once, but slow sales convinced Mike Geczi, general manager for food and beverage service at Nationwide Arena, to stick with the basics. "People here like to eat," he said. "But it's all the staple foods. We did grilled tuna, lobster rolls, and sushi, but it's always back to 'We'd prefer to get a pizza, peanuts, and a beer.'"

STANDINGS

1	Adriano Moraes	9,200 points	6	Ross Coleman	5,533 points
2	Mike Lee	7,316.5 points	7	Greg Potter	5,170 points
3	Justin McBride	7,222.5 points	8	Mike Collins	4,924.5 points
4	Mike White	6,553.5 points	9	Jody Newberry	4,900.5 points
5	Brendon Clark	5,842 points	10	Rob Bell	4,839 points

NINETEEN
ADRIANO'S
ARMS RACE

Stepping into the lobby of the Mandalay Bay Resort & Casino, rookie rider Matt Bohon stopped and took in the sensory overload. The spinning wheels of the slot machines. The clink-clink-clinking of coins dropping after a payoff. The shouts and groans from people clustered around the craps tables. The men and women standing behind the blackjack tables in their crisp white shirts and tuxedo vests, dealing cards with an effortless flick of the wrist. The cocktail waitresses sashaying through the room in sequined tops, short skirts, and spiked high heels. The shouts of big winners and the sound of money being won and lost.

Fast as he could, Bohon, a milky-faced 21-year-old from

Missouri, checked in, dumped his duffel bag in the hotel room, and headed back down to the casino. Bull riders were at the blackjack tables. Groupies were gawking. The drinks were coming. And so Bohon squeezed in at one of the tables, bought $400 worth of chips, and prepared to break Mandalay Bay.

Fifteen minutes later, Bohon's stack of chips was gone. Then he was gone, heading back to his room and trying to figure out how he'd lost his money so fast.

Middle-aged fans, easy to identify in their PBR shirts, hats, and jackets, seemed content pulling on the arms of the 25-cent slot machines. But others headed to the sports book, which already had posted odds for the PBR finals—Moraes was listed as the favorite at 7 to 2, Mike White at 4 to 1, Justin McBride at 9 to 2, and Mike Lee at 5 to 1, with long shots like Sean Willingham and Tony Mendes at 50 to 1.

In a nearby corridor, giant cowboy boots hung from the high ceilings and led the way to the PBR Fan Zone, a 400,000-square-foot exhibition hall where thousands of bull riding fans who poured in snatched up everything from a bottle of PBR "8 Seconds Hot Sauce" for $6, a PBR shot glass for $8, a Little Yellow Jacket Christmas ornament for $15, a toy model Ford F-150 with the PBR logo for $30, and limited-edition leather PBR jackets for $350. Fans also had a chance to sit on a "real bull" named Buckshot. (Wink, wink. Buckshot was really a docile 3-year-old steer that showed little interest in even standing up.) Or collect autographs from the riders who showed up for daily appearances. But on Thursday, check-in day for the PBR finals, McBride was in no mood to sign autographs. Having dispensed with the crutches he'd used after breaking his right ankle in Grand Rapids, Michigan, McBride hobbled into the hotel and headed for rider registration. It was a room set aside for the riders where they picked up sponsorship patches, got a rundown on scheduled events, and signed the contestant agreement and release form. As soon as they signed the form, a PBR official handed over a $5,000 check given to each of the 45 riders making the finals.

But McBride threatened to hold out. Unsigned contract in hand, McBride stood with fellow riders Dave Samsel and Brendon Clark in the hallway. Registration ended at four o'clock that afternoon, and the clock was ticking. None of the three riders said it directly, but the issue was obvious: The PBR had scheduled a 3-day 2005 event that conflicted with Tuff Hedeman's Championship Challenge in Fort Worth, Texas.

During the political fallout after Hedeman's resignation as PBR president, McBride, Clark, and Samsel remained loyal to Hedeman, who was planning to produce not only his events in Fort Worth and Bossier City, but also a few others, with backing from the PRCA and the CBR. If the riders signed the PBR forms and rode at any of Hedeman's 2005 events held on the same weekend as a BFTS event, they faced a 1-year suspension from the PBR. And the PBR was carefully scheduling events to overlap with Hedeman's. Only riders who'd won the PBR championship were exempt from attending BFTS events, and no one needed to test the board's willingness to enforce the rule. When rider Terry Don West failed to show for an event the week of the September 11, 2001, terrorist attacks, the PBR suspended him for a year.

This was no ordinary week, with Major League Baseball and the NFL canceling its games, and this was no ordinary rider. West had won the PRCA bull riding championship, had ridden the feared Bodacious twice, and had earned the respect of Donnie Gay, the retired eight-time world champion, who once called West "one of the top five bull riders of all time." But West also was the lone bull rider who missed the event, and so the PBR promptly suspended him for 1 year.

West sued the PBR, insisting he'd called the PBR office and explained that he wouldn't be able to make it because of travel complications. He settled out of court for $400,000, but the PBR vowed to continue enforcing the rule.

Word quickly spread among the PBR executives in Mandalay Bay about the potential problem. The PBR refused to budge: Sign the contract or forfeit the $5,000 check and the right to ride at the finals. But this was not Terry Don West. This was McBride and Clark, the third- and fifth-ranked riders. Without them, the show would go on, but not without fans wondering about their absence—and their absence potentially leading other riders to question the competition clause. It was a stare-down.

Now was not the time to take a stand, Sean Gleason, the PBR's chief operating officer, told McBride, Clark, and Samsel. Now was the time to compete for the $1 million bonus and the championship, he said, while suggesting the board would be willing to discuss the issue after the finals.

Clark and Samsel signed. McBride held out.

Again, Adriano Moraes implored McBride to sign the contract. Randy Bernard and Ty Murray waited hopefully.

Grudgingly, he gave in.

Adriano Moraes had his own beef. That day, in an interview with the *Las Vegas Review-Journal,* he'd criticized the PBR's new point system for the finals, up from 1,500 points available over the previous five-round competitions to 6,500 points available over the new eight-round competition. Next day's headline on the front page of the *Review-Journal* sports section: "Leader Upset over Points System."

"It's unfair after you worked your guts out all year long to know that if you stumble once in the finals, you might lose the title," Moraes told the *Review-Journal.* "The guy who is leading before the finals should have a better chance at winning the championship."

Fairness was beside the point. This was about drama. Television drama. The more suspenseful the finish, the higher the Nielsen ratings. The higher the ratings, the more advertisers paid for 30-second commercial spots. The more advertisers paid, the better the deal the PBR could get from NBC and the Outdoor Life Network. And in overhauling its points system, the PBR had company.

That year, NASCAR had introduced a radical new points system. Instead of using cumulative points from all of its races, the top 10 drivers after 26 races would qualify for a 10-race shootout, with points earned during those 10 races determining the champion. Like baseball purists who decried the introduction of wild card playoff teams and interleague play, NASCAR purists howled in protest. Yet the system NASCAR had used since 1975, much like the PBR's, had produced too many anticlimactic finishes. Both NASCAR and the PBR lacked the built-in drama of a postseason culminating with a World Series or Super Bowl. As the NASCAR season drew to a close, the excitement of the championship race quieted the critics. The same thing had happened on the PBR—with the notable exception of Adriano Moraes.

With the PBR's new point system, in addition to collecting the maximum of 100 points for a qualified ride, the rider with the round's top score would get 400 bonus points, with bonus points dropping incrementally for those finishing second through 10th. But the biggest change came in the overall bonus. The rider with the top cumulative score at the finals would get 2,500 bonus points, with bonus points dropping incrementally for those finishing second through 10th. The points were precious, and in an attempt at greater precision, four judges worked the event. The sum of each of the four judges' scores was divided by two, thus producing some scores with quarter points.

What it all added up to was this: The new system gave McBride, Mike Lee, and Mike White a legitimate shot to overtake Moraes, especially with the Brazilian's having successfully ridden just 46 percent of his bulls in the past seven BFTS events, compared with his 85 percent rate through the season's first eight events. In recent weeks, he'd inserted a baseball-card-size rendering of St. Michael the Archangel in the inside brim of his cowboy hat, and in Las Vegas he had at his disposal not one but two priests.

But when Moraes heard about McBride's holding out, he put aside his own concerns. McBride's skipping the finals would only have improved Moraes's chances at winning the $1 million bonus and gold buckle. But Moraes couldn't imagine the 2004 finals being held without its reserve champion and someone he admired so much. He urged McBride to sign the forms.

McBride loved Hedeman, but not enough to give up a chance to win his first world championship and the $1 million bonus. The PBR brass suspected Hedeman was behind McBride's threatened contract holdout. But Hedeman remained out of sight until six o'clock the next morning. That's when he arrived at the Mandalay Bay arena with Ross Coleman and a TV crew from the local FOX affiliate.

Bud Light, which sponsored Hedeman and Coleman, had arranged a bull riding demonstration during a live broadcast from the arena.

When Bernard heard about it, he was livid—and even angrier when he found out Denise Abbott, the PBR's vice president of public relations and marketing, was at the taping.

"You knew?" Bernard asked Abbott about the early-morning TV shoot.

"Yeah. I didn't think it was a big deal," she said.

"Not a big deal?" Bernard asked incredulously.

Twelve hours later, Hedeman returned to the arena and walked to the media room. He was there to pick up his press pass, Hedeman told the guy handling the credentials.

There was none to be found.

Empty-handed, Hedeman, no longer employed by the PBR or OLN, walked down the hall to a room serving as the PBR's headquarters office. Catie Nemeth, a ticket coordinator, looked startled to see him.

"Why can't I get a credential?" Hedeman asked.

Nemeth shrugged her shoulders and nervously walked away. Two men approached Hedeman. They were Jeff Collins, the PBR's mammoth legal counsel, and Val Jimenez, working security for the PBR. They told Hedeman he would have to leave, and, without incident, the men escorted Hedeman out of the arena.

The orders had come down from Bernard. If Hedeman wanted to get into the arena, he'd need a ticket—just like any other fan. It was a humbling moment for him. Despite his having been a force in founding the tour, despite his having remained the country's most recognizable bull rider, Hedeman had lost all of his power within the PBR. As he was escorted out of the arena, the sounds of spurs being filed, ropes being rosined, and stories being swapped filled the locker room during the preparation of the world's top 45 riders.

Clayton Cullen, vice president of production for the PBR, came into the locker room to explain where the five top-ranked riders would stand during the opening. He began diagramming the arrangement on a sheet of paper.

"That looks like a cock and two balls," McBride said.

Cullen looked up stone-faced, then continued his diagram.

A day after his tense showdown with the PBR executives on the contestant contract, McBride was back to his old self. To one passerby, he shouted, "Hey, you little fart stick."

In a rare serious moment, McBride explained to Moraes what the doctors had done to repair his broken ankle: inserted two screws in the tibia, inserted another screw across the fibula, and inserted nine other screws to hold the whole thing together. The ankle would require another 6 weeks to heal, but McBride could attempt to ride, thanks to the two-piece, clamshell-shaped boot that stabilized his right ankle. He'd wear his regular size-7½ cowboy boot over his left foot and wear a size-8½ cowboy boot over his right foot.

With McBride's crude sense of humor intact, he now had to prove he could ride as well as he could cuss. He insisted the broken ankle would be no problem. "It might affect my getaway," he said. "But I can crawl really fast."

Chris Shivers looked like he wanted to crawl away and hide when he showed up outside the locker room, wearing a dark Western-style sport coat—the first time he'd ever worn one in his life. The attire elicited hoots and wisecracks from his buddy Mike White. Grinning sheepishly, Shivers left the locker room, where he so desperately wanted to be, but, relegated to the sidelines at the finals for the first time in 8 years, he went to join the OLN TV crew. Nestlen's badgering had paid off, securing a TV gig for his top client.

It was 30 minutes from the scheduled opening for the first of eight rounds that would be held over the next 10 days. Rider Wiley Petersen called 20 or so riders together for a pre-event prayer. They bowed their heads.

"There are bull riders all over the world that want to be where we are now," Petersen said. "So let's take advantage of it."

Unsure about ticket demand for the first weekend of the expanded finals, the PBR scheduled the first three rounds to be held in the 11,000-seat Mandalay Bay Events Center. That night, waiting on the riders were more than 60 bulls and 7,000 fans.

With OLN live, Paulo Crimber greeted the audience atop Stretcher, who, like a car with engine trouble, jumped, stalled, jumped, and shifted into overdrive. Crimber hung on for the first qualified ride of the night.

The first 41 competitors would produce crowd-pleasing wrecks and rides. Zack Brown, the California surfer-turned-bull-rider, mastered Red Jacket, son of Little Yellow Jacket, for 87 points. Ross Johnson hung on as Shark launched himself off the dirt on all four hooves, the animal twisting himself 3 feet off the ground. Rubbing his backside after taking a horn to the ass on his getaway, Johnson grinned when the judges awarded him 87.25 points. Then Smooth Talker turned J. W. Hart's first ride into a rough trip, dumping the cowboy with the broken leg and smashing him against the chutes before the bullfighters could intercede. Hart scrambled up the chutes and for several seconds just leaned over the top bar, his body hanging like wet laundry on a clothesline. Looking for his first qualified ride since February, Lee Akin held on during a nasty belly roll and tamed Happy Jack for 86 points. And Brian "Pee Wee" Herman, who had made just two qualified rides on his last 20 bulls, took yet another shot on I Wanna Be Bad. He proved to be badder than the bull, staying in perfect position during a reverse and earning an 88.75 score that moved him into the first-round lead.

But the first 41 rides were the appetizers before the main course: resumption of the race for the $1 million bonus. Each night it would come down to the end of the show, the top contenders riding last.

Murray had joined the broadcast booth, only after ruling out the idea of his replacing Hedeman as the behind-the-chutes commentator. "I don't want to be no chute bitch," Murray said. So that role belonged to Shivers, who discarded his sport coat and looked comfortable and capable with a microphone instead of a bull rope in his hand.

First up: Mike White, fourth in the point standings.

Moraes saw White as his biggest threat. Since winning in Columbus, Mighty Mike had been riding with supreme confidence. Even though he stood in fourth place, it was White—not Moraes, McBride, or Lee—who had headed to New York for a round of prefinals interviews, including an appearance on the *Today* show.

At the 2003 finals, White had arrived in Las Vegas feeling tighter than Moraes's bull rope around a bull's midsection. He rode only two of his four bulls, failed to make the championship round, and watched as his best friend, Shivers, won the title.

But at the 2004 finals, White arrived feeling confident and loose. Before the first round, he told Shivers, "I'm going to do something different. I'm just treating this like any other bull riding event and trying to stay relaxed."

Climbing aboard River Rat, White began making his hand wrap when the bull lunged beneath him. White patiently hopped out of the chute and waited for the bull to calm down. "A smart move," Shivers told the TV audience.

White climbed back in the chute and steadied himself on the skittish bull, and out they went. Holding on during an early jump, White spurred the bull with his left foot, and he kept spurring until the 8-second buzzer sounded, earning him 83.5 points and giving him his ninth qualified ride in the last 12 attempts.

Next up: McBride, third in the point standings. As he lowered himself on Black Hawk, the bull thrashed and lunged in the chute. But the bull finally settled down, and McBride settled into the pocket. With his thin face tightened and blue eyes narrowed, McBride called for the gate.

Black Hawk bucked right, and McBride's injured right leg flopped against the bull's midsection. But McBride knew he could take 8 seconds of excruciating pain, and so did everybody else inside the arena when the buzzer sounded and he was still on the bull. On the dismount, he landed on his head, flipped over on his stomach, and, with the crowd cheering, speed-crawled to safety. His score of 82.75 points was almost secondary, because McBride had proved that despite the broken ankle, he was prepared to compete.

Next up: Lee, second in the point standings. He boarded Without Warning, a bull that had been ridden on four of five outs, and he coasted to an 84.5-point score. Providing commentary on the OLN broadcast, Murray praised Lee for his technical perfection, fitness, and determination. "If I'm Adriano," Murray added, "that right there is my competition."

"Ahead of McBride?" asked OLN's Brett Haber.

"I'm not taking anything away from Justin," Murray said. "Justin's one of the greatest bull riders to come along in a long time. But

Justin's injured, and Mike Lee—the guy is focused, and I think he really wants it."

Last up: Adriano Moraes.

He settled atop the bull named Larry 'Cable Guy's Git-r-Done. Faster than you could say the bull's name, Moraes hit the dirt. Gasps shot through the arena.

In the 2.6 seconds that elapsed between the moment the chute gate opened and when Moraes lost his rope, the idea that he would cruise to the championship ended. The race for the $1 million bonus and the gold buckle was on, and the crowd understood the heightening drama the next night, when White scored 92 points on Showtime while riding his fifth straight bull and his 10th in the last 13 attempts. Then the cheers went from loud to deafening.

Body jerking back and forth as if riding a bareback horse, McBride held on during a wild ride on Sudden Impact for 90.25 points. Next Lee climbed aboard a bull named Lightning, a two-time champion in Mexico, and it was more thunder. The crowd erupted as Lee rode the bull for 89.25 points. Just 2 days into the eight-round finals, Moraes was facing a pressure-packed ride on Coyote Ugly, a bull that had bucked off its last seven riders. Of the past 12 riders to board Coyote Ugly, only one had made the buzzer: Adriano Moraes.

With the pressure on, Moraes did it again, overpowering the 1,200-pound bull. But as Moraes dismounted, he grimaced and grabbed his left arm, his riding arm. In came the score—86.25 points—and out went Moraes, headed for the sports medicine room.

Tandy Freeman needed less than a minute to diagnose the injury. Moraes had ripped his left distal biceps tendon, the tendon connecting the muscle to the elbow. The muscle remained attached only by the two tendons connecting to the shoulder. As Freeman rotated the arm, already swollen and purple, Moraes grunted.

Freeman showed Moraes how the injury would weaken his grip when Moraes turned his palm upward, but not if he could keep his palm down and arm locked against his body. If not for a championship hanging in the balance, Freeman said, he would've recommended surgery that required 6 months of rehabilitation.

Moraes asked Freeman if he'd inject the left arm with something to numb the pain before his ride in the third round. It wasn't an option. Freeman explained that such medication would not only numb the pain but also numb Moraes's riding hand, making it virtually impossible for Moraes to hold on to the rope.

But Freeman did provide some painkilling pills. Licking closed the small pouch, he issued his standard warning about using the medication. "Don't drink, drive, operate heavy equipment, handle large sums of money, sign legal documents, or play with large animals."

"What about bulls?" Moraes asked.

Freeman grinned. "Not until tomorrow," he said.

A PBR official walked in to get an injury report. Freeman told her Moraes was questionable for that next night.

"Bullshit," Moraes snapped.

Freeman held up his hands to calm Moraes. "If I was going to the sports book, I'd probably put money on that you'd get on," he said.

Moraes was determined, and earlier that night Murray had seen the same grit in McBride. He sought out McBride in the locker room to congratulate him on the ride.

"Remember the sight, the smell, the feeling, and recreate it six more times," Murray said like a corner man sending his boxer into the 12th round of a championship fight. "The guys with the biggest balls and who try the hardest will win.

"They'll falter, and you won't."

Through two rounds, Moraes's lead had shrunk to 1,627 points. But even with $1 million at stake, the finals were about more than bull riding. Every day, in a parking lot outside the Fan Zone, the aroma of barbecue and chili wafted through the warm air as folks in hundreds of booths stirred their secret sauces as part of an 8-day cook-off culminating in its own championship. And as the posters leading to the Fan Zone promised: "The Fun Doesn't Stop After :08 Seconds." Every night, the PBR hosted after-event parties featuring a band and bottomless amounts of alcohol in one of the ballrooms at Mandalay Bay.

Riders, after their mandatory appearances at the parties, headed to the Palms Casino or the Gold Coast, the cowboy-friendly casino for high-stakes blackjack. Others snuck out to the strip clubs, while several gathered nightly at Mandalay Bay's Rum Jungle, where go-go dancers competed with the buckle bunnies for the attention of the riders. Unlike the regular-season events, rookies were pleasantly surprised to find more aggressive groupies and a shorter getting-to-know-you period.

"It's definitely a new experience," said Bohon, who did better at the after-event parties than he had that first day at the blackjack tables.

Lee's agent, Shawn Wiese, worried about the rider's tendency to isolate himself, took Lee out for a night of bowling with other riders. Later in the week, Lee also attended a drag-racing event as part of his endorsement agreement with the US Army. He also drove around the city in his rental car, with Pastor Todd Pierce occasionally riding shotgun. But Lee spent much of his time holed up in his hotel room, avoiding what he believed was Satan's strong presence in Sin City. "Mike has made an enemy of the devil," his father once explained. "Mike is ornery, and he likes to kind of tie a knot in the devil's tail whenever he can."

Every day in Las Vegas, Lee would meet with Pierce for spiritual talks and counseling sessions that lasted anywhere from 10 minutes to an hour. By Sunday, Lee was praying the pressure of contending for the championship would dissipate.

Sunday night. Round three. With 41 rides completed, the prelude ended and the showdown resumed.

Riding Joe Millionaire, White scored 81.75 on the sluggish bull, which earned him a reride option. In his last six rides, White looked capable of staying aboard anything. He checked to see which bull he'd be riding. Hells Bells, the back judge told him. Without hesitation, White shook his head. Though he'd ridden his past six bulls and 11 of the last 14, on White's four previous attempts on Hells Bells, the bull had thrown him off each time. So he played it safe, kept his modest score, and stayed in the top cumulative scores during the finals, worth $225,000 and, just as important, 2,500 bonus points toward the championship.

McBride followed White by riding his third straight bull at the finals. Duster whipped back like a crash-test dummy, and McBride scored only 72.5 points. Like White, he declined a reride option. He was in too much pain. Landing on his broken ankle on the dismount, McBride needed help getting out of the arena.

Aboard Waterproof Dip, Lee rode his third straight bull of the finals and scored 85.75 points. Again the night came down to Adriano Moraes, who, with a heavily wrapped left arm, climbed aboard Vegas Nights.

Resting his right arm on the outside gate, Moraes wriggled into position on the bull. He tightened his grip on the rope. His face tensed. Then came the nod.

Vegas Nights made a hard turn out of the chute. Moraes lost his balance, fell to the dirt, and grimaced while grabbing his injured arm and heading to the sports medicine room. Through three rounds, he had led the overall standings with 9,302.25 points, still 1,476.25 points ahead of his closest pursuer, Lee. But that was without factoring in the huge number of bonus points awarded for the top cumulative finishes; and through three rounds, Lee had led the cumulative standings, while Moraes was tied for 21st. Had the PBR finals ended after those three rounds, Lee would have earned 2,500 bonus points and won the title by more than 1,000 points.

But the thought of winning a championship swirled with the more maddening images in Lee's head.

"If we could see what's really going on, we'd probably pee on ourselves," Lee said after the third round. "All these demons are following us around, trying to steal our souls. . . . Angels are trying to fight them. It'll be a fight to the end."

Lee went on for 5 minutes about the unseen world. Then he abruptly chastised himself. "When I talk too much, I feel terrible," he said. "I feel like puking. I feel like a know-it-all."

Coming off as a know-it-all had never seemed to bother Moraes. But not even Moraes professed to know the answer to the most pressing question: Could he, at 34 years old, rebound from a disastrous start at the finals after tearing the biceps muscle of his riding arm?

That Sunday his wife, Flavia, took a call from a man who said he'd heard about her husband's injury. The man said he'd just attended a conference on alternative medicine in Las Vegas and, before he left town, wanted to give Adriano a package of herbal remedies guaranteed to reduce the swelling and pain in Moraes's injured arm. Flavia suggested the man drop off the package at the front desk of Mandalay Bay Monday morning.

A day later, that is where the package remained. After riding bulls for almost 20 years and suffering countless injuries, Adriano Moraes was sure of one thing when it came to doctors and alternative medicine healers.

They had no miracle cures.

CONCESSIONS

Hot dog	$5
Nachos	$2.50
Soft pretzel	$2.50

Why not deep-fried Twinkies? "That's a good question," said Erin Coleman of the Mandalay PR staff. But she had no answer—and no defense for the arena's bland concession offerings.

STANDINGS

1	Adriano Moraes	9,302.25 points	6	Ross Coleman	5,617.5 points
2	Mike Lee	7,826 points	7	Greg Potter	5,468.25 points
3	Justin McBride	7,717.75 points	8	Rob Bell	5,027.25 points
4	Mike White	7,161 points	9	Mike Collins	4,924.5 points
5	Brendon Clark	5,941.75 points	10	Jody Newberry	4,900.5 points

TWENTY

THE DELICIOUS
SHOWDOWN

Las Vegas, Nevada
Thursday–Sunday, October 28–31, 2004

A massive bull with lethal horns stood at the corner of
Third and Fremont streets, the neon-lit honky-tonk section
of town known as Glitter Gulch. It was dead—not the street,
but the bull, preserved by a taxidermist. Next to the bull,
painted letters on the side of a trailer read, "Welcome Bull
Riding Fans." Kenny Petet, a rodeo clown, had loaded the
dead bull, named Texas Red, into the trailer and driven from
his home in Mesquite, Texas, to this lonely corner in Sin
City, covering 1,207 miles without so much as a nap. In
hopes of capitalizing on the PBR fans descending for the last
weekend of the finals, he was charging $15 for a photo with

Texas Red, the dead bull, and another $5 for a key chain embossed with the photo. But pedestrians passed Petet and Texas Red without a glance as they marched up the street toward a sign that from a distance shimmered like a mirage.

Upon closer inspection, one could see it was an electronic video board above the entrance of Mermaids Casino. The looping videotape showed a woman seductively biting into a golden brown, deep-fried—at last, at last—Hostess Twinkie.

The Holy Grail. The deep-fried Twinkie of Las Vegas. The yearlong search had ended.

Inside the tired casino, among the 300 one-armed bandits, a concession worker lined up on a baking sheet 50 individually wrapped Twinkies. The woman inserted a wooden stick on one end of each confection, then slid the baking sheet into a freezer and pulled out another sheet of 50 frozen Twinkies. She peeled off the cellophane wrappers, dunked the Twinkies in pancake batter, and dumped them into the deep fryer's bubbling oil. Two minutes later, the golden brown Twinkies were ready for the final touch: powdered sugar across the top and a dusting of chocolate sprinkles.

Patrons fished dollar bills out of their pockets, took a penny's change for the 99-cent Twinkie, and hungrily chomped into a dessert disgusting to some and delicious to others. Deep-fried Twinkies two blocks from a picture bull on a casino strip the same weekend of the PBR finals? Only in America.

Though Kenny Petet had set up his bull a mere two blocks from Mermaids, Herb Pastor, owner of the casino, wasn't sure what deep-fried Twinkies had to do with bull riding or how they might help a rider stay on a bucking bull for 8 seconds. All he knew was what they had done for his business. Sitting in a cramped office, Pastor asked his business manager for the numbers. Fingers tapped on a printing calculator, and the roll of paper spit out the tally. Over the past year, Mermaids had sold 21,700 deep-fried Twinkies, but the dessert faced new competition.

Three weeks earlier, Pastor had instructed the concession workers to start deep-frying Oreo cookies. The workers had looked at Pastor like he was crazy. He loved that look.

Before long, Oreo cookie sales hit 145 orders a week, fast gaining on the Twinkie, with its weekly sales of 417 per week, and easily outpacing the chocolate-dipped frozen banana, with its weekly sales of 20 per week.

"Over the long run, who do you like?" Pastor asked Jason Babcock, the casino's director of purchasing.

"Oreos."

"Me, too," Pastor said.

"Unfortunately, the banana's left behind," Babcock told his boss. "But somebody's got to be in the dust."

The established Twinkie trying to hold off the upstart Oreo. In some ways, the battle mirrored the PBR's race for the gold buckle and $1 million.

ADRIANO MORAES FEARED IT WAS OVER. Maybe that's why he actually decided to pick up the package of herbal remedies that had been left for him at the front desk of the Mandalay Bay Resort & Casino and started applying a paste on his left torn biceps.

When things had been going well, Moraes had proclaimed himself the world's greatest rider—ever. When things went poorly, he worried he'd be unable to stay on a bull for 8 seconds—ever again. In the 3 days since he'd gotten bucked off Vegas Nights in round three of the eight-round finals, Moraes sunk into the abyss of self-doubt. His torn biceps might have contributed to his slump, but he suspected there was another problem. He just couldn't pinpoint what it was.

At 11:30 Wednesday night, the night before round four, Moraes called his two younger brothers and fellow Brazilian riders Guilherme Marchi and Paulo Crimber into his hotel suite. They gathered to study videotape of their previous bull rides at the finals, and they watched closely when the tape showed Crimber, Adriano Moraes's protégé. At 23 years old, Crimber suddenly had emerged as one of the PBR's hottest riders. During the first weekend of the finals, he won the second round and a $20,000 bonus with a 92.5-point ride on Jack Daniels Happy Hour. He covered all three of his bulls and trailed only

Mike Lee and Mike White in the finals standings based on cumulative points.

Four years earlier, when Crimber had decided to test his skills in the United States, Moraes had helped him find an apartment in Keller, Texas, not far from Moraes's house. He helped make Crimber's travel arrangements, taught him how to enter bull riding events, and tutored him with his English and the finer points of bull riding. He became Crimber's mentor, and as a tutor, he could be tough.

Moraes was hard on himself and just as hard on Crimber, because he knew the young Brazilian had enormous talent. Ceaselessly, the mentor had ordered his pupil to lean over the bull.

It took courage.

Leaning over a bull put a rider dangerously close to the horns. But it also put a rider in ideal position if a bull made a quick turn out of the chute. Lean over the bull! Crimber had heard Moraes's instructions so many times the move had become as routine as rosining his bull rope.

As happy as Moraes had been for Crimber after the first weekend at the finals, Moraes felt ashamed that a young rider he'd helped groom had surpassed him during his own slump. In the hotel room that night with the VCR whirring, Moraes studied replays of Crimber just as closely as he studied his own rides.

"That's it!" he shouted.

Startled, the four Brazilians looked at Moraes.

"That's it!" he shouted again.

The pupil had mastered what the mentor had forgotten: Lean over the bull!

More than forgetting the technique, Moraes suspected that fear was at work. Three months since he had collided with Smokeless Wardance's right horn and broken his left cheekbone, Moraes feared its happening again. He'd begun to straighten his torso in the chutes, which kept him at a safer distance from the bull's horns but made it harder to stay centered on the bull after a quick first turn out of the chutes.

"That's it," Moraes repeated.

The next day, the five Brazilians met in the hotel gym, Moraes leading them through a series of simulated bull riding moves. Seated on the floor, they visualized sitting in the chute and leaning over the bull as they prepared for the gate to open. Again and again, eyes closed, Moraes leaned forward and visualized the perfect ride—the kind of ride he needed to hold off Justin McBride, Mike White, and Mike Lee for the world championship.

By that morning, one championship had already been decided. Those who entered the PBR's Fan Zone and walked directly across the 400,000-square-foot exhibition hall to a small merchandise booth discovered the news on embossed T-shirts and embroidered caps that read, "Little Yellow Jacket. Three-Time PBR Bucking Bull of the Year."

"It's official," crowed Darlene Berger of Mandan, North Dakota, home of Little Yellow Jacket and her family's Berger Bucking Bulls.

In the annual vote by riders, Little Yellow Jacket had edged Pandora's Box. The announcement had come 2 days earlier, at a banquet for the stock contractors. Later in the week, Cody Lambert, who picked the bulls used by the PBR, declared the Bergers' star bull the greatest in rodeo history. But no one knew where the four-legged champion was headed after Vegas.

For the right price, Joe Berger was ready to sell. So Tom Teague, the co-owner of Little Yellow Jacket, sent word to Joe's ex-wife, Darlene, that he wanted to buy the Bergers' 50 percent share of Little Yellow Jacket and take full control of the bull. Darlene Berger dispatched her son, Chad, to negotiate, but she said nothing about it to her youngest son, Nevada, fearing how he might react to losing his beloved bull. Teague offered $100,000. Chad Berger wasn't sure whether to laugh or spit in Teague's face.

No deal, said Chad, and he thought more seriously about a plan to buy out Teague and Teague's partner, Bernie Taupin, and syndicate Little Yellow Jacket. By offering shares in Little Yellow Jacket to a limited number of buyers, Chad and Darlene Berger thought they could raise $1 million. So even if they agreed to sell their 50 percent interest, Darlene and Chad Berger calculated it was worth $500,000. The negotiations grew almost as intense as the bull riders' race for the championship. But by then the word had gotten back to Nevada Berger, and he wasn't happy to hear about any of it.

"It'd be like selling your own kid, you know?" Nevada said. "We've been around him since he was a baby and grown up around him every day. If I don't see him every day, I'm wondering how he's doing. I can't imagine somebody else being able to haul him. That really bothers me.

"He's not going anywhere."

THE AUTOGRAPH SEEKERS ARRIVED IN WAVES, and Mike White greeted them all with a friendly hello. But each time the crowd cleared, his scowl returned. The previous day, he'd shown up at a press conference for the five leading riders and seen a press release that read: "Lee and McBride Gain Ground in the PBR's Million-Dollar World Title Race."

Never mind that during the season's homestretch, White had been the hottest rider on tour. Never mind that during the first weekend of competition at the finals, White, Lee, and Crimber had been the only riders to cover all three of their bulls. Never mind that while White and Crimber were tied for second in the finals standings, trailing only Mike Lee, McBride was fourth. Leaving the press conference, White passed Denise Abbott, vice president of public relations and marketing for the PBR, and sniffed, "Don't ever ask me to do any more press stuff."

Abbott looked puzzled.

"Why?"

"Because of that press release."

"Your name's in there."

"Yeah, at the very bottom in fine print."

What was it going to take for him to get the respect he thought he deserved? Of course White knew the answer: win the damn championship. But he continued to carp about the press release until a tall, middle-aged brunette approached the autograph table. It was the mother of rider Cory Melton, who, like White, had been born and raised in Louisiana. She was a welcome sight in the sea of strangers.

Melton's mother made small talk, then asked White to sign pictures for a couple of her nephews.

"They'll be tickled to death to have an autograph from the next PBR champion," she said.

White grinned. "I hope," he said, referring to her prediction about his becoming the next PBR champion.

World champion Mike White. He liked the sound of that and imagined those words in bold letters across a PBR press release.

GLEAMING IN HER SIGNATURE RED AND GRAY, there she stood at the corner of Tropicana and Swenson streets—the Thomas & Mack Center. One hundred four feet tall. Forty-two thousand square feet large. From the cozy Mandalay Bay Events Center, the finals moved to a building with the look and lore worthy of the final 4 days of the season. The escalators carried men and women wearing Western shirts and cowboy hats up to the well-lit entrance of Thomas & Mack. Inside, the basketball floor sat underneath 3 million pounds of dirt freshly leveled for the world's best bull riders and the world's best bulls. It was the grand stage of bull riding, and the stage on which Adriano Moraes intended to finish the season as the PBR's three-time world champion.

That night before the introductions to round four, OLN reporter Leah Garcia walked in and saw Bobby "Jinx" Clower, the guy in charge of opening the chute gates. "What do you think about Adriano and his bull tonight?" she asked.

Moraes had drawn Crossfire Hurricane, which during the 2004 season had bucked off all 16 riders, including Moraes. "He can tape it all he wants to," Clower said, referring to Moraes's bandaged torn biceps. "He's out."

Clower was betting against Moraes, and so was almost everybody else who'd seen Moraes fall off his third-round bull in less than 2 seconds. Two and a half hours later, when Moraes climbed aboard Crossfire Hurricane for the last ride of round four, the crowd grew hushed. McBride had gotten bucked off Hotel California, and Lee had fallen off Sudden Impact, but White had kept the pressure on Moraes by riding his fourth straight bull of the finals.

Lean over the bull. Lean over the bull. It'd become a silent mantra for Moraes.

As he'd visualized and practiced during simulated exercises, Moraes was leaning forward over Crossfire Hurricane when the gate opened. In proper position, Moraes survived the first hard turn to the right and, free arm at a 90-degree angle from his body in textbook fashion, he bore down for the ensuing assault. Four hard jumps to the right. An abrupt turn back to the left. Five more hard jumps. Then came the buzzer and . . . *Yes.* Moraes had made it! Dismounting to his right, Moraes took a few steps, then dropped to his knees. He clutched his left arm. He gazed heavenward. The fans erupted in cheers.

Well, most of them.

"Oh, boy. The Brazilian's coming out in him," cracked one spectator.

With Moraes's theatrics over, the fans went silent. They were waiting on Moraes's score.

A minute passed.

No score.

Another minute passed.

Still no score.

Suddenly, over the PA system came an announcement: Jody Newberry's score of 91.25 had been readjusted to 92.5.

Murmurs spread through the arena.

Another 30 seconds passed. Finally, the announcement for which everybody had been waiting, Adriano Moraes's score.

Ninety-three points!

He'd won the round with the highest score yet at the finals. Again, the crowd erupted.

Clutching his injured left arm, Moraes wore a look of ecstasy and relief. "Holy macaroni," he boomed when he entered the sports medicine room. "It really hurts when you're riding. But when you win a round, it cures anything."

J. W. Hart, hobbling on his broken left ankle, later stopped Moraes in the hallway. "Hey, way to bear down," Hart said. "That's what it takes."

With one miraculous ride, Moraes had bumped his lead to 1,969.25 points, climbed to ninth in the cumulative standings, and reemerged as the odds-on favorite to win the gold buckle and $1 million.

While Moraes fielded questions at the press conference, Lee, who'd dropped from first to fourth in the all-important cumulative standings, took a call from his father. Dennis Lee had stayed in Texas because he worried his presence might put unneeded pressure on his son. But after watching his son's ride that night, he couldn't help pointing out a mistake: At the end of the ride, Lee had looked down, looking for a place to bail out, rather than keeping his eye on the bull and refusing to let go of the bull rope.

Gutless, Mike Lee called it, and he vowed not to let it happen again.

The next night, during round five, McBride rode Toy Tiger for 89.25 points, keeping alive his outside chances of catching Moraes, who rode King's Court for a respectable 85.25 points. But it was Lee, never so much as glancing at the ground while aboard a bull named McNasty, who scored 89.75 points and won the round. Just like that, Lee was back in the picture, closing the gap on Moraes to 1,564 points, inching up to third in the finals' cumulative standings, one spot behind contender White and three spots ahead of McBride.

Abbott brought Lee and Moraes to the postevent press conference. Moraes headed straight for the podium; Lee sat down in the back row.

"Up in the front," Abbott said, waving Lee to the podium.

Even while in striking distance of a world championship, Lee took pains to avoid the spotlight. In fact, Lee was so averse to the extra attention, he had entered small rodeos under an assumed name. It all made Moraes think Lee might actually fear winning the championship because of the spotlight that came with it—the spotlight under which Moraes naturally basked. Their relationship still appeared strained, with Lee referring to Moraes as a "pretty good" friend.

Each night, the winner of the round was required to attend the afterevent party and accept a buckle. Reluctantly Lee headed to the ballroom with his wife, mother, and brother and drifted into his own world. A world without spittoons or spit cups. With a pinch of snuff in his mouth, Lee walked across the hall and squirted tobacco juice into some potted plants. Then he walked to the back of the ballroom and behind the stage, where he got directions for the buckle ceremony. With no potted plants in sight, Lee squirted his tobacco juice on the floor. After the presentation, he rejoined his family members and headed across the street for dinner at McDonald's.

Some PBR executives who watched Lee's behavior feared his being in the spotlight as much as Lee did. But 24 hours later, Lee rode into it yet again. He scored 90 points on Paleface, taking the lead in round six. The pressure was back on Moraes.

In the chute, he contorted his face as he fought Milk Man, who squatted on his front quarters. The bull refused to budge. Lee hustled over to the chute and jabbed at the bull with his boot, trying to bring Milk Man to a standing position and give Moraes a fair shot to ride the recalcitrant bull. "Nod your head!" Lee shouted to Moraes. "You can ride him."

Here they were, battling each other for the championship, and Lee was trying to help his chief rival and offering encouraging words.

Moraes nodded. The chute gate opened. Out they went. Just as Lee had predicted, Moraes rode the bull, scoring 87.25 points.

Though Lee won the round, Moraes took another step toward winning the championship. His lead over Lee had shrunk to 1,212.25 points, but he'd climbed to fifth in the cumulative standings, three spots behind Lee. If the competition had ended and the bonus points had been awarded that night, Moraes would have won the championship over Lee by 462.25 points, with McBride and White finishing more than 1,600 points behind.

White, who rode his sixth straight bull that night, approached Moraes in the tunnel leading to the locker room with a look of resignation. "I can't win it," he said.

"Mathematically—" Moraes began, about to point out that White would have a shot if Moraes failed to cover his next bull.

White shook his head and cut him off. "I know," he said, "but you're not going to fall off."

Moraes paused. Then he broke into a huge grin. "You're right," he said.

After all the number crunching and calculations, it was clear: Lee was the only rider with a legitimate shot at catching Moraes. At the press conference Saturday night, Lee sounded spookier than ever.

"When I ride, I have to be ready to die that day," he said. "That's the way I have to ride, just to be free."

Later that night George Michael, lead commentator for NBC's Sunday broadcast, ran into Lee. "How are you handling the pressure?" he asked.

Replied Lee: "I'm not in this world right now."

Lee's vacant but calm look contrasted with Moraes's anxious enthusiasm. That was only one of the contrasts. Lee was humble to a fault. Moraes struggled to contain his confidence. Lee hardly thought about winning the world title. Moraes expected it, now more than ever.

For the seventh round on Sunday, Moraes had drawn Easy Money, considered one of the most rider-friendly bulls in the round because he was a rideable bull who produced high scores. The bull would turn to the right and spin flat, the kind of bull Moraes could ride in his sleep. In Easy Money's last five trips, White and Ned Cross, a second-year pro who hadn't even qualified for the finals, had successfully ridden the bull. Moraes was thrilled with the draw.

When the press conference ended Saturday night, Moraes left the arena with his onetime mentor, Charlie Sampson. They hadn't seen each other in years. Earlier Saturday, Sampson had flown in to Las Vegas for his induction into the PBR's Ring of Honor, and the timing was impeccable: Sampson's receiving the PBR's highest honor on the night Moraes moved closer to an unprecedented third PBR championship.

Under the dark, cloudless sky, the two men laughed and reminisced about how Sampson had discovered Moraes in Brazil more than 15 years earlier. Sampson recalled having told Moraes that he was good enough to compete against the top riders in the United States. "That's why I came," Moraes said.

Driving back to Mandalay Bay with Moraes's family, Sampson pulled out his cell phone and called his son. "I'm here with Adriano," he said.

"Did you watch tonight? Well, you got to watch tomorrow, because tomorrow is the championship and Adriano is going to win."

With Sampson having to catch a flight out early that next morning, the men said their good-byes inside the hotel.

"Ride the front end," Sampson reminded Moraes as Moraes had reminded Crimber countless times and earlier that week reminded himself.

"I did it tonight, so we do it again," Moraes said. "I love you, Champ."

SUNLIGHT FLOODED THROUGH THE LARGE GLASS WINDOWS of the 28th-floor suite in Mandalay Bay Resort & Casino. It was eight o'clock Sunday morning, and next to the two priests stood Adriano Moraes, translating the Sunday Mass for more than a dozen Brazilians and others squeezed into the hotel suite. The picture windows to the priests' backs afforded a spectacular view of Sunrise Mountain in the distance, with the pyramid-shaped Luxor Hotel to the north and the Thomas & Mack Center to the east.

For the past 2 days, Moraes and his wife had knelt and recited afternoon prayers in the direction of Thomas & Mack. Before leaving for the arena Sunday, Flavia gazed at the building one last time and offered another silent prayer.

Midway through the Mass in Moraes's room, Mike Lee slipped into the South Pacific Ballroom on the bottom floor of Mandalay Bay for the Cowboy Church service. More than 2,000 people crowded into the ballroom and listened as Lee's wife, Jamie, fighting through her shyness, belted out "Amazing Grace." Then she headed toward the back of the room and rejoined her husband, still doing his best to blend in with the crowd.

Over at the Thomas & Mack Center, the bartender at the Jack Daniel's tent served the first Jack and cocoa, Bloody Mary, and Bud Light by 9:30 in the morning. Fans began forming a line outside the arena's front entrance more than an hour before the gates opened.

Among the early arrivals were Bill and Peggy Duvall, who, instead of their matching PBR jackets, were wearing their Sunday best—Bill in a Western-style formal jacket, a beige cowboy hat, and polished brown cowboy boots, and Peggy in a black jean jacket with pink rhinestones over a black T-shirt with more pink rhinestones and beige cowboy boots. After having attended 15 regular-season events, they weren't about to miss the finals. In fact, they'd stayed all 10 days at Mandalay Bay, eager to see how it would end after having seen the 2004 season begin 10 months earlier in Jacksonville.

Inside the sports medicine room, 11 riders were receiving treatment for assorted injuries. That didn't include Cory Melton, who had withdrawn from competition earlier in the week with two cracked vertebrae, or bullfighter Rob Smets, who'd aggravated his twice-broken neck, or Justin McBride, who was sitting in a shower stall in the locker room and straining to pull a boot over his broken right ankle.

Someone asked McBride how he felt. "Like a dump truck just fell off the Empire State Building and landed on me," he said. "My ankle, my leg, my back, my head—I don't know which hurts worse."

In another locker room down the hall, Lee stood alone. He was brushing caked rosin off his bull rope when Bobby "Jinx" Clower, the gateman, poked his head into the room.

"Time to get the quarter," Clower said.

Lee allowed a thin smile.

Through 28 weekends, Lee had yet to win a single event, but his consistent riding had kept him in contention for the championship. Since the season opener, Clower had greeted Lee with the same refrain: "Nickel-and-dime 'em all year, and get the quarter in the end." To ensure he got the quarter—or in this case the $1 million bonus—Lee would need two bull rides as spectacular as the opening introductions.

Two stuntmen attached to ropes dropped from the ceiling and into a large box. An explosion rocked the arena, and smoke curled from the bottom of the box. From opposite sides emerged Lee and Moraes, who then strode toward the center of the arena and clambered up portable stairs and atop a raised platform.

The two top-ranked bull riders, with hands on hips and feet spread apart, stared each other down like gunslingers at the OK Corral. Some 16,500 fans thundered their approval.

Moraes and Lee had survived a grueling 10 months, outlasting and outdueling the world's best riders to get there: the Thomas & Mack Center on October 31, 2004, on the last day of the finals and the Professional Bull Riders season. Introductions over, the two riders descended the stairs and hustled toward one end of the arena, where fellow riders and bulls waited. When the chute gates swung open, the violent dance would begin.

Starting with the seventh round, 43 riders dropped into the chutes and rode their bulls before the real showdown began. Mike Lee versus Adriano Moraes. On Slick Willy, Lee looked effortless, but the bull looked lifeless. The result was a score of 73.25 points and a reride option. Dangling his feet over the cliff's ledge, Lee took the reride and risked disaster. Moraes climbed aboard Easy Money, and two Brazilians helped pull Moraes's rope. He wrapped the slack underneath his gloved left hand and across his palm before closing his fingers and balling his hand into a fist. But something didn't feel quite right, so Moraes unwrapped the rope. The two straining Brazilians pulled even harder and handed the slack to Moraes, who again wrapped the rope around his hand and made his fist. Twice, with his free hand, he pounded his left fist closed. He pushed down on the front of his black cowboy hat, rested his right arm atop the chute gate and . . .

Easy Money reared up. The Brazilians uttered a frantic stream of Portuguese. Moraes held up his right hand, signaling he was okay. He resettled on the bull, then gave a quick nod. The gate swung open.

Easy Money turned right and by the first jump had all fours off the ground. Moraes was sitting dead center. With his second buck, the bull made another turn, and Moraes slipped to the right. Jump three, another half turn and . . . it was only a matter of time. Easy Money, maybe the easiest bull of the round, dumped Moraes to the dirt.

Reaching his feet, Moraes cocked his fist and stepped toward the chutes as if preparing to punch the metal covering. But his arm went limp, and he slowly spun in a circle, drifting to the side of the ring, where he crashed against a signage board and slumped to the ground.

"Aarrgggh!"

Yellow mouthpiece still jammed in his mouth, Moraes let out a primal scream. It lasted almost as long as his ride—2.8 seconds.

But the round wasn't over. Lee had wiped his score off the board by accepting the reride and now had to board Geronimo, who had been ridden six out of 10 attempts during the '04 season. The way Lee was riding, they might as well have put him on a picture bull, because it was a picture-perfect ride. He scored 88.75 points to drive another nail in Moraes's coffin.

The $1 million. The gold buckle. Potential history. It would all come down to the eighth round, the championship round, featuring the 15 riders with the top cumulative scores through the first seven rounds. It was down to the final rides of the 2004 season.

During a short intermission, Lori McBride, Justin's mother, walked up to Flavia Moraes. With her son out of contention and only Adriano Moraes capable of catching Lee, Lori McBride left no doubt as to whom she was rooting for.

"Flavia, it looks like a gladiator and a pussy," she said, referring to Moraes and Lee.

Flavia giggled nervously, squeezed Lori McBride's hand, and glanced at the young woman sitting to her right.

"Well, I'm Mike Lee's wife, and I don't appreciate you calling him that," Jamie Lee huffed.

"I am so sorry. That wasn't meant for you to hear," Lori McBride said.

The two women exchanged frosty glares.

It was time for the championship round.

On the metal deck behind the chutes, Pastor Todd Pierce saw Lee tying and retying the laces of his boots. "You think those shoes are tied well enough yet?" Pierce asked.

"I don't know," Lee answered. "I just can't seem to get them comfortable."

No one on tour knew Lee better than Pierce did. Pierce had befriended and counseled the young rider since they had first met at the Tuff Hedeman Championship Challenge in 2002, and though Pierce was 12 years older than Lee, he saw a lot of himself in the young rider. The intensity. The fierceness. The struggle to quiet his mind. Now Pierce saw anxiety.

While Lee said he couldn't get his laces comfortable, Pierce knew it was Lee himself who couldn't get comfortable. Lee was losing his focus.

Pierce knelt on the metal deck, clasped hands with Lee, and prayed. Repeating after Pierce, Lee said, "Okay, Father, I'm feeling the pressure. I give it to you, and I'm just going to ride the bull like you created me to."

On the same metal deck, Moraes was pacing when Leah Garcia pulled him aside for an interview. "You know, I had the easiest bull of the whole event," Moraes moaned.

What now? Garcia asked, with Moraes just minutes away from climbing aboard Reindeer Dippin, the bull he'd drawn for the championship round. What would Moraes do? The dejection vanished from his face. He looked angry, determined.

"I'm going to try to spur his guts out," Moraes said.

Only Moraes had a chance to catch Lee, and his chances depended on Lee's getting bucked off for only the second time in eight rounds. Had the event ended after seven rounds, with the bonus points distributed, the standings would've looked like this: (1) Lee, 11,694.5 points; (2) Moraes, 10,018 points; (3) White, 9,405.25 points; (4) McBride, 8,927.5. If Lee bucked off, he was guaranteed a score of at least 10,994 points by virtue of his having secured no worse than a fifth-place finish in the cumulative standings. To catch him, Moraes would have to ride his bull and jump in the cumulative standings from his current spot of 12th to seventh. And then the championship round commenced.

Down went Dan Henricks and down went Ross Coleman before Greg Potter survived Sling Blade for 90 points. The score scarcely distracted the crowd for the moment of truth: Moraes versus Reindeer Dippin.

As soon as the chute gate opened, Moraes knew he was in for an unusual ride. Reindeer Dippin looked more like Rudolph the Red-Nosed

Reindeer. Instead of his quick spins and powerful bucks, the bull almost loped around the arena. Moraes made the buzzer and earned a score of 79.75 points but also got a reride option. Decision time. The score would've moved Moraes into seventh place in the cumulative standings, good enough to win the championship if Lee bucked off Mossy Oak Mudslinger, the 2003 runner-up for Bull of the Year. Ty Murray, before retiring, had failed to ride the bull in his only attempt. So had stars like Michael Gaffney and Troy Dunn, while Shivers had failed in his only two attempts. Lee had failed in his own attempt, that coming in 2002 and Lee's rookie year. During the 2004 season, the bull had been ridden four times in 15 attempts—twice by Moraes and twice by McBride. And at the 2004 finals, he'd already bucked off Adam Carrillo and Lee Akin.

To remain in seventh place, Moraes would need each of the next six riders to buck off, and Moraes wanted things in his own hands. He accepted the reride on a tantalizingly named Big Bucks. Moraes watched the next five riders fail to make the buzzer before Michael Gaffney boarded Little Yellow Jacket, the three-time Bull of the Year. If Gaffney bucked off, Moraes had taken a needless gamble, so maybe it was relief that prompted him to join the crowd's roar when Gaffney, at 35 the oldest rider competing in the finals, rode Little Yellow Jacket and earned 93.75 points, the highest score yet during the finals. Zack Brown, who'd already clinched Rookie of the Year honors, followed with a 93.25-point ride on Night Life.

In the chutes, Moraes boarded Big Bucks. His face looked drained. Wrapping the bull rope around his fist, he settled in, then unwrapped the rope and climbed out of the chute. He wasn't ready. Not for the biggest ride of the year. Not yet. Realizing Moraes would be delayed, the officials moved to Cody Whitney and Kid Rock. Whitney got rocked, all right, slammed to the dirt, and the athletic trainers ran to his aid and helped him off.

Now there was no more waiting. No more stalling. No more need to crunch numbers for Adriano Moraes. To jump to sixth in the cumulative standings, which if Lee bucked off would give Moraes the championship, Moraes needed a 90-point ride.

For a shot at the title, Moraes *had* to ride his bull, Big Bucks, un-ridden in five trips on the BFTS tour. Rope wrapped around his left hand, right hand pushing down on the cowboy hat before resting on the top of the chute, a quick nod, and there they went.

Big Bucks dropped his head toward the ground and bucked his hind hooves skyward. Moraes slid forward. A hard jump to the left, two more fearsome bucks, and Moraes jerked forward too far. He tumbled off the right side of the bull and hit the ground. Getting back on his feet, Moraes walked to a corner of the arena and dropped onto his right knee. He looked up at the overhead video replay board. "Over," he mouthed.

With the world championship clinched, Lee still had the finals title and another $225,000 bonus within reach. He settled onto Mossy Oak Mudslinger with the same eerie composure he'd shown in the chutes throughout the 10-day finals.

Ready to die.

Free.

Mossy Oak Mudslinger blasted out of the chutes, bucking and spin-ning with fury. Yet Lee looked like he was riding a sedated steer. Main-taining his body control, Lee made it to the buzzer and scored 93.75 points, matching Gaffney's score on Little Yellow Jacket and winning the $225,000 bonus for the finals victory, the $1 million bonus for the season championship, and the gold buckle.

In the stands, Flavia hugged Jamie Lee. And the first rider off the chutes and into the arena was Moraes, who grabbed Lee's bull rope from the gateman and handed it to the new champion. Moraes stuck his right fist in Lee's chest. "Great job," he said.

The two riders bumped fists.

Then Moraes knelt down and greeted two of his sons, 6-year-old Jeremias and 4-year-old Antonio. Jeremias was crying, and Moraes tried to soothe him with a kiss on the forehead. He scooped up the boys into his massive arms and marched out of the arena, clearing the stage for the new PBR champion.

Standing between Randy Bernard and Leah Garcia, Lee stared at the army of photographers and cameramen as if suddenly realizing that his victory came with a price—the blinding spotlight.

Bernard leaned over to Jamie Lee, standing beside her husband. "So, have you spent the money yet?" he joked about the $1 million.

She broke into a weary grin. "Mike gets upset if I buy three shirts," she said.

Bernard's last-minute plan was for the winner and his family to shake up champagne bottles and pour the bubbly over one another's head. But as soon as Lee clinched the title, he'd sent away the champagne. He knew Lee, a teetotaler, was as apt to drink alcohol as he was to drink rat poison.

Lee celebrated his victory with a can of root beer.

Packing up his equipment back in the locker room, Moraes knew nothing could wash the bitter taste out of his mouth. Not champagne, not root beer, nothing.

Bernard, standing near the oversize $1 million check to be presented to Lee, looked nervous and distracted. The fans inside Thomas & Mack had missed the TV fiasco. With the PBR championship still undecided but with NBC rushed for time after its NASCAR coverage ran long, the network cut away from the finals and sent the broadcast back to OLN with Moraes and Lee yet to make their final rides. Now Bernard looked as if he were about to walk the plank.

"I'm going to have to change my name," he joked.

By the time Bernard reached his suite at Mandalay Bay, he checked his computer and found 275 e-mails—a slew of them, he was sure, from fans angry about NBC's aborted coverage. A half hour later, sipping a Jack Daniel's with a splash of water, Bernard rechecked the e-mails. The count was up to 318.

Already late for the awards ceremony, Bernard grabbed his drink and, wife in tow, headed for the South Pacific Ballroom. There was Justin McBride, who, despite another heartbreaking finish, looked oddly content as he sat next to Jill Ericksen, McBride's former schoolmate. Their relationship had taken off since McBride's breakup with Michelle Beadle.

The Brazilians sat at a table in the back with one empty chair. Adriano Moraes was missing.

Suddenly, he reappeared.

"Two hundred thousand dollars a year," he said. "It's done."

In the works for weeks, an endorsement deal with a national company was all but finalized. It would be the most lucrative sponsorship deal Moraes had landed in his career—and a testament to his popularity, considering that Lee's agent was fielding no six-figure offers.

But Moraes's smile looked forced. Sitting next to his wife, he still felt a lump in his throat or whatever it was keeping down the emotion. His wife said she wished he could cry, but Moraes had no intention of doing so. Certainly not at the awards banquet.

Actually, Moraes told Flavia that something strange had happened in the past 10 minutes. For the first time since he'd fallen off his last bull of the season, he felt more determined than devastated. He still had to decide whether to have tendon-reattachment surgery that Freeman said would keep him out for 6 months. But between spoonfuls of vanilla ice cream and peach cobbler, Moraes predicted he'd win the 2005 championship.

"The lazy guy died tonight," he said. "Tomorrow I will start working on my championship. If no one wants to go to the gym with me, I'll go alone. I know how much I love bull riding, but I don't know how much time I have left. So I've got to get it done."

Flavia kissed him on the cheek.

"One thing. I beat the odds," Moraes continued. "No one thought I could come back. . . . I'm still the greatest that ever lived."

In the front of the ballroom, where Lee's mother, brother, and agent sat, there were two empty chairs—the ones belonging to Mike Lee and his wife. Mike and Jamie were on the dance floor. The PBR's new champion wore a black blazer his wife had talked him into buying Saturday rather than letting him wear the brown one he'd bought at a thrift shop a couple of years earlier. She wore a shiny, opalescent dress.

Locked in an embrace, the two swayed as Alison Krauss, the Grammy Award–winning singer, performed the song "When You Say Nothing at All."

"Our song," Jamie Lee called it.

She had first heard it before she and Mike got married, and she thought the lyrics were perfect. So often her husband failed to find words to express himself. But when Jamie looked into Mike's eyes and studied his face, she could see the most important thing—that Mike loved her.

During Lee's acceptance speech—when most riders heard him speak more than he had over the past three seasons—Lee thanked "my beautiful, beautiful wife."

Jamie beamed.

In the next half hour, the twelve hundred or so people at the awards banquet began trickling out in small pockets, with the crowning of the new champion and the 2004 season complete. The PBR had survived a political assault from Tuff Hedeman. Little Yellow Jacket had won his third straight Bull of the Year. Adriano Moraes had rebounded from his worst season ever. Justin McBride had proved again to be among the toughest and most determined riders in the world. And Mike Lee, in paying tribute to his wife after winning the championship, had at last found the right words.

CONCESSIONS	
Taco salad	$5
Skinny Philly cheesesteak with fruit	$6.50
Chicken fingers	$5.50
Apple-cinnamon-stuffed pretzel	$3.50

"No deep-fried Twinkies," said Maria Dos Santos, operations manager for food and beverage at the Thomas & Mack Center. "Those, they'll be interesting. Let me know who serves them." Our pleasure. Just head down to Mermaids Casino at 32 East Fremont Street.

FINAL STANDINGS

1	Mike Lee	$1,417,592	12,138.25 points
2	Adriano Moraes	$253,921	10,018 points
3	Mike White	$307,921	8,905.25 points
4	Justin McBride	$278,427	8,669.5 points
5	Greg Potter	$148,132	7,586.75 points
6	Zack Brown	$288,447	6,601 points
7	Ross Coleman	$139,279	6,358 points
8	Brendon Clark	$138,976	6,241.75 points
9	Jody Newberry	$121,712	6,078.75 points
10	Michael Gaffney	$145,354	5,942 points

INDEX

Underscored page references indicate tables.

M